MW01156489

A Soldier's General

CIVIL WAR AMERICA

Gary W. Gallagher, editor

A Soldier's General

The Civil War Letters of
Major General Lafayette McLaws

EDITED BY JOHN C. OEFFINGER

The University of North Carolina Press

Chapel Hill and London

© 2002
The University of North Carolina Press
All rights reserved
Set in New Baskerville and Egiziano types
by Tseng Information Systems, Inc.
Manufactured in the United States of America

The paper in this book meets the guidelines for
permanence and durability of the Committee on
Production Guidelines for Book Longevity of the
Council on Library Resources.

Library of Congress
Cataloging-in-Publication Data
McLaws, Lafayette, 1821–1897.
A soldier's general: the Civil War letters
of Major General Lafayette McLaws / edited by
John C. Oeffinger.
p. cm.—(Civil War America)
Includes bibliographical references and index.
ISBN 0-8078-2690-1 (alk. paper)
1. McLaws, Lafayette, 1821–1897—Correspondence.
2. Confederate States of America. Army—Biography.
3. Generals—Confederate States of America—
Correspondence. 4. Generals—Confederate States of
America—Biography. 5. Generals—United States—
Biography. 6. United States—History—Civil War,
1861–1865—Personal narratives, Confederate.
7. United States—History—Civil War, 1861–1865—
Campaigns. I. Oeffinger, John C. II. Title.
III. Series.
E467.1.M3744 M36 2002
973.7′42′092—dc21 2001054203

06 05 04 03 02 5 4 3 2 1

Page iii: Pen-and-ink sketch of Lafayette McLaws
as he appeared between 1861 and 1865.
(Courtesy of the Georgia Department
of Archives and History)

For my parents,

Jack and Sally Oeffinger,

who let me seek my own path,

and for Kathryn and Clayton,

who are my greatest joy!

Contents

Illustrations

Acknowledgments

Many people played a critical role in the evolution of *A Soldier's General.* Richard A. Shrader, reference archivist at the University of North Carolina at Chapel Hill's Wilson Library, introduced me to the Lafayette McLaws Collection #472 in October 1994. He encouraged the beginning of this project and guided me through the process. I am truly thankful for his help.

Gary W. Gallagher painted the initial picture of the potential value of these letters in published form. Gary opened doors for this neophyte historian and provided the positive encouragement needed to bring this work to life. He introduced me to several of his colleagues who then challenged my assumptions and offered advice to improve the work. Most importantly, Gary read several manuscript iterations. He provoked new ideas, directions, and additions while providing fresh perspectives and insight. The result is a more comprehensive and thorough manuscript that would not have become a book without Gary's guidance and mentoring.

Robert K. Krick, Jeffry D. Wert, and Haskell Monroe provided keen insight for development of the introduction. Bob opened his extensive McLaws files and reviewed the initial outline and subsequent drafts. He offered historical perspectives of Lafayette McLaws, James Longstreet, and the Army of Northern Virginia. His frank and comprehensive assessments strengthened the final manuscript.

Gavin J. Campbell took time to help check the transcriptions while completing his dissertation at the University of North Carolina at Chapel Hill. Gavin reviewed the first and second iterations of the transcribed letters, compared them to the originals, and suggested corrections where he found a stray word or phrase. He proved resourceful in translating many of the most difficult words.

Michael Musick provided access to the National Archives and was always gracious with his time and assistance during my several visits. David Wallace helped gather the relevant materials on West Point.

Frank T. Wheeler, Eileen A. Ielmini, Barbara P. Heuer, Susan Dick, Mandi Johnson, and W. Todd Groce facilitated several visits to the Georgia Historical Society in Savannah. There is a wealth of personal mementos in the Lafayette McLaws Collection #2087, including the cocoa nut dipper that

McLaws received from his officers on the Peninsula, some of his pistols, his saber, and a large pair of spurs.

Helen Lila Talley, Elizabeth W. Knowlton, Gail Miller DeLoach, and Andy Phrydas—all members of the Georgia Department of Archives and History in Atlanta—provided access to the McLaws files. David Baskin at the Texas State Archives and Library in Austin was helpful in obtaining interlibrary loans. Pen Bogert and Rebecca Rice provided information on the Taylor and Edwards families from The Filson Club's collections in Louisville. Heather A. Whitacre was also helpful in checking the Museum of the Confederacy's photographic collection.

Bill Kirby of the *Augusta Chronicle,* Erick Montgomery of Historic Augusta, Augusta historians Michael White and Ed Cashin, and Doris Parks, secretary of the Richmond County Board of Education, helped with research in Augusta and Richmond County, Georgia.

Dorothy Pourteau, my mother-in-law, introduced me to genealogical research and provided valuable advice. One of the most enlightening series of conversations was with Uldrick Huguenin McLaws III, who did not know how his grandfather received his name until he read the letters. Barry McLaws provided early genealogical information. Julius Huguenin, Kimberly Anne Shaw, Karen Querna, and Donna McLaws Grupp added significant and timely details to the McLaws family history. Donna, a direct descendant of Uldrick Huguenin McLaws, helped me locate additional family information and introduced me to her relatives. Kimberly and Karen are direct descendants of Abram Huguenin McLaws, Lafayette's younger brother.

David Perry, Mark Simpson-Vos, Pamela Upton, Kathleen Ketterman, and the other members of the University of North Carolina Press staff have been terrific to work with. It has been a refreshing experience to work with Mark, who always found the time to answer a new author's questions in a timely manner. Both Pam and Kathleen have always been ready and willing to provide their expertise and improvement ideas. Everyone was responsive and helped move the process along to completion. Their patience in working through the early versions helped tighten the final work. An important contribution was made by another Press reader who remains anonymous. The reader provided valued and thoughtful remarks that refined my thinking and enhanced the work. Stevie Champion proved that patience and editorial skill are all any author could ever wish for in an editor.

I owe my greatest debt to my wife Kathryn and son Clayton. Kathryn read multiple versions of the manuscript and collaborated in this work—just as she has done in our twenty-six years together. She helped think through the salient points of McLaws and his family's personality that added new dimensions to his biographical sketch. Kathryn's continued encouragement, keen insight, and computer illustration and image enhancement skills ensured the completion of the work. Clayton sacrificed many evenings and weekends for this project, yet we both gained a new discussion topic and together learned more about the war that tore the United States apart. Any errors or omissions in this book are entirely mine, as this group of family, friends, and colleagues did more than was expected.

Austin, Texas JCO
August 2001

Editor's Note

In the 1930s Virginia McLaws, a daughter of Lafayette and Emily McLaws, left her father's papers to the Southern Historical Collection of the University of North Carolina at Chapel Hill. Although readers can easily view this largely untapped source, it might take some time to adjust to McLaws's penmanship. This collection contains more than four hundred items amounting to 1.5 linear feet. Despite this wealth of handwritten material, as well as the McLaws papers at Duke University in Durham and the collection maintained by the Georgia Historical Society in Savannah, there are no published biographies of McLaws or histories of his division. In effect, the public has all but forgotten one of the earliest major general's appointed in the Army of Northern Virginia.

My goal in preparing *A Soldier's General* was to transcribe from the Chapel Hill collection, as accurately as possible, the ninety-five letters written to family members between 1858 and 1865. McLaws wrote five of these letters as a young officer in the U.S. Seventh Infantry when he was posted to the Utah and New Mexico Territories before the Civil War. He composed the remaining ninety letters between April 1861 and May 1865. In addition, this work contains thirteen extracts from letters found in volume 1 of McLaws's Letter Book, 1858–64—identified as "[LB1]" at the top of the letter. Virginia McLaws was most likely the editor of these transcriptions, which retain a fair amount of military information and summarize family issues. Finally, the book contains twenty-seven journal entries penned by the general between February 23 and March 30, 1865, from volume 2 of McLaws's Order Book, 1865—identified as "[OB2]" at the top of the entry.

The entries are rich in personal observations and McLaws's view of the Carolinas campaign leading up to the Battle of Bentonville. The result is a literal translation that is as close as possible to the original letter or entry.

McLaws was a prolific writer. The reader will find references to many letters, including those he received from his wife and other relatives, that are not among his papers in the collections at Chapel Hill, Durham, or Savannah. Family members may have kept, lost, or misplaced the letters since they do not appear in other repositories.

McLaws actively sought promotion in the early years of the war. He also exhibited a fierce determination to do his duty and ensure the welfare of his men. Dedication and concern changed to "wishing" to leave the army "if it would not disgrace his family" in the last years of the conflict.

Emily McLaws relocated the family four times and completed three lengthy trips between 1861 and 1865. In their correspondence she and her husband frequently discussed the lack of a permanent home. Because of his U.S. Army assignments in the Utah and New Mexico Territories, Lafayette McLaws spent little time with his children before 1861. The residual effect was a constant longing to help personally rear their two sons and daughter instead of passing on his standards of conduct and family values through letters. All of these elements combine to inform and entertain the general reader while they are of practical value to the historian.

I have attempted to provide a volume that is easier to read than the original material yet does not detract from its substance or flavor. Each letter or entry retains McLaws's heading style, except that all headings—and signatures—appear flush with the right margin. An editorial note in brackets identifies the day of the week and McLaws's location if it was not readily apparent. Each heading is located in the top right corner of the letter or entry.

Lafayette McLaws embedded a subtle affectation in his formal signature. Historians have generally read the signature as "L M Laws" without recognizing the difference between the two capital *Ls*. McLaws always inserted a small curling *c* as he signed the *L* in Laws. This slight curling superscript *c* is barely discernible in many instances. However, it is distinct in numerous other examples such as the letter to Emily on October 3, 1861, announcing his promotion to brigadier general.

McLaws also found little need for consistently indenting paragraphs, whereas for simplicity I have regularized paragraph indentations. He often ended sentences with commas, dashes, or periods combined with dashes or commas, generally with a space after the last word and before the final punctuation mark, or he used no punctuation at all. I retained the periods and dashes (treating all dashes as em-dashes [—]) without the extra space on either side, but changed commas to periods at the end of sentences.

McLaws used capital letters indiscriminately. He had a propensity to use a capital *S*, especially at the end of a word. He also routinely capitalized *C* and *M*. In some cases, it was difficult to distinguish between a capital and lowercased letter. McLaws's capitalization within a sentence has been retained if it does not detract from the content of the letter or entry, but for readability, all new sentences now begin with a capital letter.

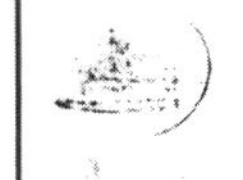

Head Quarters Division
November 22nd 1862

My dear Sweetheart

You will perhaps be astonished in seeing my address Fredericksburg Va. My Division was moved in advance from Culpepper C. H. and after a rather disagreeable march arrived here on the morning of the third day, and found that the opposite side of the river, the Rappahannock was lined with the camps of the enemy.

They had well calculated on our humanity; for their batteries were planted immediately above the town on an eminence which enabled them to command it. Their trains were ostentatiously moving under our guns, their batteries manouvered within easy reach of our shot, their troops strutted along the opposite bank, some with arms and some without. Everything was done as it were to provoke a fire from our side, they even fired upon the trains coming in & going out. But we did not return a shot, did not fire upon their trains, their troops, or their numerous Cavalry. For we all divined that this ostentatious display was made in order to

Example of Lafayette McLaws's penmanship on a good day.
(Courtesy of the Southern Historical Collection, University of North Carolina at Chapel Hill)

The general employed an extensive vocabulary, including a few Spanish words, sometimes bordering on the romantic. He combined a fair understanding of grammar and punctuation to make the letters comprehensible as well as interesting. His original spelling has been retained without the use of [*sic*] to reference misspelled words. For instance, McLaws consistently

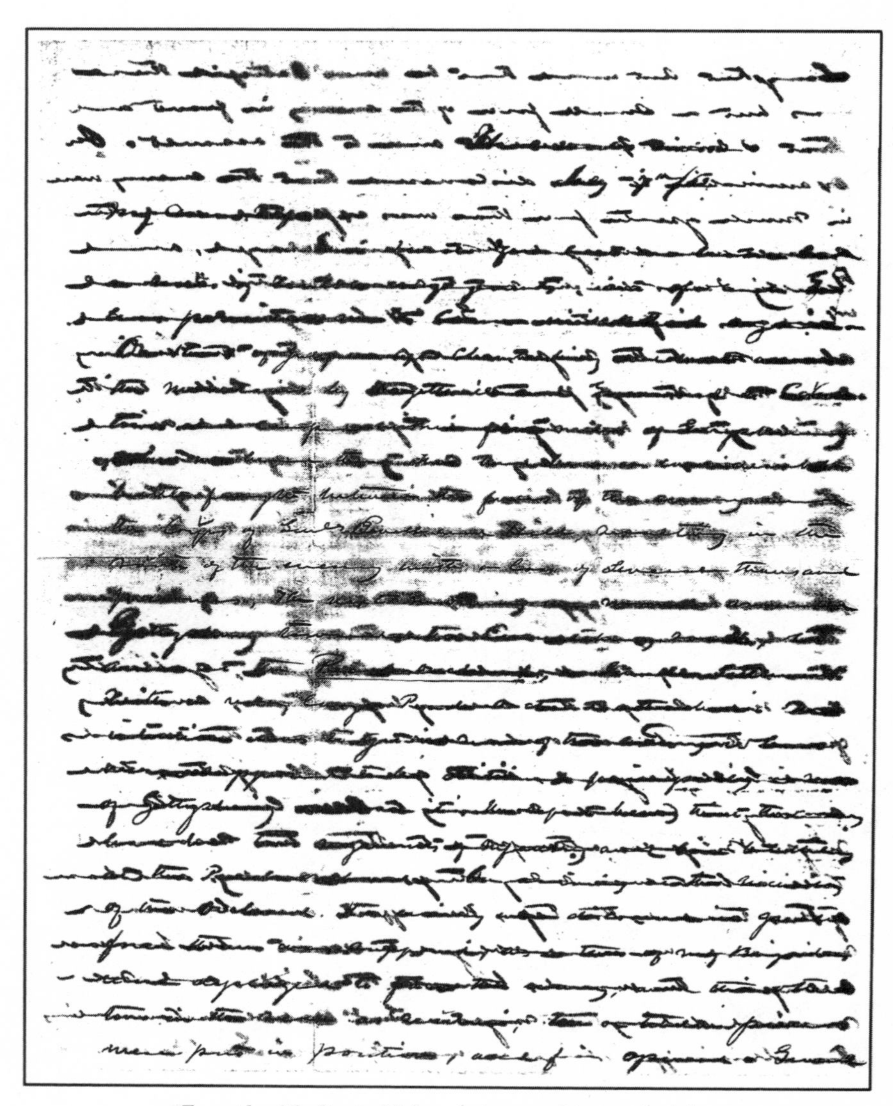

Example of Lafayette McLaws's penmanship on a bad day.
(Courtesy of the Southern Historical Collection, University of North Carolina at Chapel Hill)

misspelled Fredericksburg, as Fredricksburg, which is surprising given his role and performance in that battle. He also used abbreviations, especially in his journal. Terms like "infy" for infantry or "arty" for artillery appear in their original form. To avoid confusion, however, extraneous punctuation marks, letters, and double words (e.g., they they) have been deleted, and words that run together in the original have been separated.

The letters and journal entries illustrate the ideas, opinions, reflections, and soul-searching of Lafayette McLaws. They are a testament to his and his daughter Virginia's attention to archiving old records and add significant dimensions to the general's personality and life. The introduction, which incorporates the new primary research, is intended to provide a more complete understanding of McLaws and his family and to be a useful reference in reading the letters.

Thousands of books and articles refight the battles and assess the personalities of the Civil War. The footnotes in this volume offer practical information as background to the written material. For example, they briefly identify all but a handful of the individuals referenced in the McLaws letters—including an officer's complete name and home state, his class at the U.S. Military Academy or college attended, rank at the time, and final rank.

Readers interested in learning more about the ranking officers should consult Ezra J. Warner's *Generals in Gray: Lives of the Confederate Commanders* (Baton Rouge: Louisiana State University Press, 1959) and *Generals in Blue: Lives of the Union Commanders* (Baton Rouge: Louisiana State University Press, 1964). Joseph H. Crute Jr.'s *Units of the Confederate States Army* (Gaithersburg, Md.: Old Soldier Books, Inc., 1987) presents a useful account of regimental organization, deployment, and engagements. Robert K. Krick's *Lee's Colonels* (Dayton, Ohio: Morningside House, Inc., 1992) is an excellent biographical source of the field officers in the Army of Northern Virginia.

Historical Times Illustrated's Encyclopedia of the Civil War, edited by Patricia L. Faust (New York: Harper and Row, 1986), is a valuable compilation of battles, locations, people, resources, and terms. Jeffry D. Wert's *General James Longstreet: The Confederacy's Most Controversial Soldier* (New York: Simon and Schuster, 1993), is the most current and complete of the Longstreet biographies. Another important reference on the Army of Northern Virginia is *Fighting for the Confederacy: The Personal Recollections of General Edward Porter Alexander,* edited by Gary W. Gallagher (Chapel Hill: University of North Carolina Press, 1989).

As shown in the examples provided, McLaws obviously had good and bad days when he wrote the letters or journal entries. Readers interested in viewing the originals should schedule a trip to Chapel Hill, for there is nothing quite like seeing the real, handwritten letters. Yet even from a distance—in their typewritten and partially edited form—they remain informative, entertaining, and thought provoking.

Abbreviations

DAR
Daughters of the American Revolution

Duke-LM
Duke University, Durham, Lafayette McLaws Papers #3417

E.D.
Enumeration District, U.S. Census

ETM
Emily Taylor McLaws

GHS-LM
Georgia Historical Society, Savannah, Lafayette McLaws Papers #2087

GHS-VM Taylor Children
Georgia Historical Society, Savannah, Virginia McLaws, "Children of John Gibson Taylor and Elizabeth Lee Taylor"

GHS-VM ETM
Georgia Historical Society, Savannah, Virginia McLaws, "Emily Allison Taylor McLaws"

GHS-VM LM Sketch
Georgia Historical Society, Savannah, Virginia McLaws, "A Sketch of the Life of General Lafayette McLaws"

LB1
Lafayette McLaws Letter Book, 1858–64, vol. 1, SHC-LM

LM
Lafayette McLaws

NARA
National Archives and Records Administration

OB2
Lafayette McLaws Order Book, 1865, vol. 2, SHC-LM

OR
U.S. War Department, *The War of the Rebellion: A Compilation of the Official Records of the Union and Confederate Armies.* 128 vols. Washington, D.C.: Government Printing Office, 1880–1901. *OR* citations take the following form: volume number (part number, where applicable): page number. All volumes cited throughout footnotes are from series 1.

SHC
Southern Historical Collection, University of North Carolina at Chapel Hill

SHC-LM
SHC, Lafayette McLaws Papers #472

USMA
U.S. Military Academy, West Point

Introduction

Major General Lafayette McLaws, the lead division commander in Lieutenant General James Longstreet's First Corps of the Army of Northern Virginia, contemplated his division's most recent engagement as he prepared to write home on the evening of July 7, 1863. Torrential rain, the roads deep in mud, and thoughts of fellow soldiers left behind on Pennsylvania fields marked the long three-day march from Gettysburg. The men, weary from the thirty-five-day campaign into Pennsylvania and the intense fighting that took place on July 2, were in good spirits. These Georgians, South Carolinians, and Mississippians were hardy souls. The cowards and drifters had long since left their ranks. The true believers remained with the division, hardened by long marches with little food to keep them moving. They had just erected a series of breastworks outside of Hagerstown, Maryland, and waited for Major General George Gordon Meade, commander of the Union Army of the Potomac, to make his attack. Robert Edward Lee, the Confederate commanding general, would not have hesitated to aggressively attack Meade. Instead, the division led by the forty-two-year-old McLaws regrouped and waited behind their defensive positions. The men waited for the waters of the raging Potomac to recede enough for them to cross the pontoon bridge into Virginia and safety. They would continue to wage war with a determined spirit, long for a lasting victory and an end to the bloodshed.

July 2, 1863, the second day of battle on the ground in and around the crossroads town of Gettysburg, was one of the most important military engagements of Lafayette McLaws's twenty-three-year military career. The young general from Georgia was not allowed to wage battle in the manner he believed necessary to win. The division, comprised of four brigades, advanced under Longstreet's orders in a piecemeal manner. It crossed the Emmitsburg Road beginning at 4:00 P.M. on that hot, dusty day led by four civilian prewar brigade commanders. The 6,924 men pushed the opposing Federal units back through the Peach Orchard, Rose Farm, and the Wheatfield. "The result of the day's fighting showed us that we had driven the enemy back to their main line, the right of which was Cemetery Hill and the left Round Top, and that was all we did." The men, "had driven the forces opposed to them, from their positions, and occupied the grounds and held them unt[i]l withdrawn by order." The conduct of their corps commander, James Longstreet, not their lack of courage or aggressiveness, determined the outcome. It was Longstreet's ineffective coordination and the disjointed manner in which he committed the four brigades that led to the afternoon's incomplete results.[1]

McLaws tallied the loss to his division and the Confederacy as one brigade commander killed (William Barksdale), another mortally wounded (Paul Jones Semmes), and a long list of irreplaceable colonels, majors, captains, and soldiers. "The loss in my division was near twenty four hundred, the heaviest of the war, and many of the most valuable officers in the whole service have been killed."[2]

McLaws began to mentally question the command skills of Longstreet, a boyhood friend and West Point classmate, in a letter to his beloved wife Emily:

> My dear wife, Since I wrote you last we have had a series of terrible engagements out of which God has permitted me to come unscathed again. . . . I think the attack was unnecessary and the whole plan of battle a very bad one. Genl Longstreet is to blame for not reconnoitering the ground and for persisting in ordering the assault when his errors were discovered. During the engagement he was very excited giving contrary orders to every one, and was exceedingly overbearing. I consider him a humbug, a man of small capacity, very obstinate, not at all chivalrous, exceedingly conceited, and totally selfish. If I can it is my intention to get away from his command. We want Beuregard very much indeed, his presence is imperatively called for.[3]

This 138-year-old letter is arguably the most celebrated McLaws passage cited in American Civil War literature. Lafayette McLaws never expected other individuals, much less people in the early twenty-first century, to read his most private thoughts. In the 1930s his daughter Virginia donated the largest group of his papers to the Southern Historical Collection at the Uni-

1. Busey and Martin, *Regimental Strengths,* 130; LM, *Battle of Gettysburg,* 81, 94.

2. LM to ETM, July 7, 1863, SHC-LM. The loss in LM's division was actualty 2,217 or a 32 percent casualty rate. Hood's division, the other division from Longstreet's corps engaged at Gettysburg on July 2, reported the same rate of casualties. Busey and Martin, *Regimental Strengths,* 307.

3. LM was referring to General Pierre Gustave Toutant Beauregard, Louisiana, USMA 1838.

versity of North Carolina at Chapel Hill. These papers contain a sizable amount of unpublished primary material—except for a few quotations that pointedly describe Longstreet.

McLaws's letters to Emily and other family members, his written communications to leading figures in the Confederate army, and his Order and Letter Book entries provide new insight into the all-but-forgotten general. Apart from William Dorsey Pender, no other major general reporting to Robert E. Lee left a comparable unpublished legacy. McLaws's atrocious penmanship is the most significant reason these letters and their associated papers have never been widely circulated. Robert K. Krick tells us that the former Confederate general "spent the later years of his life writing and speaking copiously on war topics, but little of that production reached print." According to Krick, "The enormous volume of surviving manuscripts by McLaws represents perhaps the most extensive unused body of material on any Confederate major general, but his execrable handwriting renders that splendid mass of documentation difficult to retrieve." This body of surviving wartime records is clearly an important untapped resource in understanding major elements of the Confederate States Army—its battles, troops, and leaders.[4]

Now we can all share in his insights, thoughts, and struggles as McLaws wrote home about the savage war. In the final analysis, the men who served under Lafayette McLaws began to shape how history would view their commander. His engraved tombstone in Savannah's Laurel Grove Cemetery reads, "He knew when to lead us in, and he always brought us out." His troops knew him for what he was—*a soldier's general.*

Family and Early Life in Augusta, Georgia, 1821–1837

Alexander McLaws and his family were returning to Scotland from Santo Domingo when a storm wrecked their ship off the coast of Georgia, near Darien, in 1783. "After this unfortunate experience, he decided to settle in America, so Augusta was selected as their home as it was far away from the sea."[5] In 1790 Alexander's wife Janet gave birth to their youngest son, James.

James McLaws married Elizabeth Huguenin on January 24, 1815. Eliza-

4. Krick, "Lafayette McLaws," 4:131.

5. These words are inscribed on Alexander McLaws's gravestone, located near the front entrance of St. Paul's Church, Augusta; he died on April 23, 1810. Janet McLaws was born in Scotland and died about 1828 at age eighty-one. Augusta Genealogical Society, *Summerville Cemetery,* 52.

beth, the daughter of David and Elizabeth Huguenin, grew up in St. Luke's Parish, South Carolina. Virginia McLaws noted that "the Huguenins were French Huguenots who came to South Carolina from one of the West Indies islands where they owned family plantations." Elizabeth's brother, Captain Abram Huguenin, lived on the family's original plantation, "Roseland." Union major Henry Orlando Marcy described Roseland as "one of the most lovely spots he had ever seen, pen would fail to do it justice." He recorded in his diary that the plantation was located "near the Coosawatchie R [River] situated on high ground, in a splendid grove of live oaks of a centuries growth. Outhouses and all at a distance bear the look of a county village. Every outhouse was nicely whitewashed. The grounds were beautifully laid and splendidly kept. The mansion was huge and eloquently furnished."[6]

James McLaws began working as a cotton factor and moved into county politics six years later. Augusta was a rapidly growing city and the political environment changed quickly between 1817 and 1821. The citizens of Augusta sent James to the city council, where he represented the middle ward of Augusta on April 9, 1821. On January 10, 1822, the voters elected him to the newly established post of superior and inferior court clerk of Richmond County, a position he held through fifteen successive elections spanning thirty years.[7]

The political world opened up investment opportunities for James. In 1833 he helped organize the railroad from Augusta to Athens, which became the original segment of the famed Georgia Railroad. He also developed lasting political and family friendships. The future governor of the Territory of Florida, Robert Raymond Reid, mused that "among his first friends in Augusta was James McLaws, always my friend, and afterward my brother-in-law." Reid resigned his position as judge of the superior court to become district judge for eastern Florida in 1832.[8]

Elizabeth gave birth to Anna Laura, the McLaws's first child, on October 29, 1816, and to William Raymond on November 20, 1818. The couple's third child, Lafayette, was born in Augusta on January 15, 1821. Abram Huguenin, the youngest surviving child, followed on April 13, 1823. A fifth child, Janet, was born on June 15, 1826. Elizabeth died on October 8, 1848. James lived two more years; at his death on November 20, 1850 at age sixty,

6. GHS-VM LM Sketch, 1; Marcy Diary, New York.

7. For the description of changes, see Jones, *Memorial History,* 169–70; Announcement, "Slate for Councilman Election" (March 14, 1822, 3), and Election Announcement (April 18, 1822, 3), *Augusta Daily Chronicle.*

8. Jones, *Memorial History,* 229 (Reid), 170; GHS-VM LM Sketch, 1.

he was the oldest native citizen of Augusta. Their children buried James and Elizabeth McLaws in Augusta's Summerville Cemetery.[9]

Anna Laura became a scholar and never married. An avid reader, she appeared to inject the intellectual or thought-provoking questions into family discussions. Family papers indicate that she may have had an affectionate relationship with Henry Clay. Anna Laura also provided Lafayette encouragement and support, especially during and after his court-martial in 1864. She frequently wrote to her brother and joined him in Savannah in the fall of 1864. After her death on July 17, 1894, she was buried near her parents in Summerville Cemetery.[10]

William R. and Lafayette were the closest in age and attended the University of Virginia together for a year. Lafayette then moved on to the U.S. Military Academy at West Point and pursued a military career. William R. opened the political doors for his younger brother. Following his father's example, he began his career as a delegate to the June 1843 Democratic state convention. Between 1855 and 1859 he was the attorney general of Georgia. The 1872 Augusta City Directory lists William R. in a law practice with Joseph Ganahl Jr., the surgeon of the 10th Georgia Infantry and an attorney, who served as Lafayette's defense counsel at his court-martial. After the war he became a judge.[11]

On November 20, 1853, William R. married Mary Ann Boggs, who had previously moved from Monmouth County, New Jersey, to teach the Huguenin children at Roseland. The couple had three children, William Raymond McLaws Jr. (1859), Meta Telfair (July 3, 1855), and Lillie Huguenin "Bet" (1860). Mary Ann died in Augusta on December 1, 1872, and William R. in Clarkesville, Georgia, on August 29, 1880.[12]

James and Elizabeth named their third child for Marie Joseph Motier Marquis de Lafayette, the famed French general of the American Revolution. McLaws intensely disliked his name, pronounced LaFet in Georgia, preferring family names instead. In 1825 the marquis returned to the United

9. Birth Registry, Augusta: James and Elizabeth McLaws (no additional information has been found on Janet, who may have died at birth); James McLaws obituary, November 26, 1850, *Augusta Daily Chronicle.*

10. GHS-VM LM Sketch, 1; Augusta Genealogical Society, *Summerville Cemetery,* 52.

11. Georgia Attorney General's Office, *Attorneys General of Georgia,* entry for William R. McLaws, 1855–59; Haddock, *Haddock's Augusta,* entry for William R. McLaws.

12. Evans, *Baldwin County,* 45; Jones, *Memorial History,* 246; Edward J. Thomas, *Memoirs;* Burial Records for Magnolia Cemetery, Augusta: Mary Ann and William Raymond McLaws.

States as an invited guest of the U.S. Congress. "On the ocean voyage he sailed on the same vessel with Mr. King [John Pendleton King], and during the journey became intimately acquainted and a lasting friendship was formed." King succeeded Robert Reid as judge of the superior court of Richmond County. The Marquis de Lafayette visited Boston, New York, and Washington, then traveled to Augusta in the fall of 1825. "Here he was entertained by Mr. King, who accompanied him throughout the city, where he received the highest honors." Virginia McLaws wrote that the French general noticed her father "and took the young Lafayette on his knee."[13]

McLaws was able to "write when he was four years of age." Family records indicate that "as a small boy he wrote on the walls or his books, 'Gen. Lafayette McLaws,' not realizing that he would one day become a general." The practice of scribbling in books continued with his grandchildren. Numerous pages scattered throughout the SHC-LM collection contain a young child's scribbled marks.[14]

Abram Huguenin McLaws attended Georgetown and William and Mary Colleges before becoming a member of the bar. The family's businessman, he was elected lieutenant of the Richmond Blues, fought with the Georgia regiment, and was wounded in the War with Mexico. After the war he returned to Augusta and married Sarah Twiggs Porter on November 2, 1848. They lived in Sand Hills, just outside Augusta, and raised nine children: Mannie E. (1854), Sarah "Sallie" Telfair (1856), James P. (1857), Anna Laura (1859), Emily Lafayette (1863), Huguenin G. (1867), Evanline W. (1871), Adam (1872), and Raymond B. (1874). County records indicate that there may have been two other boys who died in childbirth. Hu McLaws joined his brother's staff as division quartermaster in 1862.[15]

Hu variously ran a plantation, worked as a geologist, and served as the second superintendent of Richmond County's school district, where he led efforts to build schools to meet black Augustans' needs. In the final years of his life he was a newspaper editor. Among the children of Hu and Sarah, James graduated from the University of Georgia, and in 1880 the U.S. Engineer Corps appointed him engineer in charge of a survey of the Savan-

13. Jones, *Memorial History,* part II, 31–32; GHS-VM LM Sketch, 1–2.

14. GHS-VM LM Sketch, 1–2.

15. Abram Huguenin McLaws obituary, *Savannah Morning News,* October 13, 1901; Seventh Census, 1850, Division 73, Richmond County, Ga., NARA M 432, RG 29; Eighth Census, 1860, Octavia, Early County, Ga., NARA M 653, RG 29. Hu McLaws was the assistant marshal responsible for taking the census in this enumeration district.

nah River between Augusta and Savannah. Their most notable child, Emily Lafayette McLaws, lived with Varina Howell Davis, Jefferson Davis's second wife, in New York City after her parents died. Emily Lafayette published five fictional books with Civil War themes, taking her uncle's name as a pseudonym. She died on February 21, 1944, at the age of eighty-one. Huguenin G. died at Emily Lafayette's home on November 20, 1933. Evanline taught grammar school in Richmond County and died in 1937. Raymond became a physician and lived until March 4, 1961.[16]

Young Lafayette McLaws attended Augusta's Richmond Academy. Charles C. Jones observed: "one of the oldest schools of its kind dating to 1785, it was the oldest seat of learning in the United States with the exception of Yale, Harvard, and Princeton." The curriculum included "Latin, Greek, French, German and English languages, a thorough mathematical course from arithmetic to calculus, a popular course of natural philosophy, theoretical and analytical chemistry, astronomy, geology and also a course of physiology and hygiene. The highest rate of tuition was ten dollars per quarter." James Longstreet, the nephew of prominent Georgia educator Augustas Longstreet, attended the academy at the same time as McLaws. McLaws also studied at the Georgia Male Academy, run by an ex-army officer and West Point graduate Thomas S. Twiss.[17]

The College Years, 1837–1842

When McLaws was sixteen, John P. King, who had advanced from the superior court of Richmond County to the U.S. Senate, recommended that the youth be appointed to the U.S. Military Academy. The academy deferred the 1838 appointment until it could fill the next vacancy from Georgia. As

16. Compiled Service Records of Confederate Generals and Staff Officers and Nonregimental Enlisted Men: A. H. McLaws, NARA M 331, RG 109; Richmond County Board of Education Minutes, January 11, March 15, 1873; 1880 Census, 119th District, E.D. 105, p. 18, Richmond County, Ga.; 1900 Census, Village of Summerville, vol. 59, E.D. 49, sheet 18, Richmond County, Ga.; Leonard, *Woman's Who's Who,* 527; Emily Lafayette McLaws obituary, *Tampa Tribune,* February 23, 1944; Huguenin G. McLaws obituary, *Tampa Tribune,* November 21, 1933; E. W. McLaws date of death, Georgia Deaths, February 19, 1937; Raymond B. McLaws date of death, Georgia Deaths, March 4, 1961.

17. Jones, *Memorial History,* 157; GHS-VM LM Sketch, 2; West Point Alumni Foundation, *Register of Graduates,* 222.

a result, Lafayette completed his first year of college at Thomas Jefferson's Academical Village, University of Virginia, in 1837.[18]

McLaws entered West Point on July 1, 1838. The seventeen-year-old cadet's classmates included future Civil War generals James Longstreet, Gustavus Woodson Smith, Daniel Harvey Hill, Earl Van Dorn, Abner Doubleday, John Pope, and William Starke Rosecrans. Another member of the class of 1842, James Monroe Goggin of Virginia, left the academy before graduation to fight in the Texas revolution. He later became McLaws's adjutant general. McLaws described Smith as one who "is most decidedly a reserved man on all military matters—although away from that topic he is as free as a boy, he is a classmate of mine, and has always been distinguished for his talents and sound judgment." McLaws continued to correspond and discuss the "interior workings in Bragg's Army" with G. W. Smith as late as 1893.[19]

McLaws's first year at West Point was his best at the academy. Out of 85 fourth-class students, he ranked thirty-fourth in math and twenty-fourth in French. He kept his demerits down to thirty-eight for the year, which ranked him ninety-first out of 231 cadets, and did not earn any demerits in December 1838.[20]

The second (third-class) year proved to be more difficult. McLaws ended with a rank of fifty-seventh out of seventy-six cadets. He was fifty-first in math, thirty-ninth in French, a dismal sixty-ninth in drawing, and sixty-fourth in English grammar. His demerits nearly doubled to seventy, ranking him 166th out of the 233 cadets at the academy in 1840.[21]

His third (second-class) year continued the trend, as he finished fiftieth in a class of sixty cadets. He earned rankings of thirty-seventh in philosophy, fifty-first in chemistry, and fifty-fourth in drawing. McLaws rated 176th out of 219 cadets as his annual demerit total increased to ninety-eight. He averaged a few demerits per month except for three specific months. In August he "was caught without crepe on his arm," in January he "was absent from

18. GHS-VM LM Sketch, 2; LM entry for 1837, 27, and 1838, 45, NARA M 2037, RG 94.

19. Gustavas Woodson Smith, Kentucky, USMA 1842, cadet and later Confederate major general. LM to ETM, April 25, 1862, SHC-LM (first quotation); G. W. "Trumps" Smith to L.M. "Snygss," May 24, 1893, SHC-LM (second quotation).

20. USMA, Merit and Conduct Rolls, NARA M 2037, RG 94: LM entry, Fourth Class, June 1839.

21. Ibid.: LM entry, Third Class, June 1840.

quarters," and in July he was written up for "allowing smoking." All three reports earned McLaws an extra tour of guard duty on Saturdays.[22]

The first-class cadet ranked forty-third in engineering, thirty-ninth in ethics, fiftieth in tactics, fiftieth in artillery, and forty-third in mineralogy. His demerits continued to escalate until McLaws earned 147 for the year, a lackluster performance that ranked him 178th out of 207. In January he received demerits "for visiting after taps," earning him two more tours of Saturday guard duty. Cadet McLaws accumulated 353 demerits before graduation. The academy's Conduct Roll noted "but three in his class of fifty-eight members, worse in conduct." In an interesting twist, McLaws outranked Longstreet in ethics by sixteen positions. These rankings were somewhat reversed in infantry tactics, where Longstreet ranked fortieth and McLaws fiftieth—neither turning in stellar academic performances. McLaws graduated forty-eighth in his class of fifty-six.[23]

Early Life in the U.S. Army and the War with Mexico, 1842–1848

Before the War with Mexico the U.S. Army deployed its forces in regimental posts across the frontier. By General Order No. 44 Lafayette McLaws received his commission as a brevet second lieutenant on July 21, 1842 and joined Company I of the 6th U.S. Infantry at Fort Gibson, located in the Cherokee part of the Indian Territory, on October 11. The fort, established in 1824, was designed to house five companies and sat 150 yards from the river. Rectangular in design, the two sides running north to south were 318 feet in length and held the barracks and stores. The longer east-west sides measured 348 feet. As a result of this close proximity to the river, poor quality of the water, and exposure to the miasmas of the river valley, Fort Gibson was considered one of the unhealthiest posts in the army. McLaws endured it through early July 1844, having transferred through four different companies. According to 6th Infantry returns, he had reported sick for three of his twenty-one months on the post.[24]

General Order No. 33 promoted the young officer to second lieutenant and transferred him to the Baton Rouge Barracks on July 8, 1844. The

22. Ibid.: LM entry, Second Class, June 1841.

23. Ibid.: LM entry, First Class, June 1842.

24. Bauer, *Zachary Taylor,* 99; Regimental Returns, 6th U.S. Infantry, August 1842–July 1844, NARA M 665, RG 391.

engineers had placed the garrison on rich, fertile land nestled among numerous plantations whose owners grew crops such as sugar and cotton and raised cattle. More importantly, the fort was located on the first level plain of high ground overlooking the Mississippi River north of New Orleans. It contained two ranges of officers' quarters and two barracks, both 180 feet long and 36 wide. The buildings were two stories high, included a piazza on one side, and housed eight companies of men. During a posting to the fort General Zachary Taylor complained about "the lack of a wall around the installations," which "permitted soldiers to mingle with the local inhabitants to the detriment of health and morals."[25]

McLaws joined Company D of the 7th Infantry and took temporary command of the unit on September 5. Over a four-month period the new second lieutenant accepted, then relinquished temporary command, and during his posting to the barracks he reported sick four of the nine months. This included a sixty-day leave of absence with permission to apply for an extension based on a surgeon's certificate of ill health. Widespread disease was common to forts located next to rivers, and during McLaws's tenture the Baton Rouge Barracks overlooking the Mississippi River was no exception. There the outbreak of infectious diseases was so rampant that a special military board was created to define precautionary measures needed to prevent exposure. McLaws had his first direct involvement in a court-martial in June 1845, when the army tried Captain Richard H. Ross, the commanding officer of Company D, for being absent without leave. McLaws and the other three company officers appeared as witnesses.[26]

In preparation for the War with Mexico, the 7th Infantry relocated to Fort Pickens, Florida, in July 1845, then left Florida by ship on September 17. Zachary Taylor, the commanding general of the Army of Occupation, had established the base camp on August 15. The site was located on a small, flat plain on the southern side of the mouth of the Nueces River known as "Kinney's Ranch." Colonel Henry L. Kinney had established the trading post in 1838, and by 1845 "the ranch had grown into a rambling collection of twenty to thirty houses whose inhabitants made their living largely by engaging in that most peculiar of trades common to many parts of the Gulf of

25. Bauer, *Zachary Taylor,* 42.

26. Major General Edmund P. Gaines, Division Order No. 6, Western Division, Special Orders, 7th U.S. Infantry, p. 103, and S. Cooper, vol. 1, Special Orders No. 27, p. 129, NARA M 665, RG 391; Regimental Returns, 7th U.S. Infantry, July 1844–June 1845, NARA M 665, RG 391.

Mexico—smuggling." After a ten-day voyage across the Gulf of Mexico, the 7th Infantry arrived at the camp on September 26.[27]

One of the principal advantages of Taylor's choice was the large, level plain located within a quarter of a mile of Kinney's Ranch. After the American soldiers cleared the field of scrub brush, Taylor used the natural sand surface as the perfect drill field that could accommodate large contingents of troops at the same time. The plain was ideal for unit drills, parades, inspections, and reviews. Based on the army's prewar garrison strategy, only a limited number of field grade officers had commanded battalion size or larger units on the drill field. Colonels and majors thus needed the drill experience as much as the captains, lieutenants, and enlisted men. The parade ground made an excellent field for constant drill and training. "A camp where there is not active service is a dull and stupid place," Lieutenant George Gordon Meade wrote his wife Margaretta on November 3. "Nothing but drill and parades, and your ears are filled all day with drumming and fifeing."[28]

The young men also needed outlets to expend their energy and natural curiosity beyond the army's requirements of drill and instruction. West Point classmate Lieutenant Napoleon Jackson Tecumseh Dana wrote, "about every week now an expedition of some kind or other is fitted out, and many of them volunteer and get permission to go along. Day before yesterday [November 4, 1845] one left for San Antonio de Bexar, that paradise of Texas. . . . Many officers went along for pleasure. Among other inducements for the young officers is that San Antonio is said to have pretty girls." Virginia McLaws related that on November 29 her father "joined a party of officers on a buffalo and deer hunt through as far as San Antonio and in what was then considered Comanche country. McLaws horse, a mustang which was recently caught, fell upon him after swimming the Nueces River and 'badly mashed' his foot. This confined him to bed for over six weeks."[29]

The lieutenant's luck did not improve with the arrival of the new year. Lieutenant Samuel Gibbs French, another friend, recounted the beginning of McLaws's return to Corpus Christi at San Pedro Springs, the source of

27. Regimental Returns, 7th U.S. Infantry, July–September 1845, NARA M 665, RG 391.

28. Meade, *Life and Letters,* 1:35.

29. Ferrell, *Monterrey,* 31 (Dana); Regimental Returns, 7th U.S. Infantry,, October–December 1845, NARA M 665, RG 391; LM Certificate of Disability, January 9, 1846, NARA M 567, RG 94, office mark M-30; GHS-VM LM Sketch, 2–3.

the San Antonio River. The majority of the returning officers had arrived and were marking time until the next wagon train's departure. Lieutenant William Logan Crittenden decided that a little target practice was in order. He "got up and took from his pocket what was called a pepper box pistol and fired at a tree in a line parallel to the road. Just at that time Lieut. Lafayette McLaws left the train to come where we were, and shouted: 'Quit firing, I am shot.' As he was not in range, no one regarded what he said, and Crittenden kept firing the revolver." French observed that McLaws had a "wild look" when he rode up to the officers, his shirt red with blood. Two of the bullets fired by Crittenden had ricocheted off the tree and hit McLaws as he arrived on the scene. "There was the hole where the bullet entered the breast, and he was spitting blood; and no surgeon being present he was put back in the wagon to be taken back to San Antonio." McLaws believed that his days were numbered and told French that his "whole chest is filled with blood, and I can feel the blood shaking inside as though I were filled with water." The surgeon found that one ball had hit his index finger and another lodged near his spine. The blood McLaws was "spitting up" actually came from his finger since he periodically put his fingers in his mouth. The other wound was more serious, "as the wound was probed by a surgeon and the ball discovered near the spine. It was a glancing shot that pressing against the skin followed the line of least resistance until arrested by the spine." The surgeon did not extract the ball lodged next to the spine.[30]

Meanwhile, Taylor's Army of Occupation left for Matamoras, Mexico. The 7th Infantry departed Kinney's Ranch on March 10, 1846, and began its dull, dusty march over the flat prairies of what is now southern Texas. The distance between water holes generally determined a day's march. Company D and the 7th Infantry arrived in camp opposite the Mexican town on March 28, eighteen days after they began their overland trek of 150 miles.[31]

On March 28 Taylor's army set up camp and started constructing Fort Texas, a six-pointed star earthwork designed to hold eight hundred men, opposite Matamoras. The fort was located on the road to Palo Alto and Port Isabel and within a few hundred yards of the Rio Grande River, just above the main ferry crossing. Two of the sides measured 150 yards in length and the other four measured 125 yards. "The angled walls of packed earth rose to a height of nine feet with a width of fifteen feet. Inside there were dug

30. French, *Two Wars*, 39; LM, Certificate of Disability, File M-114, March 11, 1846, NARA M 567, RG 94, office mark M-114; GHS-VM LM Sketch.

31. Regimental Returns, 7th U.S. Infantry, 79, NARA M 665, RG 391.

powder magazines and bomb shelters; cannon platforms were raised at each point of the star. Outside a moat encircled the fort, twenty feet wide and eight feet deep, spanned by a single drawbridge."[32]

Meanwhile, the Mexican army, under Brigadier General Francisco Mejía, had delayed building its defenses until after the arrival of Taylor's army. Mejía quickly set about constructing a fort with sandbags above the main river ferry crossing. He also built two redoubts, each of whose distance to the American earthen work was between 700 and 800 yards. His intent was to catch Fort Texas in a cross fire once his artillery opened fire on the American troops.

McLaws rejoined Company D and the rest of the 7th Infantry on April 14. Major Jacob Brown, the regiment's commander, moved the 7th, Captain Allen Lowd's four 18-pounders, and Lieutenant Braxton Bragg's flying field battery into Fort Texas on May 1. In all, the troops numbered about five hundred men. Taylor led the rest of his army back up the road to Port Isabel, nineteen miles away, to establish a supply base and ensure the security of the port.[33]

General Mariano Arista, the new Mexican commander, wasted no time in executing an assault on Fort Texas. He sent the 4th Infantry, the Puebla Battalion, some sappers, and two hundred light cavalry across the Rio Grande to begin the siege. The attack, in coordination with artillery fire from the Matamoras redoubt batteries, began at 5:00 A.M. on May 3. Lieutenant Dana wrote that "reveille was as usual at the earliest dawn and we had just commenced washing, etc., before going to work when the batteries of the enemy opened, and their shot and shells began to whistle over our heads in rapid succession. They had commenced in real earnest, and they fired away powder and copper balls as if they had plenty of ammunition."[34]

The next day four more guns and 1,320 men arrived to complete the encirclement. Dana wrote that on the morning of the sixth, "a howitzer shell mounted the parapet and before he could dodge took off the leg of Major Brown below the knee." Arista demanded the fort's surrender on the afternoon of May 6, to which the new commander, Captain Edgar S. Hawkins, "begged leave politely to decline his invitation." A desultory bombardment and counterbombardment continued until May 9, though the

32. Timanus, *Texas Forts,* 97–98.

33. Regimental Returns, 7th U.S. Infantry, January–May 1846, NARA M 665, RG 391; Bauer, *Mexican War,* 49.

34. Ferrell, *Monterrey,* 58–59.

Mexican army made no effort to attack. The Mexican generals concluded that their artillery was too light to breach the earthen walls and the only recourse was to starve the Americans into surrendering before Taylor returned from Port Isabel.[35]

Taylor set his 2,228-man army in motion to return on May 7. Arista, alerted to Taylor's march, moved to block the U.S. army. The Mexican army stretched across the Port Isabel to the Matamoras road at Palo Alto. The Americans won a tactical victory on May 8 since they slept on the field of battle that night.

Starting on the morning of May 9 a third and final engagement took place in a dense tangle of chaparral and trees called Resca de la Palma, where Taylor's troops were engaged in a pitched battle that lasted most of the day. The American army turned the Mexicans' flank at the end of the day, resulting in their flight of panic back across the river and into Matamoras.[36]

The fort's name changed from Texas to Brown on May 17, 1846, to honor the fallen major. The 7th Infantry relinquished control of the fort and moved outside to encamp on May 23. Taylor's army remained in camp opposite Matamoras through early September. On the sixth Company D with McLaws departed for Monterrey, Mexico. They arrived at Walnut Springs, within three miles of the city, on September 19. In 1846 the town was the capital of the Mexican state of Nuevo Leon and had an estimated population of 10,000.

The 7th Infantry took part in the attack on the Bishop's Palace on September 21. The same day the city surrendered, and McLaws's regiment moved into the central part of the town to locate quarters. Lieutenant Dana wrote that "on the morning of the twenty-eighth, the last division of the Mexican army filed past us, and the city was cleared of them. We then set to work to select quarters for officers and men. We took possession of two sides of the [city] plaza, and I had a room in the second story of a house all to myself. Gault, McLaws, Gardner and Clitz lived on the same floor." Four of the young officers, including McLaws, would become generals in the Civil War. Dana was promoted to Union major general of volunteers in November 1862. Franklin Gardner, who earned a brevet promotion to first lieutenant at Monterrey, later commanded Confederate troops at Port Hudson, Louisiana. He was confirmed a major general in June 1864. Henry Boynton Clitz

35. Ibid., p. 61.

36. Bauer, *Zachary Taylor,* 145–51, and *Mexican War,* 46–22; Ferrell, *Monterrey,* 58–64.

was brevetted Union brigadier general for actions at Gaines Mill, Virginia, on June 27, 1862.[37]

McLaws's health did not fare much better in Monterrey than it had in Texas. He reported sick beginning December 23, 1846, and remained on the sick list through February 20, 1847, when he returned to his regiment at Camp Watson, near Tampico, Mexico. McLaws received his promotion to first lieutenant on February 16 and returned to duty in time to take part in the siege of Vera Cruz from March 9 to 29, 1847. He then transferred to Company H and left for recruiting duty in New York on April 5 because of poor health. McLaws recruited volunteers in New York City, Schenectady, and Buffalo through the remainder of 1847 and into 1848. He finally rejoined his regiment after the fall of Mexico City, convoying supply trains from the United States. Family papers indicate that he repeatedly requested to return to his unit. In the end, U.S. senator John P. King had to intercede with the War Department to get McLaws transferred back to Mexico. He arrived with the supply train after the fighting was over.[38]

Marriage to Emily, a Family, and the Antebellum Army, 1848–1861

McLaws became acting regimental adjutant as the 7th Infantry departed Mexico City for the United States on June 6, 1848. On July 20 Company H arrived at Jefferson Barracks, Missouri, and on August 19 McLaws transferred to Company C as acting adjutant. He stayed with Company C one month before transferring to Company I on September 18; he remained in Company I for the balance of the year. In December 1848 McLaws relinquished command of his company to serve for the first time as a judge advocate in a court-martial.

Although St. Louis, Missouri, and Jefferson Barracks experienced an outbreak of cholera in June and July 1849, it does not appear that McLaws contracted the disease or reported sick. During his tour at the barracks he did, however, meet and marry twenty-three-year-old Emily Allison Taylor. Emily, a niece of Zachary Taylor, was the daughter of John Gibson and Elizabeth Lee Taylor of Louisville, Kentucky. According to Virginia McLaws, Emily's "father and mother were second cousins"; her mother was "pretty, witty, lively, sweet and sincere." Jefferson Davis married his first wife Sara Knox

37. Regimental Returns, 7th U.S. Infantry, September 1846, NARA M 665, RG 391; Ferrell, *Monterrey*, 141.

38. GHS-VM LM Sketch, 3–4.

Taylor on June 17, 1835, at Beechland, Elizabeth Lee Taylor's plantation home. Several of Emily's sisters had already married military officers, and while visiting one of the sisters she met McLaws.[39]

Lafayette McLaws and Emily Allison Taylor were married by Reverend Robert M. Chapman, an Episcopal priest, in Louisville, Kentucky, on August 9, 1849. Their marriage bond, dated August 7, listed Frederick Geiger Edwards as the bondsman. Edwards was the husband of Emily's older sister Anne Pendleton Edwards. McLaws had only four days to spend with his new bride before he left on detached service to Santa Fe, New Mexico. The young couple did not see each other again for more than two years.[40]

Colonel John Munroe, commander of the Department of New Mexico, requested McLaws's assignment as his adjutant and inspector general, a position the youthful officer held from October 23, 1849, to July 19, 1851. Special Order No. 117, issued on August 24, 1851, transferred McLaws back to Company D and promoted him to captain. The Western Division's Special Order No. 57, dated August 9, 1851, granted him a furlough for four months. McLaws rejoined Company D on March 25, 1852, at Fort Gibson, where he remained from 1852 to 1857. His orders sent him to Fort Smith, Arkansas, in 1857, then back to Jefferson Barracks, Missouri, for garrison duty in 1858.[41]

Lafayette and Emily McLaws started their family probably in Louisville while he was on leave from the distant military assignments. William Huguenin "Willie" was born at Fort Gibson in 1852. On November 15, 1851, shortly before Willie's birth, McLaws had applied for the 160 acres land bounty due him because of his Mexican War service. John Taylor "Johnnie" followed on September 20, 1853, at Fort Gibson and Laura in 1856, perhaps in Louisville. Uldrick Huguenin was born on November 30, 1861, in Augusta. McLaws mentions all four children prominently in his letters home. In 1861, when the Civil War began, the older boys were nine and seven and Laura

39. Regimental Returns, 7th U.S. Infantry, December 1846–July 1848, NARA M 665, RG 391; GHS-VM ETM, 1; Bauer, *Zachary Taylor,* 70.

40. GHS-VM LM Sketch, 4; GHS-VM ETM, 1; Entries for LM and Emily Allison Taylor for August 7, 9, 1849, Jefferson County Marriage Registers, Licenses, and Bonds, Louisville; Entry for 1849, LB1, 1858–60.

41. Regimental Returns, 7th U.S. Infantry, August 1848–June 1857, NARA M 665, RG 391; GHS-VM LM Sketch, 4–5; GHS-VM ETM, 1. In 1850 ETM was living with her sister Anne Pendleton Taylor Edwards. She probably stayed with the family during LM's duty in the West. Seventh Census, 1850, entry for Frederick Geiger Edwards, Jefferson County, Ky., Louisville 4th District, 343.

was under five years old. Three daughters were born after the war: Annie Lee, in 1867; Virginia Randall, on August 29, 1868; and Elizabeth Violet, on January 15, 1870.[42]

Willie, the oldest son, died in 1870 at the age of eighteen. Laura, while away at school in Virginia, contracted a fever, "perhaps typhoid," and returned home; she died in October 1877 at age twenty-one—another "great blow to her mother and father especially." In April 1890 Annie Lee died of typhoid fever, the same disease that took Emily Allison Taylor McLaws's life the next month, on May 22. McLaws buried his wife and daughter in Savannah's Laurel Grove Cemetery.[43]

John Taylor McLaws became a post office clerk for his father and then a purser on the steamship *Nacoochee.* He died on August 17, 1921, and was buried in Bonaventure Cemetery, Savannah. Uldrick Huguenin attended North Georgia College and became a prominent Savannah lawyer. He was the captain commanding Savannah's Oglethorpe Light Infantry between 1896 and 1897. Uldrick's wife was the former Gertrude Livingston Hobby, a direct descendant of Philip Livingston, president of the Provincial Congress in 1775. Uldrick died on November 24, 1934; he was buried in Bonaventure Cemetery near his older brother. Virginia, who never married, became an artist on the Art Department's faculty at Sweetbriar College. *Who Was Who in American Art,* compiled from the original thirty volumes of the *American Art Annual* (1898–1933) and its subsequent four volumes also under the title *Who Was Who in American Art* (1935–47), contains several of Virginia's citations. The last surviving child of Lafayette and Emily McLaws, she died on August 11, 1967, and was buried beside her parents and sister. Elizabeth, the youngest daughter, became a children's librarian and for a brief period worked for the Georgia Historical Society. She later married her younger cousin, Edward Postell King Jr. of Atlanta. Elizabeth died on September 28, 1954, and was buried beside her husband in Hendersonville, North Carolina.[44]

In 1858 the army sent Lafayette McLaws to the Utah frontier, where troops from Camp Floyd and Fort Bridger patrolled the immigrant trails

42. LM, Application for Land Bounty for Mexican War Service, NARA RG 15, Records of the Veterans Administration, Unindexed Bounty Land file, Mexican War Pension file; GHS-VM LM Sketch, 4.

43. GHS-VM ETM, 2.

44. Ibid.; LM obituary, SHC-LM; Uldrick H. McLaws obituary, *Savannah Morning News,* November 25, 1934, p. 2; Gertrude Livingston Hobby McLaws, DAR ID: 72800,

during the 1859 traveling season. McLaws, now in command of several companies, protected the immigrants proceeding west through the Fort Hall region.[45]

The distance between McLaws and Emily increased the difficulty in raising a young family. Virginia described her mother as "a strong, persevering woman who was devoted to her husband, and children." Emily brought the children west to see their father on at least one occasion. They were traveling by stagecoach to meet McLaws when they came to a river or creek crossing and "as it was late and getting dark, the driver thought it wiser to wait until the next morning, when they began to drive on, but the river was too full to cross. A big storm had come up during the night and it was not considered safe." Emily and her children sought lodging in a small house nearby and waited a week before crossing the river. "Always there was danger on account of Indian tribes." Emily and the children moved to Louisville, Kentucky, because "it was not considered safe in the part of the country where her husband had to be."[46]

McLaws could see the country begin to unravel even at a distance from the political events taking place in the United States. On February 27, 1860, he wrote, "Debates in congress show no mitigation of sec. feeling." The notation continued: "Conservative papers of the North do not blame her for it. I think it would be better not to be so fanatical on any subject, the extreme pro-slavery man is as bad as that type of anti-slavery, John Brown. I do not consider slavery an evil by any means, but I certainly do not think it the greatest blessing. The abolitionists think it is the greatest curse, a good deal worse than Cholera or the plague—with the South it is a practical question—with the North it is all theory & fanaticism."[47]

On March 20 he observed, "Brigham Young still rules the country." Later in the passage he wrote: "The Utah question is such an apt one to suit the principles of the Rep. Party & break down squatter sovereignty that both

---

National Society, DAR, *Daughters,* 73:285; Falk, *Who Was Who,* 410; Ninth Census, 1870, Augusta, Richmond County, Ga., 31; Tenth Census, 1880, Savannah, vol. 4, E.D. 28, sheet 21, Chatham County, Ga.; Bonaventure Historical Society, *Bonaventure Cemetery,* Records for John Taylor, Uldrick Huguenin, and Gertrude Hobby McLaws. Major General Edward Postell King Jr. surrendered the Bataan Peninsula to the Japanese and spent the remainder of World War II in a Japanese prison camp.

45. GHS-VM LM Sketch, 5–6; Unruh, *The Plains,* 218.

46. GHS-VM ETM, 1.

47. Entry for February 27, 1860, LB1, 1858–60.

Rep. & Dem. will keep it to electioneer upon." McLaws believed that the Democratic Party would "not allow Congressional interference in the Territories for that will give the majority to abolish slavery in them whether the inhabitants are willing or not—Douglass Dem. against it on abstract principles—Southern Dem. from principles of interest & the others because it is contrary to the Rep. doctrine." He concluded: "The Dem. will be afraid to move troops because Mormons will so behave that humanity will cry for gov. protection & martial law will be tacitly admitted. Rep. say slavery is as bad as Mormonism. Sutlers, merchants & gentiles have invested money in hopes of getting gov. contracts. Their interest to retain army—if army moves, these fail."[48]

On April 24, from Camp Floyd, McLaws commented that "about this time Charleston Convention in full blast." He thought that the "squatter sovereignty doctrine" espoused by U.S. senator Stephen Arnold Douglas was, "though not orthodox according to extreme Southern notions, can do us no harm, but on the contrary the only [one] under which the south [can stay] in the union, can have a shadow of a shade in maintaining her 'peculiar institutions' in the territories to be formed out of the Cherokee Creek & Choctaw nations. These people if left to themselves will of course decide to have slavery. The old whigs who are attempting to organize an independent party are playing into the hands of the Rep. [Republican] party." Douglas, a native of Vermont who had built his national reputation in Illinois, was a longtime opponent of Abraham Lincoln. He believed that the country's frontier residents should decide for themselves whether to allow slavery to exist in their territory. On June 7 McLaws noted, "If leave of absence is granted, more desirable to get it from El Paso than Sante Fe because of difficulty which may be expected in carrying our servants through Kansas."[49]

McLaws learned who the 1860 presidential nominees were on July 4. "I am informed of the Pres. & Vice Pres. nominations," he wrote. "I like Breckenridge & Lane best—Bell and Everett stand no chance against Douglas [in] the north, nor B. & L. in the South." He went on to describe the camp near Denver City: "We have been traveling along the base of the Rocky Mts. Long's Peak, still white with snow, constantly in view over 2⅓ miles high. Scenery magnificent, climate delightful, gold seeks & land speculators everywhere—gold not plentiful for diggers—owners of quartz mills may

48. Entry for March 20, 1860, ibid.
49. Entries for April 24, June 7, 1860, ibid.

be making money. Every little stream dotted with squatters principally from Ohio, known by their brazen faces & exceeding course manners[,] a better lot from Ind. & Ill."[50]

The detached duty without leave and long marches began to take its toll on McLaws. On July 26 he wrote: "To-day reached here within 26 ms. of Fort Garland. We expect in two days to be in immediate vicinity of this fort to repair wagons, harness, exchange oxen & get a supply of provisions." He stated: "I intend writing to a friend of mine; Maj. [James] Longstreet who is paymaster at headquarters to use his influence in getting a leave granted to me." It took McLaws and his command three days to reach Fort Garland, on July 29.[51]

He did not receive the leave and instead prepared an expedition. "Mexican spies & guides will accompany the column," he wrote. McLaws and his men were "busy arranging packs & fitting saddles to mules—are to move with pack animal only, no tents." He closed with the observation, "The Navajos are terrifying people, stealing all their stock etc. near Albuquerque." McLaws described Colonel Thomas T. Fauntleroy, the "officer in charge of dept. of New Mexico (incapable)." As he prepared for the expedition, he repeated, "Navajos a terror to country."[52]

McLaws left Fort Craig on September 10 "with two companies of infantry and one of mounted rifles." On returning from the expedition, he camped in Canon Bonito near Fort Defiance. "I have been busy preparing 3 companies of Infantry for field service. Col. Canby has not arrived. All in doubt about campaign"; he observed that the distance between Fort Craig and Fort Defiance was 250 miles. On October 17 Brevet Lieutenant Colonel Edward Sprigg Canby directed McLaws to lead one of three columns in the Navajo expedition. His command would be "composed of 5 companies, 2 of mounted rifles, 3 of Infantry."[53]

50. Entry for July 4, 1860, ibid. In 1860 the major political parties offered four presidential tickets. The Republican ticket included Abraham Lincoln of Illinois and Hannibal Hamlin of Maine. The Constitutional Union Party, a Whig and Unionist coalition, offered John Bell of Tennessee and Edward Everett of Massachusetts. The Democratic Party split over slavery: Stephen A. Douglas of Ilinois and Hershel V. Johnson of Georgia were nominated in the North and John C. Breckinridge of Kentucky and Joseph Lane of Oregon in the South.

51. Entries for July 26, 29, 1860, LB1, 1858–60.

52. Entry labeled September 1860 and entry for September 1, 1860, ibid.

53. LM to sons, October 17, 1860, SHC-LM; Entry for October 17, 1860, LB1, 1858–60.

Canby did not arrive at Fort Defiance as expected. McLaws's column "left this place with 252 men completely equipped & well ready for the fray" on October 20, 1860. "I had marched only 11 miles the first day, halting at La Joya for the night when about 10 men from Col. Canbys command came galloping into camp." They brought orders that changed the column's objectives. In an order originally dated October 19, Canby informed McLaws:

> There are indications that the Navajos, in large bodies, are making their way to North & South of the Moqui villages. This may change and extend operations. To meet the contingency I have ordered 12000 rations to be advanced on that road. If the column is not usefully employed you may employ it in the direction of Moqui after a few days. Of course I can not judge of this as you can. Use your discretion in the matter. If the express meets you on the road, open all the communications addressed to the com. officers of Fort Defiance.

McLaws observed, "A disappointing order, it broke up the planned Nov. expedition." He returned to Fort Defiance while Canby continued operations against the Navajo Indians.[54]

On November 7 McLaws noted: "Col. Canby has left with his column, another has gone—I remain in command of this place—charged with making out estimates for the expedition, organizing recruits into companies as they arrive & then to put on foot an expedition against the Indians, composed of men from my column."[55]

McLaws told Emily on December 10 that he had just returned from a twenty-two-day scout. The opening paragraph conveyed his most important thoughts: "my command and myself in good health, and have but time to write you that I am here. And to say that Colonel Fauntleroy has granted me permission to avail myself of the leave of absence given by the War Department when the Navajo Expedition terminates."[56]

The third column departed Fort Defiance, and McLaws's men camped near West Spring on December 17. He informed Emily: "I will send you a copy of my report [on the Navajo expedition], although it is eighteen pages of writing. . . . When you have read the report, please send it to WmR to whom I intend writing. . . . I wish to ask his advice to the course I should

54. Entries for October 18–20 and November 1860, ibid. The date of the entry for October 19 is crossed out with "Nov.?" inserted above it, but the entries are consistent in describing the sequence of events.

55. Entry for November 7, 1860, LB1, 1858–60.

56. LM to ETM, December 10, 1860, SHC-LM.

pursue if Georgia secedes from the Union. My present idea is to go with my State as a matter of course. To offer my services as a military man." McLaws also provided an assessment of his commanding officer: "Colonel Canby is endeavoring to do his duty through good and evil report, and in spite of a great many unexpected obstacles, caused chiefly by the want of supplies."[57]

McLaws led another column as 1860 ended. On December 23 he wrote: "yesterday I received orders to move with my command tomorrow morning on a 16 days scout *to open* a wagon road from here down the Puecos to Bealy road running by Zuni to California & to examine the country west of the Puecos so as to make a road thence to the Moqui villages on the Moqui road coming from Fort Defiance. On my return from that Col. Canby says he will relieve me." He learned of the secession proceedings on January 16, 1861. Canby finally granted McLaws the six-month leave of absence promised in September 1860. He began his homeward journey from New Mexico to El Paso and then to Fort Davis, Texas, where he caught a stage to Jefferson, Missouri, and ultimately Louisville, Kentucky. True to form, he retained a duplicate receipt in turning over his 7th Infantry ordnance in Albuquerque, New Mexico, on January 20. He left behind one Colt revolver pistol and three dragoon holster pistols, all in "good" condition.[58]

Meanwhile, William R. McLaws set about securing a position in the Georgia infantry for the about-to-be-resigned officer. He sent Emily a circular dated February 2 stating that Captain L. McLaws "will be offered a position relative to his position in the U.S. Army." After a brief visit with his family in Louisville, Lafayette traveled on to Augusta, Georgia. From there he sent his letter of resignation dated March 14, which the army approved on March 23. He retained the notice from the Treasury Department's Auditor's Office on which he noted that the "clothing return for the following quarters—3d and 4th 1860 . . . 1st 1861 has been received, examined, and found correct & closed." On the reverse side he added: "I was about in the Rocky Mountains and did not get to Georgia until last of March, although I started from fort Bear Springs on 16th January, the fort being in the heart of Rocky Mountains—snow 2 feet deep, thermometer 10 degrees below zero." McLaws then enlisted in the forces organized by Governor Joseph Emerson Brown of Georgia.[59]

57. LM to ETM, December 17, 1860, SHC-LM.

58. Entry for December 23, 1860, LB1, 1858–60; GHS-VM LM Sketch, 7–8; LM transmittal letter, Ordnance Report, January 31, 1861, SHC-LM.

59. William R. McLaws to ETM, February 2, 1861, Circular—An Ordinance Con-

Special Order No. 27 directed Confederate Major Lafayette McLaws to Savannah, Georgia, in March 1861. He reported to Brigadier General Alexander Robert Lawton as an assistant quartermaster and commissary on April 18. The new major relinquished the staff duties to command Thunderbolt Point on April 26. He then set about organizing three underequipped companies into a fighting unit capable of defending an important section of Savannah's defensive perimeter. Brigadier General William Henry Talbot Walker wrote McLaws on June 4 asking him to join Walker's staff in Pensacola, Florida, since McLaws sought "more active service" and Walker believed that he would be assigned to Virginia. McLaws did not join Walker's staff, although he did receive the desired orders twelve days later. Special Order 58 relieved McLaws from duty in Savannah and ordered him to report to the adjutant general in Richmond. On June 21 McLaws left behind the tedious details of organizing Savannah's defense and boarded a train to command the 10th Georgia Infantry.[60]

Special Order No. 79 directed McLaws to Yorktown, Virginia, on June 24. The order promoted him to colonel and instructed him to report to Brigadier General John Bankhead Magruder, commander of the Army of the Peninsula. He found the 10th Georgia in need of his organizational talents, as the regimental leaders elected to establish the unit did not have the command skills necessary to prepare it for battle. McLaws, with his antebellum army training and recent work in Savannah, immediately assessed the situation. He put a regimental command structure in place and began to mold the unit into an effective infantry unit. The 10th Georgia would go on to garner fame and attention throughout the war.[61]

Magruder recognized McLaws's attention to detail and his ability to orga-

---

cerning Officers of the Army and Navy, SHC-LM; LM to Treasury Department, March 22, 1861, SHC-LM.

60. On May 30, 1861, LM was appointed assistant adjutant general and assistant inspector general for the District of Savannah to report to Alexander Robert Lawton. General Order No. 6, RG 109, GHS-LM; L. P. Walker to LM, Appointment of Lafayette McLaws as Major of Infantry, April 2, 1861, SHC-LM; W. H. T. Walker to LM, June 4, 1861, SHC-LM.

61. LM was appointed colonel and commander of the 10th Georgia Infantry on June 17, 1861, and reported for duty at Petersburg, Va., on June 24. The 10th Georgia was formed in Jonesboro, Ga., and Petersburg, Va., with men from Bibb, Chattahoochee, Clayton, De Kalb, Fayette, Pulaski, Richmond, and Wilcox Counties. Special Order No. 79/1, NARA RG 109.

Photograph of Lafayette McLaws as he appeared between 1861 and 1865.
(Courtesy of the Georgia Historical Society)

nize troops. In him he found an officer willing to tackle the details involved in forming new units and oversee the building of defensive fortifications—tasks that did not interest the brigadier general. Magruder's strategy was to build a line of redoubts and forts spanning the Virginia peninsula between the James and York Rivers. McLaws excelled in these tasks and assumed increasing responsibilities for the defensive line's completion. Though not officially in command of a brigade, McLaws oversaw a combination of regiments that exceeded the charge of a brigade commander.

McLaws became increasingly concerned that his actions and leadership would go unnoticed by individuals responsible for appointing major unit commanders. Worse, he feared the influence of officers who were also politicians. He believed that they would gain control of the regiments he led, negating his chance to become a brigade commander. He should not have worried. Magruder exerted efforts on his behalf, and McLaws received his promotion to brigadier general on September 25, 1861.[62]

Constructing the Williamsburg fortifications was time-consuming and tedious. On June 12, 1862, Henry Lord Page King, McLaws's aide-de-camp, recounted in his diary that "last night the Genl. [McLaws] and several of us of the staff trifled with a rifle shell of about 20 pounds—took out the fuse plug & set it off with a piece of paper put near the magazine. It exploded with terrible force—breaking window panes &c. God's mercy we were not killed." The by-the-book McLaws and his staff thus found a means to relieve their boredom on at least one occasion.[63]

The short-lived Battle of Williamsburg was the next command stepping-stone for McLaws. Lieutenant General Joseph Eggleston Johnston, now in command of the Army of Northern Virginia, had absorbed Magruder's Army of the Peninsula. Determining that Magruder's defensive lines were not the best place to fight Major General George Brinton McClellan's Army of the Potomac, Johnston ordered an evacuation of the Yorktown and Williamsburg defensive lines on May 3. McLaws's brigade was beginning its retreat on May 4 when Union brigadier general Phillip St. George Cooke's cavalry brigade attempted to cut off the line of retreat at Fort Magruder, a large bastion fort that McLaws had built.

The timing was perfect. McLaws knew the ground better than anyone

62. General Order No. 89, issued by the Headquarters Army of the Peninsula on October 3, 1861, organized the brigade structure of the army. GHS-LM. LM was placed in command of the First Brigade, consisting of the 10th Georgia Regiment and the 2nd Louisiana Regiment.

63. King Diary, June 12, 1862, SHC.

else; he also knew where to bring fire to bear on the Federal units making the attack. He immediately sent Colonel Joseph Brevard Kershaw's 3rd South Carolina Infantry back into the fort. The combination of Kershaw's advance and the other small unit deployments McLaws made into the low-numbered redoubts stopped the Union attack cold. Johnston wrote in his report that McLaws "made his dispositions with prompt courage and skill, and quickly drove the Federal troops from the field, in spite of disparity of numbers." The commanding general remarked, "I regret that no report of this handsome affair has been made by General McLaws."[64]

McLaws did, in fact, write a report dated three days before Johnston's. In it he called "attention to the promptness with which Kershaw placed his men into the various positions he was directed to occupy and the readiness with which he seized on the advantages offered by the ground." McLaws made a habit of recognizing officers and men in his reports and giving them the credit for their actions. He wrote that Kershaw's "command obeyed his orders with an alacrity and skill highly creditable to the gallant and obedient soldiers composing it." Meanwhile, Longstreet's division moved up and assumed responsibility for defending Fort Magruder. Longstreet's troops were engaged with Union troops throughout May 5, allowing the remaining Confederate units to retreat up the peninsula toward Richmond.[65]

Johnston saw McLaws's quick and decisive action. On May 23, 1862, he wrote McLaws, "I have seldom performed a more agreeable duty then forwarding to you a letter of appointment to the grade of major general, upon which your troops are to be congratulated." Lafayette McLaws now outranked such Army of Northern Virginia luminaries as Ambrose Powell Hill, John Bell Hood, George Edward Pickett, James Ewell Brown Stuart, Jubal Anderson Early, and Richard Heron Anderson. On May 26 Johnston placed McLaws "in command of the troops heretofore commanded by Major-General Magruder, the latter having been relieved" on the twenty-third.[66]

Division Command

The army assigned Magruder to the command of Department 2 of the Trans-Mississippi District on May 23, 1862. The order was recanted on May 26, and he was told to report to Johnston for his assignment. Once again McLaws

64. *OR* 11(1):275.
65. Ibid., 443.
66. Special Order No. 117, NARA RG 109; *OR* 11(3):551.

reported to Magruder, who commanded several divisions. On the morning of May 31 Johnston launched an attack against McClellan at Seven Pines (Fair Oaks); he purposely left Magruder's troops out of the way, as his plan unfolded and unraveled. After Johnston was wounded by Federal troops, General Robert E. Lee assumed command of the army on June 1.[67]

When Lee launched the Seven Days campaign on June 25, "Magruder's command was composed of three divisions of two brigades each" and played a relatively minor role in the campaign. His troops were engaged late in the day on July 1 at Malvern Hill. Lee then made the first of several leadership changes, and Magruder found himself packing his bags for Galveston, Texas. Magruder's departure opened up new opportunities for McLaws. Lee transferred McLaws's division to Longstreet's command, and McLaws now led four brigades commanded by Brigadier Generals Howell Cobb, Paul Jones Semmes, William Barksdale, and Joseph Brevard Kershaw.[68]

According to Robert K. Krick, "The division that General McLaws led for more than two years consisted of two Georgia brigades and one each from South Carolina and Mississippi. None of the brigadiers who commanded McLaws's brigades for extended periods—Semmes, Wofford, Kershaw, and Barksdale—had training or experience as a professional soldier." Krick, perhaps the most knowledgeable authority on the Army of Northern Virginia, observed: "the norm in the army was a mix of about one-half professionals among the brigades of most divisions. No other division operated for any extended period with all-amateur leadership at the brigade level. Despite that considerable disadvantage McLaws put together a solid record as a division commander." In the most extensive biographical note on McLaws to date, Krick commented, "only Ewell, and D. H. Hill among the familiar division commanders in the Army of Northern Virginia outranked McLaws, and both of those officers were away from the army for extended periods." The fact that McLaws was able to weld the four headstrong brigade commanders into an effective infantry division was no small feat and is a testament to his leadership ability.[69]

Artillerist Edward Porter Alexander, one of the South's most talented commanders, was referring to McLaws's troop positioning when, long after the war, he wrote, "McLaws was about the best general in the army for

67. *OR* 11 (3):540, 551.

68. Dowdey, *Seven Days,* 170; *OR* 11(3):648–52.

69. Krick, "Lafayette McLaws," 4:129. William Tatum Wofford assumed command of one of McLaws's brigades after Brigadier General Thomas Reade Rootes Cobb died at Fredericksburg.

that sort of job, being very painstaking in details, & having a good eye for ground." Alexander stated, "I have always, since the war, spoken of him as, perhaps, the very best division commander with whom I was ever brought in contact—for the thorough organization and discipline of the division, for the care of his men, and for his untiring personal zeal and energy in the study of the ground around him, and in his foresight and preparation for all contingencies." Moreover, "I know of few men better qualified for executive authority, both from personal character, ability and dignity, and from long and extensive and varied experience."[70]

Alexander described their first meeting somewhat differently. As a young officer in 1862, he commented, "among the first troops I met was Gen. McLaws' division & somehow I was commissioned to deliver him some order from either Gen. Longstreet or Gen. Lee, but cannot recall what it was. . . . I only remember that he [McLaws] did not relish it for some reason &, although he obeyed it, he exhibited his distaste of it, which I thought at the time to be in bad taste." Lieutenant Colonel Alexander continued: "I think it must have required some extra marching for his men for I afterward got to know him more intimately, & to appreciate that few of our generals equaled him in his care for their comfort & the pains he took in many matters of little detail. It gave him the reputation of being slow, but he made up for it in having his division always in the best possible condition."[71]

Robert Stiles, one of McLaws's officers from Mississippi, characterized him as "rather a peculiar personality. He certainly could not be called an intellectual man, nor was he a brilliant and aggressive soldier; but he was regarded as one of the most dogged defensive fighters in the army. His entire make-up, physical, mental and moral, was solid, even stolid." Further, Stiles wrote: "in figure, he was short, stout, square-shouldered, deep-chested, strong-limbed; in complexion, dark and swarthy, with coal-black eyes and black, thick, close-curling hair and beard. Of his type, he was a handsome man, but the type was that of a Roman centurion; say that centurion who stood at his post in Herculaneum until the lava ran over him." McLaws was, in fact, five feet nine inches tall with dark complexion, hair, and eyes.[72]

McLaws's concern for his men was sometimes not fully recognized. He

70. Alexander, *Fighting,* 170; E. P. Alexander to Executive Committee of Chicago World's Fair, July 19, 1890, SHC-LM.

71. Alexander, *Fighting,* 136.

72. Stiles, *Four Years,* 223; LM Oath Sworn to the United States of America, October 26, 1886, SHC-LM.

was not "popular with his raw troops, who generally designated him by the sarcastic title of 'Marse Make-Laws.' But after the first engagements on the Peninsula they became enthusiastically attached to him, appreciating his abilities and his constant care for their comfort and welfare."[73]

Lafayette McLaws led his division in most of the major actions of Lee's Army of Northern Virginia through December 1863. He did not take part in the Battle of Second Manassas, as the division was responsible for guarding river fords. His first leadership test took place during Lee's Maryland campaign between September 4 and 22, 1862. Lee called McLaws to his headquarters on Tuesday, September 9, and told him that "the whole army would move the next morning (Wednesday), taking the Hagerstown road, and that Gen. R. H. Anderson of South Carolina would be directed to report to me, and that I would follow with Andersons' and my own division in the rear of the army, until reaching Middletown, I would take the route to Harpers Ferry, and by Friday morning, the 12th, possess myself of Maryland Heights, and endeavor to capture the enemy at Harper's Ferry and vicinity." McLaws replied that he "had never been to Harper's Ferry, nor in the vicinity." Lee stated, "It did not matter." He believed that the enemy was smaller than reported and intimated that McLaws would have no trouble dealing with the "3000 or 4000" Federal troops.[74]

Shortly afterward Lee issued Special Order No. 191 directing Major General Thomas Jonathan Jackson's command to lead "the advance, and, after passing Middletown, with such portions as he may select, take the route toward Sharpsburg, cross the Potomac at the most convenient point, and by Friday morning take possession of the Baltimore and Ohio Railroad, capture such of them as may be at Martinsburg, and intercept such as may attempt to escape from Harper's Ferry." From the outset McLaws clearly understood his role. The report he submitted after the campaign began, "In compliance with Special Orders, No. 191, of September 9, 1862, from your headquarters, I proceeded with my own and General Anderson's division, via Burkittsville, to Pleasant Valley, to take possession of Maryland Heights, and endeavor to capture the enemy at Harpers Ferry and vicinity." Historians have generally described the actions McLaws took as those needed to support Jackson. Joseph L. Harsh recently observed, "Jackson and McLaws are depicted as operating separately against the enemy 'at each place.'"

73. Unidentified newspaper article, "General M'Laws: Some Incidents Recalled by His Recent Visit Here," SHC-LM.

74. LM, *Maryland Campaign*, 5.

McLaws believed, "So long as Maryland Heights was occupied by the enemy, Harpers Ferry could never be occupied by us. If we gained possession of the heights, the town was no longer tenable to them."[75]

On September 12 the brigades of Kershaw and Barksdale climbed the 1,400-foot Elk Ridge, the southern portion of which was designated Maryland Heights. The men traversed the narrow ridgeline without benefit of water. The next day Kershaw launched his attack with "a very sharp and spirited engagement through the dense woods and over a broken surface." He did not have the use of a road to help organize his troops. Instead, Kershaw moved through the woods and encountered "two abatis, the last quite a formidable work, the east and west sides being precipices of 30 or 40 feet, and across the ridge were breastworks of heavy logs and large rocks." The two brigades routed Colonel Thomas H. Ford's Union brigade late in the afternoon despite the apparent strength of their position. The Union troops escaped down a logging trail and across a pontoon bridge into Harpers Ferry. The town, "entirely commanded by Maryland Heights, from which a plunging fire, from musketry even, can be made into the place," was now the center of McLaws's attention.[76]

McLaws later wrote, "The engineers, who had been examining the mountain during the evening before, had reported that night it was impracticable to carry cannon to the top, owing to the steepness of the ascent and the numerous walls of rock that could not be passed." Abram Huguenin McLaws located "an old wood road, which wound up a part of the way" while returning from Kershaw's brigade. Lafayette assigned his brother the task of cutting the road, "and by using ledges and hauling them by hand in other places, the difficulties were finally overcome and by 2 P.M. we had two guns each from the batteries of [Captain John Postell Williamson] Read and [Captain Henry H.] Carlton in position overlooking the town."[77]

McLaws now had units spread out five miles between Crampton's Gap and Sandy Hook, at the base of the heights. He ordered Howell Cobb to take his brigade from Sandy Hook and reinforce J. E. B. Stuart's cavalry screen and the small detachment left to protect his rear at Crampton's Gap. Cobb set his troops in motion about noon on September 14.

McLaws remained on the "Maryland Heights, on top of the elevated 'look-

75. *OR* 19(2):603–4, 19(1): 852; Harsh, *Taken at the Flood,* 192–93.

76. Maryland Heights is 1,400 feet above sea level. The top of the heights tower over Harpers Ferry 240 feet above sea level. U.S. Geological Survey, *Map of Harpers Ferry.*

77. LM, *Maryland Campaign,* 12; *OR* 19(1):853–54.

Harpers Ferry with Maryland Heights in the background.
(Robert Underwood Johnson and Clarence Clough Buel, eds., Battles and Leaders of the Civil War, *vol. 2 [New York, 1887–88])*

out' erected by the Federals, directing and observing the fire of our guns," when he heard artillery fire coming from the direction of the gap. "General Stuart, who was with me on the heights and had just come in from above [Crampton's Gap], told me he did not believe there was more than a brigade of the enemy." McLaws immediately sent his adjutant general, Major James Monroe Goggin, with "directions to hold the gap if he lost his last man in doing it," then followed with Stuart. They covered the five miles quickly, only to see Howell Cobb's Georgian brigade streaming down the hillside. McLaws arrayed the troops he brought with him across Pleasant Valley. Union major general William Buel Franklin's Sixth Corps had started its attack from Burkittsville, only to stop after it passed through the gap. Franklin feared that the Federals confronted a much larger force than their own and called off the attack as darkness fell.[78]

That night McLaws faced a complex decision. He needed to hold Franklin in place with roughly the same number of troops as the Federals had on hand. McLaws would fail if Franklin cut McLaws's two divisions off from Lee,

78. LM, *Maryland Campaign,* 13; *OR* 19(1):854.

who had started to concentrate the army at Sharpsburg. He also needed to complete his assignments. His ineffective communication with both Jackson, his senior commander, and Lee added to his dilemma. McLaws had received intermittent handwritten messages from Lee. Jackson had attempted to initiate contact by use of a signal system. "Captain Manning, who had charge of the signal corps, being unable to attend to his duties from a sudden attack of erysipelas in the head," was of little help in communicating with Jackson and relinquished his duties to Captain Ellison L. Costin, one of McLaws aides-de-camp. It took Costin time to effectively establish communication with Jackson, even though he was able to maintain communication with McLaws in Pleasant Valley.[79]

McLaws bluffed Franklin into thinking that he faced a much larger concentration of troops than were present, and the Union general did not advance during the early morning hours of September 15. After McLaws received word from his signal station that Harpers Ferry had surrendered to Jackson about 10:00 A.M., he gradually removed his troops from Pleasant Valley and Maryland Heights and completed all but one assignment. Roughly 1,500 Union cavalry escaped from Harpers Ferry on the night of September 14 using an unguarded trail.

Jackson immediately marched his corps toward Sharpsburg, leaving to A. P. Hill's division the task of paroling the Federal troops. McLaws and his commissary chief, Major John F. Edwards, crossed the bridge over the Potomac River only to find that Hill's troops had requisitioned all of the food supplies. McLaws's men had been without food or water for the better part of the two previous days. Edwards, a nephew of McLaws, was the son of Emily's sister Anne Pendleton and Frederick Geiger Edwards. His brother, Lieutenant Alfred Edwards, was McLaws's ordnance officer. McLaws prominently mentions both brothers in the letters.

"I formed a new line across Pleasant Valley, still holding Maryland Heights and Weverton Pass, and waited until 2 o'clock A.M. of the 16th, when most of the paroled prisoners having crossed to the left bank, my troops were withdrawn to the right bank, and marching through Harper's Ferry, camped near Hall Town, about four miles distant, on the 16th inst." McLaws charged his brigade commanders with getting their units through the small town choked by Hill's detainment and release of the Federal soldiers. Meanwhile, he and Edwards set out for Charlestown to locate food for their hungry troops. Unable to locate any measurable quantity, the fatigued men re-

79. *OR* 19(1):855–57.

sumed the march to Sharpsburg, crossing the Potomac River in the early morning hours, and arrived on the field at sunrise on September 17, 1862. McLaws sought out Lee, who ordered McLaws to bivouac his division near Lee's headquarters, about two miles from the battle.[80]

Called into action at 9:00 A.M., McLaws led his division in fine style as they slammed into the left flank of Union major general John Sedgwick's division and drove back Major General Edwin Vose Sumner's Second Corps in the woods west of the Dunkard Church. They hit the Federal troops with great force at exactly the right time. The Union assault stalled, forcing McClellan to begin anew, this time attacking the Confederate center. The investment of Harpers Ferry and McLaws's action in the West Woods gave the division commander added confidence in his ability to prosecute a battle.[81]

On September 17 H. L. P. King wrote in his diary that he "Met Gen. Jackson & he & Gen. McLaws had a conference. Shell fell at our feet, wounding one of Gen's Couriers—did not explode or it would have killed both Gens." Once again, McLaws luckily escaped an artillery shell with King nearby.[82]

McLaws's division recouped after the short but intense Maryland campaign. When it arrived at Fredericksburg, Virginia, on November 19, Longstreet assigned "McLaws's division upon the heights immediately behind the city and south of the Telegraph road." McLaws again put the knowledge he had gained on the Peninsula to work, paying particular attention to how he positioned the division at Fredericksburg.[83]

McLaws's "division occupied the front of defense from Hazel Run along the ridge of hills to the right and through the point of woods extending to Mr. Alfred Bernard's field, one brigade in reserve." He directed his left-hand brigade to construct "an extended rifle-pit at the foot of the main ridge, from the left of Telegraph road to a private road near Mr. Howison's barn." The center brigade constructed "rifle-pits along the foot of the hills in front of its position, and others on the crest of the hills." The brigade on the right "constructed rifle-pits and breastworks of logs through the woods, with abatis in front of them." Finally, McLaws arranged the artillery on the crests of the hills.[84]

Colonel Henry Coalter Cabell, McLaws's chief of artillery, wrote, "The position of our artillery and infantry made by Major-General McLaws was

80. LM, *Maryland Campaign,* 18–19.
81. LM's report, *OR* 19(1):857–60.
82. King Diary, 40, SHC.
83. *OR* 21:568.
84. LM's report, *OR* 21:578.

certainly most happy to counteract the disadvantages of our position." Cabell made several recommendations that McLaws agreed to. He concluded, "It is but an act of simple justice to Major-General McLaws to say that the disposition of the artillery in other respects was such as he had chosen." Artillerist Alexander observed that a "sunken road, for a part of the way, gave the infantry a beautiful line, &, where that was lacking, McLaws, with his usual painstaking care & study of detail, had utilized ditches & dug trenches & provided for supplies of water & of ammunition & care of the wounded."[85]

McLaws's division held despite the six significant attempts to push his men off Marye's Heights on December 13. The stalwart defense helped to force Major General Ambrose Everett Burnside's Army of the Potomac to accept another major defeat, which ultimately led to his removal as commander.

Typically, McLaws recognized the officers who merited attention and, in doing so, singled out Alfred Edwards, an "ordnance officer, who was active and efficient in supplying ammunition to the troops." He also recognized "Surgeon [John T.] Gilmore, chief surgeon of the division, [who] had his field hospital in readiness, and his arrangements were so complete that there was no detention or unnecessary suffering of the wounded." Gilmore made sure the 1,186 wounded officers and men "who could not remain in camp were sent at once to the hospitals in Richmond." Significantly, McLaws did more than construct extended rifle pits and build abatis and breastworks to reinforce the defensive position. He made sure that water and ammunition was nearby. More important, he ensured that the wounded troops received medical attention immediately. These tactical characteristics are reminiscent of World War I, some fifty-two years in the future.[86]

William Allen Blair has written that "scholars credit Longstreet with encouraging the use of entrenchments, thus contributing a tactical innovation to the army." Moreover, "Longstreet's appreciation of the power of the defensive probably matured at Fredericksburg on December 13, 1862, when his soldiers repulsed numerous Federal assaults while losing only eight hundred men behind strongly fortified positions on Marye's Heights." According to Longstreet, "Much credit is due Major-General McLaws for his untiring zeal and ability in preparing his troops and his position for a successful resistance, and the ability with which he handled his troops after the attack."

85. Cabell's report, *OR* 21:585; Alexander, *Fighting*, 176.
86. *OR* 21:582–84.

McLaws should have received credit for the tactical innovations at Fredericksburg, although it was not in his nature to seek public recognition.[87]

Lafayette McLaws returned from his first leave home on April 10, 1863, to find Longstreet on detached service with Hood's and Pickett's divisions. Longstreet's absence changed the command structure, for during the May 1863 Chancellorsville campaign McLaws reported directly to Robert E. Lee. At the outset of the battle Lee sent Stonewall Jackson's corps and the divisions of McLaws and Richard H. Anderson to meet Major General Joseph Hooker's Army of the Potomac. Hooker, the new Union commander, attacked the flank and threatened Lee's rear. McLaws and his men marched from their fortified positions in Fredericksburg up the Plank Road, moving into position just short of Chancellorsville. On May 2 both McLaws's and Anderson's divisions formed a blocking position. Lee wanted their troops to threaten Hooker's units with enough force to hold the Federals in place. While this occurred, Jackson completed his famous flank march and secured Lee's victory at Chancellorsville. McLaws and Anderson became the anvil and Jackson's troops the hammer as they caught Hooker between them.

The plan worked as Jackson rolled up the Federal right flank, only to have dusk overtake his attack. The combination of a continued night attack and the dense underbrush helped stall the attack's progress. The night's work also brought disastrous results for the Army of Northern Virginia. Jackson's own troops shot him while he reconnoitered the next phase of his attack. His death cost Lee one of his top two field commanders.

The next day, May 3, Sedgwick's Sixth Corps crossed the Rappahannock River, pushed through Fredericksburg, and threatened Lee's army from the rear. Lee assigned the defense of Fredericksburg to Major General Jubal A. Early. Barksdale's Mississippians remained with Early to keep Sedgwick's wing from catching Lee's men between two Federal pincers. McLaws arrived at Salem Church, roughly midway between Chancellorsville and Fredericksburg, in time to help Brigadier General Cadmus Marcellus Wilcox stop the Federal advance. Kershaw's South Carolinians were put in as they arrived on the field and helped blunt the Federal attack as the rest of the division deployed on Wilcox's flanks.[88]

87. Blair, "Longstreet," 92; Longstreet's report, *OR* 21:571.

88. LM believed that he salvaged the engagement at Salem Church on May 3, 1863,

Many Civil War commanders had days that they wished they could change, particularly when they did not measure up to expectations. McLaws's performance at Salem Church might have been one of those days. Defensive opportunities made the best use of his strengths. He could take the time to choose the ground on which to fight and properly align his troops. He took painstaking efforts to deploy troops and take advantage of terrain features. Noted Lee biographer, Douglas Southall Freeman, described McLaws as a "professional soldier, careful of details and not lacking in soldierly qualities, but there was nothing daring, brilliant, or aggressive in his character." Freeman explained, "An excellent division commander when under the control of a good corps commander, he was not the type to extemporize a strategic plan in an emergency." In the case of Salem Church, McLaws's lack of initiative tarnished his reputation and accentuated the perception that he was slow to engage in battle.[89]

Jubal Early and McLaws exchanged messages between each other and Lee on the night of May 3. Early's intent was to begin an attack at daybreak on the fourth. He wanted McLaws to press forward, extending his right when he heard that Early's troops had begun their attack. McLaws contended that Kershaw started this movement but did not find Early's men on his right and pulled back to his earlier position. Ever careful in the face of greater strength, McLaws requested additional troops. By midday Lee arrived with Anderson's division to supervise the attack. It took Anderson's men more time to move into position than initially expected. In the meantime, McLaws did virtually nothing until late in the afternoon, when it was almost dark. He then began to press his troops forward before stopping them when darkness descended over the field. Lee had looked for offensive action but relied on one of his most cautious commanders. McLaws, much better suited for defensive action, did not aggressively attack as Lee had hoped.

Perhaps McLaws mentally calculated his division's losses and held the troops back instead of pushing through the dense underbrush and steep ravines in the growing darkness. Whatever the reason, the attack did not proceed, and Sedgwick was able to evacuate his troops over Bank's Ford during the night. When McLaws, Anderson, and Early renewed their attacks the next morning, the Federal troops were safely across the river. The delay thus cost Lee the opportunity for a more complete victory.

---

and that Wilcox received the recognition in error. In lectures and articles after the war, he described in detail the actions of Kershaw, Semmes, and Wilcox.

89. Freeman, *R. E. Lee,* 2:551.

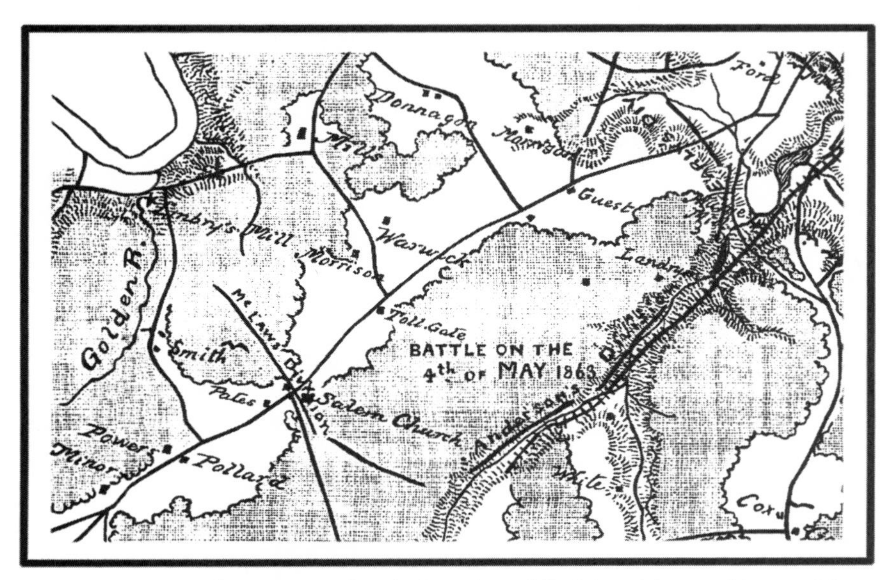

Lafayette McLaws's map noting his, Anderson's, and Early's positions on May 4, 1863. (Courtesy of the Southern Historical Collection, University of North Carolina at Chapel Hill)

McLaws, ever the detail commander, provided little insight in his report. He remarked, "The darkness of the night, ignorance of the country, and of the events transpiring on the other end of the line, prevented that co-operation which would have led to a more complete success." In the end, he concluded, "I believe all was gained that could have been expected under the circumstances." In an address after the war, McLaws wrote a ten-page description of the engagement at Salem Church and Sedgwick's advance from Fredericksburg. In his thirty-one-page review of the battle, however, he reduced his comments on this part of the fight to one line. In his own report Robert E. Lee indirectly criticized McLaws for his inaction when he wrote that "the speedy approach of darkness prevented General McLaws from perceiving the success of the attack until the enemy began to cross the river a short distance below Bank's Ford." Gary W. Gallagher describes McLaws's performance as "inept," since he spent May 4 as a "bystander" at Salem Church. In the end, McLaws's offensive shortcomings reinforced Lee's desire to have Longstreet more closely supervise McLaws in future battles.[90]

90. *OR* 25:802, 824–29; LM, "The Battle of Chancellorville: The Most Remarkable One of the War," SHC-LM; Gallagher, *Chancellorsville,* 58.

In June 1863 McLaws settled a feud stemming from his perceived tardiness in relieving Major General John Bell Hood's division at Sharpsburg. The Reverend Nicholas A. Davis, chaplain of the 4th Texas Infantry, had recently published *The Campaign from Texas to Maryland,* in which he and Hood were highly critical of McLaws's delay. Hood insinuated that the wait had cost Lee a major victory and led to a greater loss of men in Hood's division. In many cases, the information was inaccurate, especially regarding McLaws's arrival in the field. Based on second- or third-hand information, Davis's book was heavily biased to the Texan's perspective. Most significant, Davis did not take part in the battle, for his publication duties in Richmond delayed his return until after the troops returned to Virginia. McLaws finally received an apology from Hood on June 3. Davis, who did not return to the army until after Gettysburg, sent his admission of regret to McLaws on July 30. (For the relevant letters to McLaws from Hood and Davis, see the Appendix.)

McLaws had other things on his mind besides clearing his name and his division's honor with Hood. On June 3 Longstreet wrote him: "You spoke of going South the other day. If you wish to go I expect that I may make the arrangement for you that I was speaking of for myself. That is for you to go there and let Beauregard come here with his Corps. We want everybody here that we can get and if you think of going South you must send us every man that you can dispense with during the summer particularly. I understand that Beauregard is anxious to join this army and if he is I believe that I can accomplish what I have mentioned."[91]

The recent promotions of Richard Stoddert Ewell and Ambrose P. Hill to lieutenant general and command of the two newly created corps may have started McLaws thinking of home again. Nevertheless, he was in good spirits as he led his troops into Pennsylvania. McLaws worked to keep his men in line and enforced Lee's orders to not treat the citizens of Pennsylvania as Union troops treated the families of Virginia.

His upbeat demeanor changed in the early morning of July 2. McLaws had brought his division up on July 1 and "arrived at Willoughby Run about 4 miles from Gettysburg, at 12 at night and camped there. During the night I received orders to march on at 4 A.M., but this was countermanded, and I was directed to be ready to move early in the morning. The sun rises about half-past four in the first days of July." Leaving shortly after dawn, at 4:30 A.M., the division continued its march toward Herr's Ridge. When McLaws reported to Lee at roughly 8:00 A.M., the commanding general

91. James Longstreet to LM, June 3, 1863, SHC-LM.

"was sitting upon the trunk of a fallen tree, with a Topographic Map of the country about Gettysburg before him. Gen. Longstreet was walking up and down a little way off, apparently in an inpatient humor. Gen. Lee, calling my attention to the map, said, 'Gen. McLaws, I wish you to place your command in this position.'" Lee directed McLaws to locate his division at a spot "perpendicular to the Emmettsburg road, 'Can you do so?' I replied, 'General I do not know that there is anything to prevent it, but can I reconnoiter and see.' Before Gen. Lee could reply, Gen. Longstreet joined us and said, pointing to the map, and speaking to me, 'General, I want you to place your division there,' drawing his finger along a line parallel to the Emmettsburg road. 'No General,' said Gen. Lee, 'I want his division perpendicular to the Emmettsburg road.'" Lee then told McLaws that he had ordered one of his staff officers, "Capt. Johns[t]on, to reconnoiter in that direction." McLaws asked to go with Johnson, but Longstreet said no and Lee did not interfere. Instead, Longstreet ordered McLaws to wait for the results of a reconnaissance conducted by Captain Samuel R. Johnston, an engineer on Lee's staff.[92]

Lee wanted McLaws to take every precaution so that the Union signal station atop Little Round Top did not detect the approach of his division. Specifically, Lee wanted McLaws to be perpendicular to the Emmitsburg road and ensure that his attack would roll up the Union left flank. Major General George G. Meade, the next in a line of generals commanding the Army of the Potomac, had just taken command.

In spite of Longstreet's order, McLaws did complete a limited reconnaissance. The ever-careful McLaws wanted to be prepared to meet the spirit and intent of Lee's order. Indeed, he may not have wished to repeat his lack of reconnaissance at Salem Church. Longstreet waited until 1:00 P.M. to begin the march. McLaws's division led the advance, followed by Hood's men. The corps's third division, under the command of George B. Pickett, had just left Chambersburg, Pennsylvania, en route to Gettysburg.[93]

McLaws and Johnston crested the hill beyond Black Horse Tavern and, to McLaws's surprise, realized that the Union signalmen on top of Little Round Top could see the Confederate troops as they marched toward the Emmitsburg road. McLaws immediately halted the column of troops. Longstreet, who had been riding with Hood, came up to determine the cause of the delay. He realized that Johnston's reconnaissance had not uncovered this

92. LM, *Battle of Gettysburg,* 68–69.
93. Ibid., 69.

problem and ordered a countermarch. In the meantime, Hood's troops did not completely stop their march and overlapped with McLaws's men. This created a good bit of confusion in the ranks. At this point there was a spirited discussion regarding which division would now take the lead. Ultimately, both McLaws and Hood turned their troops around and countermarched. McLaws had located a path near Willoughby Run during his "against orders" reconnaissance. Both divisions marched along the run, avoiding the hill and detection, with McLaws at the front.[94]

At about 3:00 P.M. McLaws's lead brigade under Kershaw crested a small rise that overlooked the run. Kershaw wrote, "examining the position of the enemy, I found him to be in superior force in the orchard, supported by artillery, with a main line of battle intrenched in the rear and extending to and upon the rocky mountain to his left far beyond the point at which his flank had supposed to rest." McLaws and Kershaw realized that they were not on the Federal left flank, as Lee had anticipated. Major General Daniel Edgar Sickles, commander of the Federal Third Corps, had pushed his troops out to what he thought was higher and better ground. He was concerned about defending his position and completed the move shortly before Longstreet's corps arrived. The Federal line stretched from Little Round Top, on their left, down the Wheatfield road to the edge of the Peach Orchard, where it then extended up the Emmitsburg road a short distance.[95]

Kershaw understood what he must do as soon as his troops crested the rise. He placed his brigade behind a stone wall parallel to the Emmitsburg road and across from the Peach Orchard. Semmes positioned his brigade behind Kershaw's in support. Barksdale placed his brigade across the Wheatfield road, partially behind a stone fence and partially sheltered by trees. Wofford situated his brigade behind Barksdale's in support.

Sickles's action caused Longstreet to rethink a part of the attack. Hood's division continued marching behind McLaws, extending the Confederate right, in the hope of finding the new Federal left flank. Some of Hood's Texas scouts did find a way to continue around Big Round Top and roll up the Federal left. Longstreet determined that he needed to press the attack, as it was getting late in the day. He ordered Hood to commence the assault despite Hood's protests. Hood started the en-echelon attack shortly before 4:00 P.M. Longstreet ordered Kershaw to begin his advance on the enemy

94. The sources for the march and countermarch are LM, *Battle of Gettysburg*, 69–70, 75, and Kershaw's report, *OR* 27(2):366–67.

95. Kershaw's report, *OR* 27(2):367.

a short time after 4:00 P.M., and it was almost 6:00 P.M. before Longstreet released the last of McLaws's brigades.[96]

Longstreet's uncoordinated action and micromanagement of the division's attack did not deter McLaws's men from delivering one of their best assaults for the Confederacy. The men's stamina in dealing with the two days of marches and lack of water did not inhibit their ability to push Sickles and the Union divisions sent to his relief back to the edge of Little Round Top before darkness stopped the attack.

Gettysburg and Longstreet's action in not allowing McLaws to do what McLaws felt was rightfully his duty on July 2 opened a deep chasm between the two officers and friends. Even though McLaws had taken Magruder to task in his letters home, he remained cautious in what he committed to paper. The July 7 letter to Emily was the most serious break McLaws had with a superior. He sharply criticized and questioned his commander's leadership ability. Gettysburg also was the only major engagement where McLaws did not file a report as a division commander in Lee's army. July 2, 1863, thus represented a significant turning point in McLaws's career and in how he viewed Longstreet.[97]

After Gettysburg the Army of Northern Virginia returned to regroup near Orange Court House. Longstreet was growing restless and sought independent action. In September he and his corps were detached from Lee's army and transported by railroad to East Tennessee to help Lieutenant General Braxton Bragg's Army of Tennessee. The delays caused by inadequate railroad rolling stock detained McLaws and two of his brigades in Atlanta, Georgia. They caught up with Longstreet as the Battle of Chickamauga was ending. The Federal commander, Brigadier General William S. Rosecrans, a West Point classmate of McLaws, had pulled his troops off the Chickamauga battlefield on the night of September 20, but Bragg, Longstreet, and the other Confederate commanders did not realize this until later the next day. Rosecrans wanted to move his troops back to the relative safety of Chattanooga, Tennessee, and almost lost the battle.

Longstreet attempted to dictate the army's combat strategy to Bragg on his arrival on the battlefield. He continued to try to take control of the army in late September with D. H. Hill and Major General Simon Bolivar Buckner.

96. The sources for LM's deployment and the battle that followed are LM, *Battle of Gettysburg*, 75–81, and Kershaw's report, *OR* 27(2):367–70.

97. LM also did not file a report after Chickamauga, but this was probably because he was not an active participant.

Confederate president Jefferson Davis had to personally intervene and prevent the attempted coup by traveling to Tennessee to meet with the generals. The distance and alienation between Longstreet and McLaws continued to grow. McLaws conspicuously elected not to join with Longstreet, Buckner, and Hill in their attempt to have Bragg removed from command.

The clash in leadership styles came to a head during the Knoxville campaign in December 1863. Bragg sent Longstreet to drive Ambrose E. Burnside's Army of the Ohio out of East Tennessee. Central to this effort was Longstreet's need to attack Burnside before he reached Knoxville. McLaws viewed Longstreet's attempts to take Knoxville in a timely manner as a bungled job and his lack of action at Campbell's Station as a decisive missed opportunity.[98]

Longstreet's misgivings about McLaws had increased as well. Longstreet assigned McLaws the task of taking Fort Loudon, a Union bastion protecting Knoxville. Faulty reconnaissance—this time on the part of Longstreet—again came into play. McLaws put his troops in motion late on the night of November 28 after a three-day delay caused by Longstreet. The attack took place in the early morning of November 29 with the barefoot troops pushing over the cold, frozen ground to reach the fort's earthwork. The Federals took several men prisoner as they advanced over the top of the work. The supporting troops could not get through to push the Confederates into the fort. After only twenty minutes Longstreet called off the attack, ordering McLaws to lead his division back to its starting point.[99]

Longstreet regarded the aborted attack as an opportunity to change two of his division commanders. On December 17 he relieved McLaws of command because he had failed "to make arrangements essential to success" in the attack on Fort Loudon on the early morning of November 29. Instead of facing McLaws directly, Longstreet instructed his aide, Major Gilbert Moxely Sorrel, to deliver the message. McLaws was devastated by the turn of events, especially since he had always prided himself on his attention to detail. The accusation, especially in light of Longstreet's actions at Gettysburg, cracked the controlled, thoughtful approach that was characteristic of McLaws.[100]

98. LM, typed manuscript beginning with November 4, 1863, SHC-LM; *OR* 31(1): 482–83.

99. LM to Cooper, January 17, 1864, SHC-LM. For LM's Knoxville report and court-martial statements, see *OR* 31(1):481–508.

100. Longstreet also maneuvered to force the resignation of Brigadier General

McLaws lashed back at Longstreet. He copied documents that passed back and forth between Sorrel, a fellow Georgian from Savannah, and himself. In the end, he wrote his brother William R., "I *demanded* a court martial which is the reason why I am ordered for trial." Rather than address his men before leaving for Georgia, McLaws chose to send word that "it was not proper for me to make remarks upon the campaign, which I would probably be compelled to do . . . as it tended strongly to destroy confidence in the leaders, and one against humanity as it was not necessary, in any point of view and was uncalled for at the time." He believed that the court would vindicate his honor and the adjutant general would restore his command.[101]

McLaws first sent a copy of his Knoxville report, including Longstreet's communications and his preliminary report, to Adjutant General Samuel Cooper. Within hours of receiving the charges and specifications, he launched a campaign to gather reports and information from members of his command. He extended the search for information to Richmond and Braxton Bragg and gathered reports from regimental commanders and other participants involved in the attack on Fort Loudon. McLaws also enlisted the help of family members and friends as he began to build the case to defend his honor.

Special Order No. 21, dated January 21, 1864, directed, "A general court-martial to consist of seven members—a greater number cannot be convened without manifest injury to the service." The seven-member board was to assemble in Russellville, Tennessee, on February 3 or shortly afterward. Two trials were to take place, one for McLaws, the other for Brigadier General Jerome Bonaparte Robertson. McLaws's court-martial board would include Simon B. Buckner, who would preside, and Brigadier Generals Charles W. Field, James L. Kemper, John Gregg, F. T. Nicholls, George Thomas Anderson, and Benjamin Grubb Humphreys. Major Garnett Andrews, assistant adjutant general, would serve as the judge advocate. Field (USMA 1849) would later become a major general. Kemper, a graduate of Washington College, was recovering from wounds he received at Gettysburg; he also attained the rank of major general. Francis Redding Tillou Nicholls (USMA 1855) would later serve as chief justice of the Louisiana Supreme Court (1892–1904). Anderson had attended Emory College. The USMA had dismissed Humphreys in 1826; he was the only member of the court who had

---

Evander Law, who held temporary command of Hood's division, and replace him with Brigadier General Micah Jenkins. Law ultimately returned to his brigade.

101. LM to Joseph Ganahl, July 23, 1894, SHC-LM.

reported to McLaws and had taken command of Barksdale's brigade after Gettysburg. McLaws would be the ranking general officer, and one of two major generals, to be court-martialed between July 1863 and April 1865.[102]

McLaws's search for facts and details started to bring results. In a series of letters to Emily in early March 1864, the first days of the on-again, off-again trial, his comments on his progress to have his name cleared were positive, if not somewhat enthusiastic. E. P. Alexander, one of the initial prosecution witnesses, provided testimony that vindicated McLaws. Unfortunately for McLaws, he won the battle but lost the war to regain his division. The court-martial board found him not guilty of the first two specifications. On the third specification, which accused McLaws of "failing in the details of his attack to make arrangements essential to success," the court delivered a guilty verdict and recommended a suspension from rank and pay for sixty days.

In his review of the case, Adjutant General Cooper criticized the board's proceedings and Longstreet's attempt to manipulate the court: the "irregularities are fatal to the record." Cooper also found that the court could not substantiate its case based on the evidence and reversed its decision on the third specification. He concluded: "The proceedings, finding, and sentence of the court are disapproved. Major-General McLaws will at once return to duty with his command."[103]

Longstreet began to press Cooper to name a replacement for McLaws. On March 4 he recommended that one of his new protégés and a member of McLaws's court-martial board, Charles Field, command McLaws's division. On April 3 Special Order No. 81 extended a leave of absence granted to McLaws for seven more days. McLaws had returned to Sparta, Georgia, to await the outcome of the court's decision. Also on April 3 McLaws wrote Cooper to determine if he was still under arrest and asked what action the court had taken in his case.

Longstreet, unable to install Field as commander of McLaws's division, recommended Joseph B. Kershaw to Cooper on April 22. Clearly, Longstreet did not want McLaws to return, as he followed the Cooper recommendation with one to Lee on April 23. Longstreet wrote that Kershaw should continue to command the division: "as Genl McLaws is not well suited for the command of a division in active operations in the field[,] it is desir-

102. Withers, Special Order No. 21, 4:50, NARA RG 109.
103. *OR* 31(1):480–508.

able that the place should be filled at once [and] that the new Commander may have the benefit of the position in the execution of his duties, and to avoid the trouble that sometimes spring up from jealousy amongst aspirants." Kershaw, the interim division commander, was perhaps the best brigade commander McLaws had developed. On April 28 Cooper sent a telegram to McLaws, first in Abingdon, Virginia, then in Sparta, Georgia, informing him that "a major-general is required at Savannah for the command of the defenses of that city." The telegram ended: "Do you desire the assignment? Answer at once by telegraph."[104]

Special Order No. 107, issued on May 7, contained the notation that "Major-General Lafayette McLaws will immediately rejoin his command." McLaws was traveling to resume his command in Virginia when he passed through Richmond in late May. He had already prepared two drafts of a speech that he planned to make before his soldiers. Both began with the statement, "It is a great pleasure under any circumstance to meet again with friends after a long separation." One continued, "But to meet with fellow soldiers after such a long absence, and under the circumstances which I was relieved from command, affords double satisfaction." The other described home events before McLaws wrote: "For me to meet you all fellow soldiers and friends after such a long separation, after the many efforts until now futile to resume my rights and my position, give much more pleasure than if I had been away but for a short period & upon my own application. With your permission I will give you a short synopsis of the different efforts to gain my command again." In both versions, McLaws laid out the events that had transpired from the time of his dismissal, through the court-martial, to his return to command.[105]

Longstreet continued to be concerned about McLaws. McLaws wrote Ganahl the month before his (McLaws's) death, "Mr. [Jefferson] Davis whom I called upon [in Richmond] when on my way to resume command of my division told me there was such a bitter feeling in the corps & especially among my old soldiers, that Gen Lee was of the opinion it would be better if I was put on duty elsewhere." Lee also left the door open for McLaws to return when he told Davis that if McLaws "insisted, I of course he said had a right to go back." The conversation with Davis took place with several other individuals in the room. Davis told McLaws "that he was sorry Longstreet

104. *OR* 35(2):453.
105. Two undated manuscripts, SHC-LM.

had not taken my advice, and had refrained from assaulting Knoxville at the time he did."[106]

After asking to see McLaws, Braxton Bragg offered him Major General William Henry Chase Whitting's command under Beauregard. Since McLaws "had no mount, no staff, I declined the offer unless ordered." Jefferson Davis then sent for McLaws and told him that the District of Georgia, which extended halfway to Charleston, South Carolina, needed a new commander. "General Gilmer, then in command was to be relieved because of sickness; and as Gov. Joseph E. Brown of Georgia, so he had understood, was friendly to me & I to him, he felt constrained to order me there, and hoped I would go willingly." Major General Jeremy Francis Gilmer was responsible for the defense of Savannah. Both Davis and Bragg assured McLaws that his "record was clear, and there could be no reflection against me because of my transfer to another command."[107]

Apparently Longstreet was not only concerned about McLaws's return, he was even more worried about the effect McLaws would have on his old division. McLaws learned later that if he returned, there "would have been a grand demonstration of welcome . . . and I was warned that if in my response to the welcome, I should do, or say anything reflecting upon Genl Longstreet, it was his intention to re-arrest me." On May 18 Longstreet's work paid off, as Special Order No. 115, "issued in accordance with instructions from his Excellency the President," specified that "Major-General L. McLaws, Provisional Army Confederate States, will proceed to Charleston, S.C., and report to Major-General Samuel Jones, commanding, &c., for assignment to the command of the defenses of Savannah, Ga." In a letter of May 20, 1864, to Confederate secretary of war James A. Seddon, McLaws wrote, "whatever grounds of complaint may have been against me have been dismissed and my right to restoration of my proper command remains undisputed." He concluded, "if I am severed from command permanently, the decision in my case as announced in Genl Orders No. 46, gone for naught, my accusers will have gained their ends, and in so far as this action is taken in my case, I will stand convicted."[108]

Lafayette McLaws's Confederate military career had come full circle. He

106. LM to Joseph Ganahl, June 27, 1897, SHC-LM.

107. Ibid.

108. Ibid., Withers, Special Order No. 107, 4:288, NARA RG 109; Special Order No. 115 and LM to Secretary of War, May 20, 1864, both in NARA M 437.

began anew where he had started four years earlier in Savannah. Union major general William Tecumseh Sherman now led his army away from the smoldering ruins of Atlanta in a march to the sea and Savannah. Lafayette McLaws, the general known for his defensive tactics and emplacements, attempted the impossible, for the burden of stopping Sherman's advance into Savannah rested largely on his shoulders.

When Lieutenant General William Joseph Hardee assumed command of the Department of South Carolina, Georgia, and Florida in September 1864, McLaws watched and prepared as Sherman left his mark on Georgia. He does not seem to have given up hope for a Southern victory, but he became increasingly concerned about the financial condition of his family during Sherman's march to the sea.

Hardee made the decision to evacuate Savannah lest it suffer the same fate as Atlanta. On December 20 McLaws helped oversee the army's late-night departure to South Carolina. It was an army made up of soldiers crippled from the war's early years, elderly men, and young boys. On February 22, 1865, at Fort Steven's Depot, McLaws began making daily notations in his journal. His entries continue uninterrupted, with the exception of four days, through March 30, 1865. Sherman's advance continuously placed McLaws in a defensive position as the army under Hardee, and later under Joseph E. Johnston, retreated through the Carolinas. They provide personal observations he made as the Confederates desperately tried to stem the tide sweeping through their countryside. One last battle took place at Bentonville, North Carolina, on March 19 through 21, 1865.

But McLaws's service did not end at Bentonville. On March 9, Beauregard sent a note to Johnston seeking a replacement for the current commander of Augusta, Georgia. He wrote: "A good major-general should be sent there [Augusta] at once to replace General [D. H.] Hill, who is now in command. I am informed he would not be acceptable again to the people." On March 17 Hardee drafted a cryptic note to Johnston stating that he "thought it best not to mention the order to anyone until McLaws arrives." On March 21 Beauregard asked Johnston, "Whom will you send to Augusta, McLaws or Wright?" Major General Ambrose Ransom Wright, like McLaws, was a native Georgian who had also served in the Army of Northern Virginia. On April 10, in Special Order No. 26, Johnston made the assignment official. McLaws was to assume "command of the Military District of Georgia, comprising so much of that State as is not included in the Department of Tennessee and Georgia." McLaws's last official act was to publish Johnston's announcement "to explain to the Southern people the state of things which compelled me [Johnston] to put an end to the war," on May 11, 1865.[109]

The Postwar Years, 1865–1897

In a February 1863 letter to Emily, Lafayette McLaws wondered what he would do after the war. He recognized that his only training was that of a military officer—he had no farming, artistic, or business skills. The conclusion of the war and the devastation that faced Southern officers and men as they returned home must have weighed heavily on his mind. McLaws's homecoming revived echoes of his military career. He found Augusta an unconquered city, bypassed by Sherman on his march through the South. On the morning of May 1, 1865, three hundred discharged Southern soldiers started a riot when they pillaged the former government's quartermaster stores. Charles Jones wrote: "The May Day riot made it necessary for McLaws to declare martial rule the next day, to restore order until Augusta was formally occupied by Federal troops. Each ward was put under a general, then in the city. . . . Orders printed in the newspaper required everyone to remain off the streets except for business. Women, children, and Negroes were forbidden to loiter on danger of being fired on where there is a mob by cannon or small arms."[110]

As time went on, McLaws's future became even more uncertain. In 1866 voters elected McLaws to his father's old position as clerk of the superior and inferior courts of Richmond County. In short order, the local Federal military officers who did not want Southern sympathizers in government positions turned him out of office. But U.S. president Andrew Johnson restored his post, and he served out his original two-year term as clerk.

H. W. Graber, a former Texas scout for McLaws, recalled that "after spending a few days in Augusta, I found that one of my old commanders, General Lafayette McLaws, was then acting clerk of the Superior Court, with his office at the court house." Graber, a member of the 8th Texas Cavalry, had scouted for McLaws from Savannah through the Carolinas to Bentonville. He "found him wearing his old Confederate gray, with buttons and trimmings shorn off, and in conversation, referred to his love of the old uniform, still preferring it, but he said it was not a matter of choice, but of necessity." The court's fees and salary were insufficient to meet the needs of

109. *OR* 47(2):1353, 1410, 1445, 779, 874.
110. Jones, *Memorial History*, 94.

the McLaws family. McLaws told Graber that he expected Foster Blodgett, the mayor of the city, to remove him from office. "He seemed to be at a loss as to his future; said he was educated a soldier, which he had always been and never tried to make a living as a civilian, in fact, didn't know anything else."[111]

One option might have been to obtain the help of former West Point classmate, now Union major general John Pope, who commanded Georgia. Pope, raised in Louisville, Kentucky, had asked McLaws to pay him a visit. By-the-book McLaws "was afraid to accept, fearing unjust criticism by leading men of the State of Georgia, who would suspect that the object of this visit was to get office and join the Radical [Republican] band." McLaws told Graber that he would never change parties, yet he also "thought the State of Georgia had treated him badly and especially his rich acquaintances, at one time friends, and he seemed to feel he was an outcast with no prospect of ever re-entering the army, therefore, not knowing what to do." McLaws did write Pope's office to verify that the positions of magistrate in the 123rd District and surveyor in Richmond County were still open.[112]

McLaws purchased 1,572 acres in Effingham County in January 1870, the month and year of his daughter Elizabeth's birth. According to Virginia McLaws, the plantation was "named Egypt, because of the fine corn raised there. The house was quite large, two stories and a very high attic—a nice porch downstairs and upstairs with columns." The house was located forty miles north of Savannah. It "had eight large rooms with high ceilings, large closets in each, and every one with a nice fireplace. In those days there were no toilet facilities, no electric lights. There was an outdoor kitchen, also one on the large back porch." McLaws made the purchase, as the trustee for his wife Emily, for $2,500—$500 down and the balance with interest to be paid in two years.[113]

In addition to engaging in farming, McLaws attempted to sell life insurance for the Carolina Life Insurance Company, whose president was Jefferson Davis. Davis held "reasonable hope that southern men would prefer to insure with us rather than a northern company." McLaws believed the same; Davis wrote him, "your unwillingness to accept the idea of failure is the best

111. Graber, *Sixty-Two Years,* 299.

112. Ibid.; Lieutenant John E. Hosmun to LM, October 17, 1867, SHC-LM.

113. GHS-VM ETM, 2; Edmund C. Corbett to LM as trustee for ETM, Effingham County Deed of Sale, January 27, 1870, Effingham County Records.

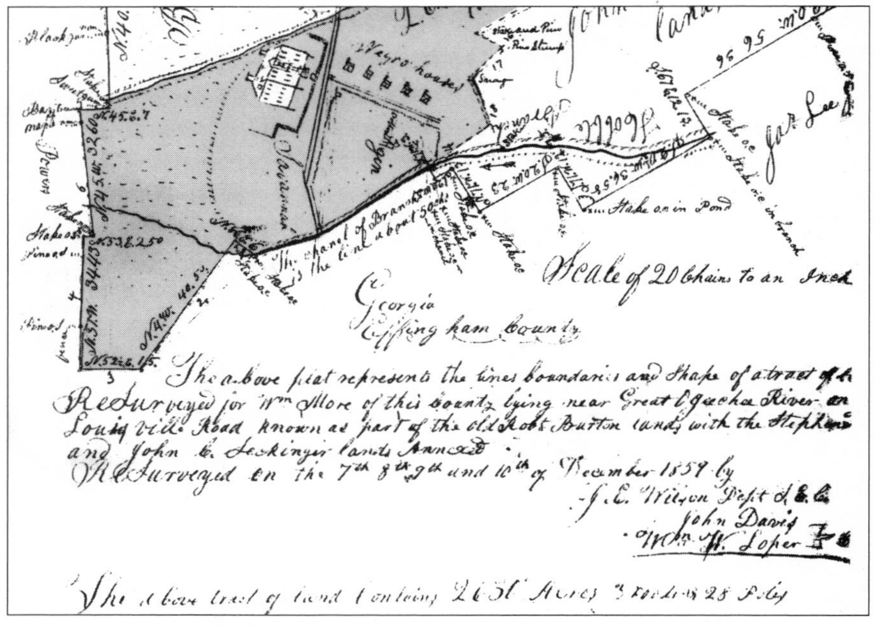

Copy of Egypt deed plan. (Public domain, Effingham County, Ga.)

guarantee of success." But McLaws could not find a way to make a living selling insurance or real estate.[114]

His hardships deepened in 1870, as he failed to succeed in business, his planting did not progress satisfactorily, and questions developed regarding clear title to Egypt. In a note to his older brother William in September 1872, he lamented: "I have been waiting here, waiting for proper titles before exerting myself to improve the premises. I have lost money and time and all from [Edmund C.] Corbett not furnishing proper titles according to agreement. . . . I have been suffering much with Vertigo again, and with a numbness in my fingers and extremities, which annoyed myself and family exceedingly but have been much better today."[115]

In 1871 McLaws initiated a correspondence with Joseph E. Johnston. His former commander wrote: "of all those associates there is no one whose official opinion and esteem I more respect than yours. You can understand, therefore, that your letter was *highly* gratifying and will be carefully preserved."[116]

114. Jefferson Davis to LM, November 19, 1870, SHC-LM.
115. LM to William R. McLaws, September 3, 1872, GHS-LM.
116. J. E. Johnston to LM, November 9, 1871, SHC-LM.

As his financial situation continued to worsen between 1872 and 1875, McLaws realized that he was not a farmer and would have difficulty securing a steady income. He therefore renewed his efforts to find an administrative or elected post. Ambrose R. Wright, owner of the *Augusta Chronicle and Sentinel,* assured him that "I will cheerfully give you my vote and whatever influence I may be able to wield to enable you to procure the Office of Comptroller General of the State."[117]

McLaws balanced his need for a steady income with a willingness to write or speak about Civil War battles. In 1873 he started the first of several exchanges with other former commanders, opponents, and fellow officers. Former brigadier general William Nelson Pendleton, the nominal Army of Northern Virginia chief of artillery, gave a lecture that dealt with Lee's alleged order to Longstreet to attack at sunrise on July 2, 1863. McLaws, on his own initiative, offered a written response to the lecture, with a copy to Longstreet, that formed the factual foundation that ultimately disproved the supposed order. Some historians have regarded this document as a defense of Longstreet's actions. In reality, McLaws detailed the events leading up to the attack to show why it could not have happened at sunrise. He also established the sequence of events demonstrating that his men arrived on the field of battle as early as possible and met their commander's expectations. Conversely, they could not have attacked at sunrise since they were not in position to do so.[118]

In 1875 McLaws traveled to Washington City to see former West Point friend and then current U.S. president, Ulysses Simpson Grant. The meeting took place after a delegation from Savannah had approached Grant for funding to clear the military obstructions in the Savannah River. Grant inquired about his "old friend" McLaws and learned that he was in dire financial circumstances. After dinner, McLaws wrote, "the general led the conversation so as to find out as to my private affairs asking what I was doing, how getting along, if I lived comfortably &c. I told him that I was then farming in a small way & living precariously." Grant paused and then asked, "McLaws have you any objection to holding office under me?" McLaws "told him that I could not perceive where the objection is in my doing so, that I resigned to follow my state when Georgia seceded as my education led me to believe that my citizenship of the U.S. came through my state." (McLaws's first alle-

117. Ambrose R. Wright to LM, October 16, 1872, SHC-LM.

118. LM to James Longstreet, June 10, 1873, and Longstreet to LM, July 20, 1873, SHC-LM.

giance was to his state.) He continued, "if I had not gone with my State, I would have regarded myself as a foreigner . . . that as my State had been restored by her own consent to the former relations with the Union, it was my duty to put myself back to follow her fortunes, so far as I was able to do so . . . & I do not know of any reason why I should not take office under my government." Consequently, Grant appointed McLaws as the collector of internal revenue for the Third District of Georgia. He worked in Savannah, where he boarded in a house on Congress Street, and returned to Egypt by train on the weekends.[119]

In 1876 Grant appointed McLaws postmaster for the city of Savannah, and the entire McLaws family moved to the first of four rented houses on South Broad, then Liberty Street. His daughter Virginia recounted a Savannah newspaper comment during this time: "The Post Office in this city is administered by Gen. McLaws. He has reformed many irregularities, and appointed a corps of assistants who are efficient and courteous. The people of Savannah are indebted to them for the best managed office in the state." McLaws, ever the detail person, brought new efficiencies to the office. President Rutherford Birchard Hayes reappointed McLaws to the postmaster position, though President Chester A. Arthur declined to do so in early 1885.[120]

McLaws also led the formation of the Atlantic and Mexican Gulf Canal Company, charted and approved by the state of Georgia on February 23, 1876. The legislation created the corporation to "build, construct, own and maintain a canal . . . from the St. Mary's or Big Satilla River, through the Okefenokee Swamp, or along its southern border, and thence westward by the most direct and practicable route . . . to the waters of the Gulf of Mexico." The canal's objective was to "open an artificial line of water communication" for the purposes of transporting timber, lumber and other products to market.[121]

The company's founding board of directors included "Joseph Shepard, G. A. Swain, and Philip Raiford of St. Mary's; Gen. Joseph E. Johnston and Gen. Lafayette McLaws, John R. Bachlott, S. L. Barnes and William Rogers of Savannah, Georgia." Meeting on April 20, 1876, the board elected Mc-

119. Undated manuscript on meeting with President U. S. Grant in Washington City, GHS-LM; GHS-VM ETM, 2.

120. GHS-VM LM Sketch, 14; William H. Taylor to LM, November 28, December 2, 1884, Duke-LM. Taylor summarized his attempts to influence the new assistant postmaster to retain LM.

121. Copy of Atlantic and Mexican Gulf Canal Co. charter by Georgia, Duke-LM.

Photograph of Lafayette McLaws as he appeared after the Civil War.
(Courtesy of the Georgia Historical Society)

Laws chairman and Shepard secretary and issued 10,000 shares of stock for a total of $1 million. McLaws received a salary of $2,500 per year plus $500 for travel expenses. The board also awarded 1,000 shares of stock for "services rendered & expenses incurred by Lafayette McLaws in forming the company, obtaining the charter & passage of a bill through Congress ordering a survey (for the above mentioned Incorporaters)." At a meeting following the board's actions, the stockholders elected McLaws president of the company. He was "authorized to negotiate with capitalists in the United States and Europe for the necessary funds to construct the canal."[122]

The Atlantic and Mexican Canal Company remained in operation through February 2, 1884, and continued to seek capital funding in New York City, England, and France. Florida governor William D. Bloxham approved a legislative measure on March 1, 1883, granting the company certain privileges in that state; the act had received unanimous endorsement in the senate and only two nay votes in the assembly. Despite extensive efforts to sell stock subscriptions and obtain additional funding from the U.S. government, the board voted on February 2, 1884, to authorize the "sale or otherwise dispose of all rights, privileges & franchises & grants which" the company had acquired.[123]

In 1886 McLaws opened a series of lectures by southern and northern military leaders organized by the Grand Army of the Republic in Boston. This marked his last career change. The former army officer wrote many articles and delivered a considerable number of lectures. He engaged in extensive correspondence with former friends and foes. Eighty-three of the 113 postwar letters found in SHC-LM are dated between 1886 and 1897. Moreover, this collection contains a substantial number of articles, lectures, copies of selected portions of Official Records (OR), and galley proofs of articles with handwritten notations. In his quest for assembling facts, understanding the late war, and earning a living, McLaws thus became a prolific writer.

The 1890s and the last seven years of McLaws's life may have been both his best and worst years. During this period he began to gain recognition for his articles and lectures, and he became the first honorary president of the Confederate Veterans Association of Savannah, an association he had previously helped organize and served as the first president. In 1893 the board of governors of the Chicago World's Columbian Exposition elected McLaws to the executive committee, though his service ended before the exposition opened when he refused to place an *R* beside his name demonstrating a Republican Party affiliation. He argued that Georgia governor John Brown Gordon had not requested a political party affiliation before he

122. Ibid.; Atlantic and Mexican Gulf Canal Co. board minutes, April 20, 1876, and stockholders minutes, April 20, 1876, Duke-LM.

123. Approval of Florida act, March 1, 1883, Duke-LM; Atlantic and Mexican Gulf Canal Co. board minutes, February 2, 1884, Duke-LM.

recommended McLaws's appointment. McLaws stood on principle and refused to renounce his membership in the Democratic Party, knowing that he was sacrificing what little income he could count on from the fair. Ironically, Longstreet was his alternate and he too resigned his position following McLaws's lead. McLaws's ability to make a comfortable living remained questionable.[124]

McLaws's financial situation continued to deteriorate. While many of his friends and family managed to survive the war and grow in political and financial stature, McLaws appears to have never asked for help. Indeed, several friends strongly encouraged him to approach Grant regarding a political appointment. Perhaps his most difficult task was to apply for a Mexican War pension, for this would reveal to his friends and the men who served under him how destitute he had become. He would have to file several affidavits and ask individuals to write about his physical and financial status. This would have forced him to swallow a good bit of pride.

McLaws's application for the pension was received on June 21, 1887, and the government issued a certificate from Knoxville, Tennessee, on October 14 for eight dollars per month. McLaws's sworn affidavit was supported by affidavits sworn by two of his former commanders, Alexander R. Lawton and James Longstreet, both on May 30, 1887.

On November 13, 1894, and again on December 7, 1894, McLaws asked for an increase due to his disability and current financial situation. On the application for an increase he explained, "In March last, I had my left eye extracted and am still under treatment because of it." Furthermore, "my right eye was injured when I was young and the sight seriously impaired because of the old wound or injury and from age." McLaws also described other physical disabilities, including his pepperbox pistol wound: "I am in constant, more or less pain all the time from either rheumatism in my hip joint or from the ball, just mentioned, and I am wholly disabled from manual labor." He wrote that he had no means of subsistence except for support from his children and that "I do not own any property, real or personal, but my clothes, books and papers, from which no income is derived." With the pension application were affidavits from Brantley A. Denmark, president of the Citizens Bank of Savannah; A. R. Lawton, his former commander, now president of the Augusta and Savannah Railroad Company; and Dr. Montague L. Boyd, his physician. Lawton wrote, "I know that he is very poor; that

124. LM to Commissioners of the Worlds Fair from Georgia, April 1893, SHC-LM; Thomas E. Garvin to LM, October 16, 1893, SHC-LM.

his present pension of eight dollars per month, taken in connection with his income from all sources, is utterly insufficient, in my opinion, to provide him with the necessities of life." The government granted the pension increase on December 11, 1894, backdated to commence on December 6, 1894.[125]

It took Longstreet until October 20, 1892, to personally acknowledge to McLaws that he had treated him dishonestly. Although he never offered a personal apology, Longstreet did admit in a letter to McLaws: "I think I have made clear it was I who caused the failure at Knoxville. It is after the same course as pointed out in my Knoxville address two years ago." McLaws considered the remarks too little too late. One month before his death, he wrote: "Since my report of Knoxville, was published [in the OR], Genl Longstreet, in an address he made at a re-union at Knoxville, exonerated me from all blame for the failure at Knoxville, taking it all himself. But my report exonerates me, so his generosity comes too late." He concluded, "I have written the foregoing, in order that you may have a statement of certain things, that never will appear in official reports—but which will enable one to form an opinion as to the motives of action, of certain men of high renown, and perhaps lead to a more just conception of their real merits, than the general public entertains for the want of such information."[126]

McLaws exchanged letters on the subject with his court-martial counsel, Joseph Ganahl, in 1894. He reflected at length on the dissension among senior commanders when Longstreet, D. H. Hill, and Buckner attempted to remove Bragg from command of the Army of Tennessee, viewing their acts as a disservice to the Confederacy. He wrote Ganahl, "I declined to prefer charges against Longstreet because I did not wish to be a party to dissensions among Confederates." He continued, "I once wrote Longstreet that he had laid himself open to very severe criticism & that I had been urged to retaliate by bringing his conduct under review; but I had refrained as it was not in my nature to bear malice, & I thought it would be detrimental to the Confederate cause, to keep creating dissensions."[127]

On April 19, 1895, the Confederate Veterans Association of Savannah sponsored a series of six lectures, published by the association's president

125. LM Application for Mexican War Pension Survivor Benefits, Application 14421, Certificate 9514, October 14, 1887, NARA RG 15.

126. James Longstreet to LM, October 20, 1892, and LM to Joseph Ganahl, June 27, 1897, SHC-LM; LM to James A. Seddon, May 20, 1864, NARA M 437.

127. LM to Joseph Ganahl, July 23, 1894, SHC-LM.

Photograph of Lafayette McLaws as he appeared late in life. (Courtesy of the Georgia Department of Archives and History)

in its 1896 annual report. McLaws spoke on "The Maryland Campaign" on April 19, 1895, and "The Battle of Gettysburg" on April 27, 1896. The forty-one-page essay on Gettysburg presents a detailed, systematic sequence of events that led up to the battle and its conclusion. It also takes Longstreet to task and questions the actions of Lee's subordinates on the field.

In the essay McLaws recounts the events that took place after the failure of Longstreet's attack of July 3, 1863, and spent three pages dissecting his corps commander's behavior. "Shortly after the repulse," McLaws received a request from Brigadier General Evander McIvor Law, who had taken command of Hood's division, "asking if he could spare a brigade to put in place of one from his division which had been drawn out from his line to meet the enemy's cavalry." McLaws sent back word that he "could not spare a man" as "the enemy were close to my line and might attack at any moment, although there was no sign of it as yet, but it was to be expected." G. Moxely Sorrel showed up within a few minutes with "an order from Gen. Longstreet for your [McLaws] command and that of Hood to retire at once to your position of yesterday." McLaws was "astonished" by the order and suggested a delay until it could be reconfirmed. He could not believe that an order to retire had been issued when the enemy was not advancing against his or Hood's front. But Sorrel insisted that "the order was positive, and there was no use in discussing it." McLaws then withdrew his division in an orderly manner and reestablished his line where he had begun at 4:00 P.M. on July 2. "So soon as my command retired, the enemy advanced to occupy the positions I had left, having a cloud of skirmishers in front." Sorrel then returned and asked McLaws if he could "re-occupy the ground" he had just vacated. McLaws responded that he "would dislike to undertake it, as the enemy was occupying it in heavy force." He asked Sorrel if he remembered the earlier order to retire; he also wanted to know why the new order was issued to "retake the abandoned position." Sorrel answered, "Because, Gen. Longstreet now denies that he gave the order for this command to retire."[128]

After the campaign McLaws asked Longstreet for an explanation "because it was not pleasant to be under the command of any one who would deny giving an order after it was found out that existing circumstances did not imperatively call for such an order—as it afterwards appeared." In "The Battle of Gettysburg," he concludes the section on Longstreet with the observation that "it was unpleasant to think that the reputation of my command and myself were dependent upon—shall I say—a bad memory?"[129]

In the last two pages of the piece, McLaws reflects on Lee, his senior subordinates, and the battle's outcome. He repeats Longstreet's published comment "That Gen. Lee was excited and off his balance, as was evident on this afternoon (July 2), and that he labored under that oppression until enough

128. LM, *Battle of Gettysburg,* 89–90.
129. Ibid., 91.

blood was shed to appease him." Yet, McLaws notes, "The evidences I have given seems to show that it was not Gen. Lee, but his leading lieutenants, [who] were off their balance, either that or had never possessed that capacity to determine the most salient points in the positions to be attacked. . . . So that now, as in the past, and as I believe will be done in the future, we can, with sentiments of profound admiration and respect, [say] 'Hurrah for Gen. Lee.'"[130]

McLaws then relates three stories that deal with command and control of men in battle, providing examples of how Generals Winfield Scott and Zachary Taylor involved their senior officers in decision-making councils:

> It was the practice of Gen. Winfield Scott, who commanded our armies and captured the City of Mexico, in the Mexican war, to call his principal officers, and many others of lesser rank, to meet him, before undertaking any important movement. When assembled, he would tell them he had called them, not to ask their advice, but to give them an outline of a movement he was about to make, and to hear their views about it. He wished them to talk freely about it, and discuss it. By doing this you will have clearer ideas, he told them, each one, of his special duties, when the order to execute is issued, and I may get ideas or information from your conversation which will assist me, when issuing the final order, by showing me in what particulars I should be the most clear and the most positive.

McLaws cites Taylor's council after the Battle of Palo Alto and another story by F. X. Aubrey, a French Canadian trader he met in New Mexico. He offers the three accounts to "strengthen his suggestion and belief" that if Robert E. Lee had called a council of his senior generals on July 1, he might have found a better solution than the one he selected. Since a council was not called, Lee "adopted the course which, if it had been intelligently and energetically carried out by his subordinates, would have produced the very best results."[131]

McLaws remained constant in his views on Longstreet to the end of his life. Shortly after Longstreet's memoir was published in 1895, McLaws wrote: "so it looks as if Gen Longstreets crucial test of the fitness of any one to command was his compliance or non-compliance with Longstreets 'suggestions'—It was a sort of mania of his, and there can be no doubt that he

130. Ibid., 95.
131. Ibid., 96.

was honest in that belief—for it seemed to make the difference, who it was he advised—if he followed his advice he was worthy, if he did not he was not worthy."[132]

On July 24, 1897, at the age of seventy-six, McLaws died suddenly at 12:20 in the morning. The *Savannah Morning News* reported: "His death was a great shock to his family, none of whom had the slightest idea until a few minutes before it occurred that his end was near. Except for an apparently slight attack of indigestion from which he suffered during the last few days, Gen. McLaws appeared to be in his usual health." According to the Savannah press, "he wrote with terseness and vigor." McLaws "had only recently been selected by General Clement A. Evans to write the history of 'Georgia in the Confederate War.'" The writer of the obituary made the astute observation that "it will always be a matter of profound regret that he should have died before this task was performed."[133]

Concluding Thoughts

Lafayette McLaws attempted to apply personal values of duty, honor, and service to his state and country in his everyday life. Commanders found that he carried out their orders, even if he disagreed with them. Though in several cases he may have delayed the execution of a task, his record shows that he took his duties and assigned responsibilities seriously. In the same way, McLaws expected his subordinate officers to complete their assignments. In recommending officers for promotion, he generally cited the phrase "competent to the discharge of the duties" or similar wording. The proper discharge of duties was a prerequisite for military unit discipline, and McLaws excelled in fostering such discipline.[134]

His concept of honor can be best demonstrated by what he thought was right, his high principles by how he dealt with others, and his integrity. He believed that an officer must be consistent, honest, and sincere in his dealings with colleagues.

Perhaps his most impressive trait was keeping meticulous records. He combined attention to even the most minor details with a methodical approach to decision-making. This focus on details may have contributed to

132. Manuscript marked "9," SHC-LM.

133. LM obituary, *Savannah Evening News,* September 24, 1897. Clement Anselm Evans, Georgia, a former Confederate brigadier general, published the *Military History of Georgia* (1895) and edited the twelve-volume *Confederate Military History* (1899).

134. Record for James Monroe Goggin, NARA M 331.

the perception that McLaws moved too slowly. Finally, McLaws was convinced that fulfilling the needs of his men helped ensure their success in battle. He did not sacrifice his men on the field, and concern for their welfare often placed him in conflict with his commanders. Virginia McLaws concluded that "some of his most prominent characteristics were extraordinary firmness and determination to do his duty, regardless of all selfish aspirations."[135]

The letters and journal entries of Lafayette McLaws illuminate the thoughts and actions of an important Confederate general who has remained virtually invisible over the last century. Whereas other Civil War generals have had biographies, autobiographies, diaries, or letters published, McLaws's body of work has not seen the light of day. His July 7, 1863, comment on Longstreet has received the most circulation. Periodically historians cite other letters, but few individuals outside the core group of Civil War historians realize the wealth of information that exists in the McLaws collections. McLaws adds both military insight and human sensitivity to his letters—ones that focus attention on many key leaders and the struggles of their troops in the war that tore this nation apart.

135. GHS-VM LM Sketch, 15.

Antebellum Army

Camp on North Fork of the Platte
Three Miles West of Scotts Bluff
[Nebraska Territory]
Aug. 8th 1858 [Sunday]

My dear wife

Although we came twenty four miles to day, & must march early tomorrow I cannot resist the pleasure of writing to you my darling to let you know how much more I am in love with my wife as distance has become so great as to be precluded from my thoughts when thinking of you. I have nearly given up any hope of returning, and therefore have become more reconciled to my fate. The uncertainty of our position, and the continual false reports that were continually reaching our ears in regard to our return, was the cause of my unhappiness being so much more acute than ever before—but now since we are out of the reach of all mails and all news, I can think calmly of my position and beg to form plans for the future. In all of which, [b]e assured my dear wife, the hope of seeing you stands prominent, and is the chief end and aim. How much I do wish your likeness was by me and those of the children. They would be great consolations.

To day we marched across Scotts Bluffs and are now camped three miles on the side towards Laramie. The day has been pleasant and the roads good. The men & officers are all healthy.

We expect to be at Laramie within three more days, where we will halt for two or three days, prepatory to our final start towards Utah. We have heard that both Major Lynde and Maj Gatlin will go on with Col Morrisons column, which left Laramie last Monday or Tuesday. Their idea in starting so early is, I have heard, to get through the mountains with their families at as early a day as possible so as to avoid the cold weather; for which I am very sorry for, as I was in hopes of having Major Lynde to command this column, Major Whiting being totally unfit for such business. being inert, absent minded ignorant and indifferent.[1]

1. Isaac Lynde, Vermont, major; Richard Caswell Gatlin, North Carolina, USMA 1832, major, later Confederate brigadier general; Pitcairn Morrison, New York, colonel,

You are of course in receipt of a good many letters as I send home one or more by every conveyance. I wrote last evening & last night a long letter to Willy & Johnny which you will explain to them of course & in doing so please, urge them to learn to read and write, so as to answer me.[2]

An officer whom we met the other day going to Kearney [Fort Kearny, Nebraska Territory] with some troops, cavalry, that had been ordered back, said that it was the general impression at Laramie that we would go on and to Oregon, but of course they do not know anything more about it than we do. I am really sorry that I should be so uninformed about the movements of the 7th Infy [Infantry] as to be unable to give you even a faint notion of what will probably take place & where we will go to, for I know how anxious you must be. As I do not expect to know anything[,] never hear anything until we arrive in Utah, let me advise you to take the Washington Star, in addition to the Missouri Republican, and also the New York Herald and if you like the Missouri Democrat. All those papers have correspondents in the army, and keep themselves better informed in regard to army movements, than any others. We see no indians and but little game. I however killed two grouse this evening, one of which was for dinner[,] the other I gave away.[3]

I am writing this in rather too great a hurry my own darling to give you all the little incidents and excitements which sway our little society. They are hardly worthy of note, but when I am at leisure and feel in a very good humor, I will try and answer you by some account of ourselves.

I hope you have bought your sewing machine and have become such an adept at it, as to be able to be no longer annoyed by poring over the boys clothes. Sticking your fingers and bleeding or dimming those soft dear eyes that know how to look so loving on me. When I have been behaving myself, those little "footsy tootsies" of yours must not be supposed to go beyond 2½ and those hands must be more carefully nursed than formerly, and besides you must be very careful of yourself, of your person and your dress, and be nothing *less* than the wife I left behind me, when we meet again, some time to come, be it soon or late, and in addition do not cease to love me.

I must now close with the old song, it is getting late and I must rise at 4 tomorrow. At Laramie I will give a long letter.

How selfish this letter is, to speak only of myself and of my desires—but

---

later brigadier general; Daniel Powers Whiting, New York, attended the USMA in 1828, major, later lieutenant colonel.

2. William (Willy or Willie) Huguenin and John (Johnny or Johnnie) Taylor McLaws were LM's oldest children.

3. The grouse is a bird similar in size to a quail.

what else can I say? excuse me if it is unpleasant and I will promise to be different, when you wish it. Good by & God bless you my dear wife, I must to bed to indulge myself undisturbed, as I do for hours in thinking of you & the children. Kiss the children for me and give my love to all.

your husband L M^c^Laws

((( )))

Camp On Timpanogos River
[Utah Territory]
May 21st 1860 [Monday]

My dear wife
An opportunity offering I hasten to send you a few words, to state my whereabouts.

We are now but ten miles up the Timpanogos thirty nine (39) from Camp Floyd, and this is our sixth day.[4] The river is too high to ford, too swift to be bridged unless with great labor and many inconveniences, and the road way has been so much washed, it would be nearly an impossibility to return. So here we are, doing nothing but grumble, that is the grumblers grumble. I do nothing but laugh at them and have my own amusement. The ladies are of course very much annoyed at the delay especially in this Cañon [canyon], as the mountains all around us are covered with snow, and the sun is visible from about 9 oclock A.M. until four P.M. So narrow is the way through which this river passes to the lake, and so high and close upon us are the mountains. Consequently the temperature is not agreeable, being uncomfortably cold during the night and in the early morning and late in the evening. I pity them, and so does every one, but here we are. The evil must be endured for it cannot be remedied.

It will be at least twelve days before we reach Fort Bridger [Utah Territory]. Our march is very slow and annoying as we are compelled to regulate our motions to accord with those of the oxen. As yet unbroken and with drivers totally unskilled.

Write as heretofore to Denver City [Nebraska Territory] with the usual indorsement. Give my love to the boys and to my daughter & my best regards to those with you. The opportunity now offered was totally unexpected and I have no time to write fully.

I will try and be ready in future. Up to this time everything has been in

4. The Timpanogos River is located near the Great Salt Lake. Camp Floyd was on the western side of the Great Salt Lake in the Utah Territory.

confusion. Occasionally the train does not arrive until long after dark.[5] On one occasion, not until after one A.M. Two wagons have been upset in the river, as the road winds immediately along the bank.

Good by and God bless you.
As ever your devoted husband
L McLaws

((( )))

Fort Defiance New Mexico [Territory]
October 17th 1860 [Wednesday]

My dearly beloved boys

I have been thinking of you so much that I have determined to write you, it being the only way to satisfy myself for not being able to have you talking to me. It does not satisfy me to be sure, but tis better than keeping quiet and being dissatisfied. This is my experience and you will find out, if you learn to write me, that you will feel much more satisfied after you have written me a letter, than you would be, if you did nothing else but wish I would come.

Well you will want to hear about my present occupation and what I have been doing.

I left Fort Craig [New Mexico Territory] on the 10th of last month, with two companies of infantry and one of mounted rifles and after travelling along the Rio Grande del Norte for forty three miles, left the river and turned my course to the west, up the dry bed of a stream called the Salada, or Salt Creek.[6] About six miles from the river following the bed of the Salada, the country changed in character very much, for on both sides of us, the sides of the creek were composed of coarse sandstone rising perpendicularly some two hundred feet, occasionally narrowing so as not to be more than fifty yards across with the sides full of "gullies" and holes and narrow ravines, presenting most beautiful places for the indians to conceal themselves and fire upon us. But no Indians were seen, not even a fresh trail and we passed through without being in the least disturbed— The first day we came nineteen miles and camped near a fine little spring bursting from the side of a hill. The water however was quite salt but yet twas drinkable, or we thought so as the day was very warm & we had had no water on the road.

5. LM is referring to a wagon supply train.

6. The Rio Grande del Norte is the northern part of the Rio Grande. Salada probably refers to the Salado River, which merged with the Rio Grande just north of present-day Socorro, N.Mex.

The next day we travelled on still in the bed of the Salada and finding no water there except such as was so salt that nothing could drink it. We turned up the dry bed of a mountain torrent and after following it three miles up to its head in the mountains came to a spring in the mountains, the water of which smelled so bad that it was difficult to drink it. But every one[,] both animals and men were so thirsty that they very soon drank it in quantities. We found that after boiling it & letting it cool, the sulphur & other odors it had were driven off and the water was very fine. Our camp this night was high up in the mountains, and as the sun went down it became very cold, which was made evident next morning for I had ice in my basin more than a quarter of an inch thick. You must recollect that on this trip no one had tents, we made our beds, the men in line & I in front of them, in the same order as when the company was formed in line, all on the ground and went to sleep looking at the stars. I did so every night and often wished that I could read something in their bright twinkling looks, to tell me about my wife and children.

The next day, I sent my spy company,[7] which was composed of twenty Mexicans ahead, to look about for water as no one knew anything of the country, and I moved down the mountain two miles to a spring which a Mexican had found the evening previous. The spy company soon returned and reported that they had come across the tracks of eleven indians with forty head of cattle coming from the direction of the Rio Grande. I at once sent the orderly sergeant of the company of rifles with twenty men and the spy company to follow up the trail, which was reported as being very fresh. About five oclock in the evening a party came back from the sergeants party and reported that he was twelve miles ahead at a spring & that he had found out there that the trail was older than had at first been supposed & therefore he had not pursued it further.

The next morning I moved on to the spring where the sergeant was, which was about four miles off the road & again up in the mountains. The water was however good. The night was again cold, with ice in the morning.

The next day, turned North and in about five miles found myself again in the dry bed of the Salada, and near three high peaks which can be seen for a long distance, called by the Spaniards or rather by the Mexicans "Los Tres Hermanos" or the three brothers. I named one Willie, another Johnny and then not being another boy I made the third peak a girl and called it Laura, it was a little fat looking mountain and seemed as if it had its head on one

7. The spy company and its men were scouts.

side talking to the other two, her brothers.[8] The head of the creek was so dry that I began to be fearful about obtaining water, and after digging in the best looking place to see if there was any appearance of moisture, & finding none, I went on feeling more anxious. However in about sixteen miles, I saw the spy company ahead halt and turn out their horses to graze & on reaching this place found a hole of water about one yard wide & two long[,] about enough for the men to have a good drink from, but none for the animals. On searching over the wide bottom we were then in the guards found another pool, out of which five ducks flew. I immediately shouted out for the men to watch the ducks, which every one did, and after they had described many circles very amazing to us anxious expectants, the kind birds were seen to disappear in the midst of some tall weeds about a ½ mile distant. I at once galloped over there and found a long narrow "gully" full of rain water. I was so delighted that I let the ducks go & thanked them as they went, as they had proved my best friends in this time of need, although I could have shot some if not all of them, as my double barrel gun was loaded & you know I can kill ducks. The water proved sufficient to give the animals one drink, and for the men during the rest of the day and to fill their canteens in the morning.

Ahead of us we could see a high sierra or mountain range which being on our course, it was supposed we must climb. It looked, the country did, as if we might go around the chain of mountains but no none knew what would happen if we should turn from our course, so I decided to keep straight ahead[;] after travelling about ten miles, I had the pleasure of finding myself & command on the top of the mountain & before me stretched a broad table land, with fine grass, and fine large pine trees to give beauty to the scene beneath. Now lay the whole country I had transversed/travelled over during the three days previous & up to this time the fourth. Far off to the ~~North~~ East was the Albuquerque Mountain, and to the South East, not so far, was a noted mountain called the "Sierra de los Ladcones" or the "Robbers Mountain," so named because tis a favorite resort of the Navajos, who hiding themselves in the numerous ravines, & kanyons, and among the thick cedar growth which covers the slopes, make sudden decent upon the flocks ranging along the river, not twenty miles distant, and before pursuit can be made are far away in their mountain hiding places, or have had too much start towards their own country—(around and where I now am), to be afraid

8. LM named the three peaks after his three children, William Huguenin, then age eight; John Taylor, age seven; and Laura Taylor, age four.

of pursuit.[9] Away down South and to the West I could see detached ranges of mountains, the names of which no one [k]new[;] they appeared denseley covered with either pine or cedar, and I have no doubt are like the Sierra de los Ladcones [Ladrones], hiding places for numerous small bands of thieving indians or Mexicans or perhaps Americans.

After enjoying the scenery and resting my animals, the march continued for twelve miles futher, when after descending some steep bluffs, we travelled along the side of a beautiful valley for two or three miles, and towards evening went into it & in a mile or two, found water in holes, much to our gratification and made camp. Again it was quite cold with ice in the morning.

The next morning I started early and within eight miles struck a beautiful spring of water called the "Savaya," which means onion, the named being significant of the fact that the wild onion is found in abundance in the meadow land about the spring. Here I halted and remained all day.

Early the next morning ascended a considerable sierra, and travelling eight or ten miles, with the Dragoon Company a mile or thereabouts ahead was suddenly startled by hearing numerous shots fired to the front.[10] I put the infantry command on their guard, and riding forward found the mounted rifle company halted, and the men in that state of excitement which showed something had occured to disturb their usual equanimity of the soldiers nonchalanca [nonchalance].

On inquiry I found out that the company, while dismounted & walking their horses, had suddenly come upon a Navajo Indian, who was riding carelessly along, to all appearances totally unsuspicious that any one was near, that upon discovering the presence of each other, the indian fled & our men gave pursuit. The soldiers discharging their pistols, and the indian his arrows. The pursuers & the pursued were a long ways out of sight when I arrived, and I contented myself with sending a party to support the one that had gone after the indian and continued the journey. On the way I learned that the Indian had shot two arrows[,] one into two horses, one in each, and one arrow into a dog of the company that had pursued him, neither of the horses or the dog were badly hurt, and the officer in command of the company Assistant Surgeon McKee (whom I had placed in command there being no line officer present), said that he was certain that the indian had been

9. The Albuquerque Mountain, now called the Sandia Peak, has an elevation of 10,678 feet. LM wrote that the "Navajo's are terrifying people, stealing all their stock etc. near Albuquerque." LB1, September 1860.

10. A "Dragoon Company" was a company of mounted infantrymen who used the horse for transportation to the battlefield and then dismounted and fought as infantry.

shot five or six times, and his horse as often.[11] But still he ran on within five miles of that place, we commenced descending, and after going for more than a half mile down a very crooked and steep path, winding among large rocks and trees, came to a beautiful stream of water coming from a spring on the mountain side, and losing itself in a beautiful valley called "La Savajette" or "Little Onion"[;] here I halted for the day.[12]

Within an hour the party that had gone in pursuit of the indian and the one sent in its support both returned and reported that the indian & horse were both undoubtedly killed, as the men had repeatedly ridden within pistol shot and discharged their revolvers hitting either the indian or the horse, many times but that arriving to a steep precipice which the Navajo horse had gone at full speed & where the American horse could not follow. Sufficient time had been gained before our men had dismounted & gone down on foot to enable both Navajo horse & Navajo indian to disappear in the thick growth of cedar, pinoñ [pine] & underbrush.

My next letter will give the continuation of my trip to this place. Now, as tis late, and I am to be up early in the morning, I bid you good bye and good night.

My dear children, my boys & my dear little daughter you must love one another and love your mother & try always to be obedient & good. And I will always love you & try & write you all about myself. Good night.

Your father L M^c^Laws

You must all go and give Ma a plenty of kisses and tell her how much I love both her and you.

((( )))

Camp Near Fort Fauntleroy[13]
[New Mexico Territory]
December 10th 1860 [Monday]

My dear darling wife
I have just returned from a twenty two day scout. My command and myself in good health, and have but time to write you that I am here, and to say that Colonel Fauntleroy has granted me permission to avail myself of the leave

11. James Cooper McKee, Pennsylvania, surgeon, later brevet lieutenant colonel.

12. During the time of LM's service, the Navajo represented one of the largest Indian nations in the Utah and New Mexico Territories. His notes listed 12,000 Navajo, 5,500 to 7,000 Apache, 5,000 Utah, 2,400 Moque, 2,000 Kayugua, 2,000 Arrapahoe, 1,500 Cheyenne, and 1,200 Commanche Indians. Entry for September 1, 1860, LB1.

13. Fort Fauntleroy was to the east of Fort Defiance in what is now New Mexico.

of absence given by the War Department when the Navajo Expedition terminates. But the Expedition has not as yet terminated and I am as far off as ever from my sights which General Johnston first violated, and by so doing has caused my present condition.[14]

Col Canby intends prosecuting the war for some time to come, and I am to be one to carry it on.[15]

The mail leaves tomorrow morning and I am very tired, so my dearly beloved wife I bid you adieu and will defer answering your sweet letters until the morrow. Three letters came from you, one from WmR. Laura writes despondingly.[16]

Give my love to all with you. To the boys and my sweet little daughter a plenty of kisses. My dear wife I sympathise sincerely with you because of your afflicted sister and while hoping for her recovery cannot but feel grateful that come what may. She is so good and pure that the worst can have no terror for her.[17]

I am very much inclined to sleep my dear wife and so you must excuse me for this time.

Good bye & God bless you
Your devoted husband
L. McLaws

P.S. I send some precious stones, garnets and emeralds picked up through the country. They are pretty to look at by candle light— Give them to Laura as a Christmas present from me.

Your husband
L McLaws

14. Colonel Thomas Turner Fauntleroy, Virginia, was later brigadier general of Virginia state troops. Albert Sidney Johnston, Kentucky, brigadier and later Confederate general, led the Utah Expedition from 1858 to 1860.

15. Edward Richard Sprigg Canby, Kentucky, USMA 1839, brevet lieutenant colonel, later major general, accepted the last Confederate surrender.

16. WmR. was LM's older brother, William R. McLaws. Laura was LM's older sister.

17. LM is probably referring to ETM's older sister, Josephine P. Taylor. When the 1850 census was taken, ETM and Josephine lived with their older sister Anne Pendleton Taylor and her husband Frederick Geiger Edwards. Seventh Census, 1850, entry for Frederick G. Edwards, p. 343, Louisville—Fourth District, Jefferson County, Ky., NARA 432, RG 29; GHS-VM Tayor Children, 1; Taylor Family Records, Record for John Gibson Taylor Family, The Filson Club, Louisville.

((( )))

Camp 3^d Column near West Spring
Two miles from Fort Fauntleroy
[New Mexico Territory]
Dec 17th—1860 [Monday]

My darling wife

Tis now the 17th day of December. Seven days from Christmas and I am camped in the Navajo Nation, waiting for supplies in order to go upon another campaign. Very different indeed from my expectations when I left Utah. But it only shows how long an injustice works evil, before good can come of it. General Johnston by his gross partiality for others, seeking to make popularity by giving leaves to others, not entitled to it, thinking that they by going to Washington and speaking in his praise would bring something to his advantage is the sole and only cause why I am not with you now. Colonel Canby is endeavoring to do his duty through good and through evil report, and in spite of a great many unexpected obstacles, caused chiefly by the want of supplies. He has done more with fewer than was ever done before by any other officer commanding a campaign. But he has not done so much as he desired, and does not wish to leave what he has been ordered to do until it is completely performed.

I have just returned from a campaign with three companies of infantry and nineteen Mexicans. My course was down the "Rio Puerco of the West" as it is called on the maps and the Rio Colorado Chiquito, and then up to Lurin and Fort Fauntleroy where I now am.[18] On my second day out a part of my command under Lieut Brooks had a considerable skirmish with about fifty Navajos killing three men, capturing four women, and nine horses & equipments, buffalo robes &c &c, and destroying a considerable amount of cooking utensils and other property.[19] The same day a Mexican boy came in and asked for peace representing that he had been sent by a chief of a large band of indians. I did not send him back. But kept him for three or four days treating him well, and then asked him which he would rather do, stay with me and act as my guide and receive pay from the government while doing so and then be sent to his friends if he desired it. He at once declared that he was tired of living with the Navajoes, and would come with

18. Rio Puerco and Rio Colorado Chiquito are rivers in what was the New Mexico Territory.

19. Edward J. Brooks, Michigan, second lieutenant, later lieutenant.

me. I accordingly gave him back his horse and saddle & bridle and bows and arrows, and he has been riding along apparently contented ever since. He was taken from his parents when quite a child by the Apaches and sold by them to the Navajoes over ten years ago and with whom he has been ever since. I gave him a suit of old clothes and got some old shirts from others and had his hair cut, bought a pair of boots & comb, and soap and make him wash his face and hands and comb his hair every day and he has improved wonderfully, fattening like a pig. So much so that even *my* clothes are not too large for him. There is another boy along, a Navajo, who is under charge of Lieutenant Brooks. He has discarded all that there is of a Navajo about him, is dressed in soldiers clothes, has his hair cut, and washes himself regularly. He is constantly laughing and singing. Indeed he is so noisy that I have had to direct the guard to stop him in his pranks on two or three occasions. He is a nephew of the late great Chief Sarcitto Langos, but in the skirmish under Lieut Brooks he made straight up to one of his own people and shot him through the side with a pistol. One of the women taken is a niece of a Chief Arunijo, and is young and pretty, more costly dressed than any woman we have yet seen among the Navajoes, and shows that she is a blooded animal by doing nothing.[20] The two others are common people, and work willingly for the niece of the chief. We call the pretty one who is fat, El Gordo or the fat one. The next thin, Delgadita or the thin one, and the small one a girl of twelve or thirteen "El Chiquito" or the little one. They appeared very much frightened when first brought into camp but I gave them some presents, such as buttons, needles & thread, and gave "El Gordo" a piece of money with a hole through it to hang on her belt, where they carry all their trinkets and charms and told her mother who was also a captive that I would take good care that not one molested her. I gave the old woman a horse saddle and bridle and let her go to her people, telling her that if she wanted her daughter again, she must bring horses and sheep to exchange for her. Since then nothing has been heard of her. A few days ago I called on the captives, and El Gordo looking very sad. I sent for the interpretor and asked what was the matter. "She said that she was "Triste[,]" the Mexican word which signifies that a person is annoyed or sad about anything. "Triste about what?" I asked. She said that the Mexican man who has no teeth (Captain of the spy com-

20. The late Navajo chief was Zarcilla Largo, and the second chief mentioned was Armijo.

pany) had squeezed her legs. I told her that if he did it again I would have his hand cut off. With which assurance she seemed perfectly satisfied and dropped her "Triste" air at once. As they were troublesome in camp, it being necessary to have a special guard for them day and night, I asked Colonel Canby and he permitting, sent the women into the garrison of Fort Fauntleroy to be kept there. The Mexican boys name is "Jesus" which in Spanish is pronounced Hay Suse and is called by the Navajoes "Harcisse." One of the Navajo women, the one I have called "Delgodita" is a very fine worker, and Lieut Brooks was anxious to take her to fort Craig with him but Colonel Canby will not permit it. Saying that she must be sent back to their own people.

On my day out had another skirmish, capturing four horses, but the indians fled precipitously.

I will send you a copy of my report, although it is eighteen pages of writing if time will permit.

I am writing you to save the mail, if an opportunity should offer. Everything here is very irregular.

When you have read the report, please send it to W^{m}R. to whom I intend writing so soon as I have time—[21] I wish to ask his advice as to the course I should pursue, if Georgia seceeds from the Union. My present idea is to go with my State as a matter of course. To offer my services as a military man and a native born and do all in my power to keep the Union dissolved. If your State should not join the Southern Union I suppose you would ask for a separation, because of a difference of political opinions. If you should[,] if you have made up your mind to it[,] [l]et me know beforeabout, and I will endeavor to fortify my mind to the chances of fate. Of course I will have first choice for the children, and will take the one that leaves me best and has been the best behaved, so you will be a party to the choice. Great will be the tribulation and many the heart breakings. But be prepared for the struggle. I certainly will not be in the Northern Confederacy and let me beg of you, not to prejudice the children beforehand. Good bye. I will keep on writing as the opportunity offers. Will write tomorrow & next day.

I will leave in a few days I expect upon another expedition but will write you more fully to day. At present a train is to leave for the river and I cannot let an opportunity go by.

I have sent a pay account to Washington and will send another by this

21. LM's report to his brother is not found in SHC-LM.

mail.[22] Give the children many Merry Christmas & New Years. Merry Christmas from me.
[letter ends here without signature]

22. "Washington" refers to the War Department, Washington City (now Washington, D.C.).

1861

For the Crisis of Our Existence Is Now Approaching

Fort Pulaski[1]
[Savannah, Georgia]
April 17th 1861 [Wednesday]

My darling Wife

Your very kind and welcome [letter] was received to day. I have however but little time to reply. A letter from Wm R was also received. The books also. In regard to your sewing machine, I intend to buy one in Savannah as there is an agency advertised with all the latest improvements. What is meant by your bundle I am unable to say. Write to Rich at once and ask about your boxes.[2] If they have not been already sent, it will be very doubtful when you will get them. And even if sent it is not improbable that they are delayed on the road because of some tariff regulation.

I am in command of this post during the absence of Colonel Williams.[3] I found it and the command not in such condition as I had been led to expect, but am doing all in my power, of course, to be prepared for any emergency. The movements of the enemy are very mysterious, or they would have taken some prominent position in this section a long time ago. It could be done even now, with no great sacrifice. Before the twenty day[s], however, which has been granted for us to disperse have transpired, I hope we will be ready for the seventy five thousand.[4]

Commodore Tatnall is here, living in an old steamboat, panting for the

1. Fort Pulaski commanded the sea approach to Savannah at the mouth of the Savannah River.

2. "Bundle" may refer to ETM's pregnancy with Uldrick Huguenin McLaws. Richard Hancock Taylor, born March 11, 1816, was ETM's brother. GHS-VM Taylor Children, 1; Taylor Family Records, Record for John Gibson Taylor Family, The Filson Club, Louisville.

3. Charles J. Williams, Georgia, colonel and commander of the First Regulars Georgia Infantry.

4. In response to the surrender of Fort Sumter, S.C., the U.S. cabinet approved President Abraham Lincoln's call for 75,000 militia volunteers.

fight against all odds, how I wished when looking at him that we had at least one good man of war for him to command.[5]

If Mr Porter will bring Willie with him to Savannah, and Willie is willing to leave his brother and sister and his mother, I will have no objections to his paying a flying visit, but he need not think of remaining here with me, for the quarters are not only very limited, three and four officers living in a small room together, with the prospect of the number increasing—I am living in the mess with others. If you can manage to send me a *boy* to wait on me I would be glad to get one as at present I have none.[6]

It has been raining very plenteously every day but this, since my arrival—to day is beautifully clear and cool.

I have heard nothing from Montgomery Alabama, concerning my position here.[7]

Governor Brown has been dilatory in regard to this fort. He is more parsimonious than the times require, or he has not been properly represented.[8]

Events are crowding each other so closely that tis impossible to predict what will occur a week ahead; What I am to do tis impossible to say, from day to day even, until then my dear wife you must learn to be content or at least not fret very much at my absence.

There are three companies in garrison. Young Twiggs is in command of one.[9]

Three companies on Tybee Island, two or three miles away, under Major Smith, all however under my command.[10]

I am certain that Johnnie would wonder and be delighted at the sea, more

5. Commodore Josiah Tattnall, educated in England, was later a Confederate naval captain.

6. Henry J. Porter was the brother of Sarah Twiggs Porter McLaws, Hu's wife. He would later enlist and serve as a second sergeant of the 10th Georgia. Porter was elected second lieutenant on June 1, 1862, after he transferred to the First Georgia. He was killed at Second Manassas, Va., on August 30, 1862. Henderson, *Roster,* 2:9. A mess was a group of between five and twenty men who worked, ate, and fought together. The *boy* was one of LM's or his brother's slaves.

7. Montgomery, Ala., was the first capital of the Confederate States of America.

8. Joseph Emerson Brown was born in South Carolina, graduated from Yale Law School in 1846, and was governor of Georgia. LM and Brown appear to have known and worked with each other; however, there is little correspondence between them.

9. H. D. D. Twiggs, Georgia, first lieutenant, later lieutenant colonel.

10. Tybee Island, located five hundred yards across the South Pass of the Savannah River from Fort Pulaski, was under the command of George A. Smith, Georgia, major, later lieutenant colonel.

I think than any other of the children.[11] I think however that every one would enjoy a walk along the beach, and I long for the time when we will have peace and all can amuse ourselves picking up shells and wondering over the vastness of the ocean.

I will write in haste as all my duties are now done.

Give my love to all with you, and kiss the children for me.

Tell Willie that goods of all kinds are cheaper in Augusta [Ga.] than in Savannah, and if he will wait until I draw my first pay in the new army I have enlisted in[,] I will send him money to buy a gun; you may dissappointed in not hearing from me frequently but do not be alarmed for my health never was better, and I have a great deal to do.

Write to Hugh, give my love to Laura, give Laura, the little one, two more kisses which came to me from the sea through a port hole.

Adios. Your devoted husband
L M^c^Laws

((( )))

Savannah, Georgia
April 26th 1861 [Friday]

My dear darling wife
No letter from you or from any one there and this is my fourth day from you. I came away, you know leaving Willie not well, and you had been sick. So the not receiving a letter makes me very downspirited. I do not go to my work with a will nor with a love for it—as my thoughts are running after you, and far away from my business.

To day I was relieved from the operation of the order directing me to do duty in the Quartermaster and Commissary & Paymaster Departments, and I am now the commanding officer of Thunderbolt Point, a place on San Augustine Creek, about five miles from this city—[12] I went there this morning and found three companies of the Volunteer force viz

1 The Cherokee Brown Riflemen—Captn Dickerson
2 Wrights Infantry " Glenn
3 Buena Vista Guards " Butt

and not one had cartridges
the 2 & 3 had no arms, accoutrements or ammunition— No[.] 3 had no

11. John Taylor McLaws would later become a steamship purser.

12. Thunderbolt Point was southeast of Savannah on San Augustine Creek below Wassaw.

tents and but the cooking utensils they had bought for themselves. One company had a Surgeon with it.[13]

Now do you not think that there must be some outrageous mismanagement somewhere, is not somebody to blame? But I have to take things as I find them so I only amuse myself at the total defenceless condition of men who have allowed themselves to be placed in charge of an important military position. It is really ridiculous especially as it so happens that no enemy is expected.

I am making inquiries as to the way of living at *Thunderbolt* and find very little to encourage me. I suppose that for some days I will be compelled to live in a half starved condition and for the rest of the time, take what chance may offer, with the certainty that chance will not give anything good.

However I am free from the Quartermaster business and will not probably be stuck here forever, or for a very long time as I would have been, if I had been complicated with contracts and property of all kind.

I have been talking with gentlemen here about Marietta [Ga.], and they praise it for its fine climate, healthyness and fine water but they say the land is poor.

Major Hardee recommends me to buy in south western Georgia, as the most promising country in the state.[14]

I wish you would ask W^{m} R to advise about converting all our stocks into money, and placing *on deposit* in bank, or all in state stock, perhaps in that of Georgia, Kentucky? or Missouri— I think that if the money was on deposit that there would be quite a chance for speculation as I have no doubt but that stocks will go down very much, even where the security is of the very best standard—inquire my dear Em and write.

I sent off my pay and transportation accounts to Montgomery Alabama,

13. The Cherokee Brown Riflemen from Cherokee County, Ga., included seventy-four men and mustered in as Company F, 2nd Georgia Volunteer Regiment, on April 18, 1861; Thomas E. Dickerson, Georgia, captain, commanded the company. The Wright Infantry, from Whitfield County, Ga., consisted of seventy-nine men and mustered in as Company H, 2nd Georgia Volunteer Regiment, on April 20, 1861, under Jess A. Glenn, Georgia, captain, later colonel. The Buena Vista Guards, from Marion County, Ga., had sixty-four men muster in as Company I, 2nd Georgia Volunteer Regiment, on April 15, 1861, under Edgar M. Butt, Georgia, major, later colonel.

14. William Joseph Hardee, Georgia, USMA 1838, major, later lieutenant general. Hardee was author of *Rifle and Light Infantry Tactics, for the Instruction, Exercises and Manoeuvers of Riflemen and Light Infantry,* a manual to update army tactics as technology began to change battlefield operations. LM reported to Hardee in 1864.

on yesterday by express, and hope to get an answer within a few days. When I will send your [sewing] machine. I have looked everywhere for a good gun for Willie but cannot find any at all suitable—not one that he could carry.[15]

I saw some pretty canary birds for sale at five dollars the pair, & one dollar & a half for the cage. —I was tempted to buy but am afraid of giving out of money—what do you think of the purchase for Laura[?]

Johnny is so small that tis difficult to find anything suitable for him, something however may turn up.

If you hear of a good place in Atlanta or rather in Marietta suppose you go up and see it.

I called on Mrs Huguenin and find her to be a very talkative old woman.[16] —She appeared glad to see me, called me Lafayette and asked me to tea. I went to tea and eat some good waffles—some brandy peaches and some orange preserves. Staid till eight & a half and came away feeling sleepy.

Have not been asked to any private house, but have been introduced to the Club by Captain McAllister and others.[17]

Dont like Savannah, but think I would if you were here with the children—would like you to come and see me, but could not remain long with you—as my *Thun*derbolt duties are pressing.

Lincoln may contemplate conquering us but I doubt it, as the weather is too hot[;] that will be the only impediment unless something more is done than is doing.

I will write Willie and others when I have the slightest time. What little is employed doing this ought to be in looking after my "*bhoys.*"

Good bye and do write me Em often as it has a wonderful effect to receive a sweet letter from you.

Kiss the children for me, and if you think it proper & he cannot be persuaded into anything else, buy the gun for Willie, if you should decide on going to Hughs or to W^mRs.

Your devoted husband L McLaws

15. This was the second sewing machine that LM sent money for or purchased, as he had sent $150 to ETM to buy a sewing machine in July 1858. Entry for July 15, 1858, LB1.

16. Eliza Huguenin, LM's aunt, resided at 34 Liberty Street in Savannah.

17. Matthew Hall McAllister was a leading member of the Savannah Bar Association.

((( )))

Oglethorpe Barracks[18]
Savannah, Georgia
May 29th 1861 [Wednesday]

My dear boy
I received a letter from Aunt Laura this morning, telling me you were better and that both Ma and brother Johnny were doing as well as could be expected and that little Laura was as usual dressing herself up fine.

I was glad to hear that you missed me, because I did not wish any one to tell me that you did not care whether I was gone or not. But here I am and busy enough at present, in a few days however I expect to be more at leisure and will look around town to see what I can find for you. In the mean time I will be very glad to hear that you are so sorry that I am away, you are doing all in you power to get well enough to come down and see me or at least to go fishing with me in two or three weeks, and take a bath in Buggs Mill Pond, where I and uncle William learned to swim. When John comes home I will put you and Johnny under his charge and let him learn you to, both shoot and hunt & fish.[19] To get well you will have to be very particular about your eating, not to eat too much, or to eat cake and candy and such *trash* as the doctor calls such things—and you must not take too much exercise, or exert yourself in any way so as to bring on the fever— I know you will do these things for me, because you will make me feel much happier than I would if I should think you were doing otherwise.

There is nothing to do here, but to muster in volunteer companies, and those for thirty and sixty days only.

The Georgia Regiment is to go over to Tybee Island,[20] and the volunteers to occupy Fort Pulaski, I mean volunteers from Savannah— The volunteer regiment that I spoke about so much, a part of which was under my com-

18. Named in honor of James Edward Oglethorpe, one of the founders of the colony of Georgia. Completed in 1834, the site was never occupied by Federal troops. Instead, the barracks housed local volunteer military companies. The same troops took formal possession of the governmental post on January 26, 1861.

19. Buggs Mill Pond was located south of Augusta and west of the Savannah River in Richmond County. John H. Jefferson was a slave owned by William R. McLaws. Ninth Census, 1870, Augusta, Ward 1, entries for William R. McLaws and John H. Jefferson, sheet 40, NARA M 593, RG 29.

20. Tybee Island is on the outer banks of the Georgia coast where the Savannah River enters the Atlantic Ocean. Brunswick is on the coast of Georgia, south of Savannah.

mand at Thunderbolt, are to leave in a few days for Brunswick, about ninety miles south from here—and will erect a fortification there.

No one here has heard of any enemy in these parts, but the people are anxious and must be kept doing something. I wish you when you feel well enough, to [go] over to Buggs Mill Pond with Ma, and look out for a place on the other side—you have heard me speak of the side opposite from your uncle William as being a pretty place to live. But I may be mistaken, for I recollect only about things according to my fancies as a boy—it might look to be a very poor place to me now. I am afraid it would but I wish your opinion about it.

For the next month or so, you will have to be very careful of yourself—but when in the country, where the air is dry and healthy, you can be out more than you were in town, and can sit under the trees and wander through the woods, and take walks on the rail road at early daylight or late in the evening, without any such fear of bad odors and catching fevers as you have in town all the time.

Good by and take care of yourself, and be kind and obedient to your Ma, if the old fever will let you, and send Pa word how you are every day or two. Give my love to Johnny and tell him I hope he will not be afraid of Terrapins [turtles] so much, or a big one might take him on his back and carry him under some log when [he] goes in the country.

Kiss Laura for me, and your Ma & Aunt Laura, and say that I will write them in a few days.

Remember me to Caroline and Hannah.[21] God bless you.

your father
L M^c^Laws

((( )))

Savannah, G^a^
June 1st 1861 [Saturday]

My dear Wife
I commenced working in my office this morning at eight oclock, and remained until two P.M.—now at four I am at it again, but not to complain now for I am writing to you.

No letter this morning from you which makes me fear a little that you

21. Caroline Walker was a slave of William R. McLaws. In 1870 she lived in LM's home and was Uldrick Huguenin's maid. 1870 Census, Augusta, sheet 31, Richmond County, Ga. Hannah is believed to have been another of William R's slaves.

overexcited yourself before—but of course I hope not; hope so strong at least that yourself and the children are still improving that I know it is the same or I hope it will be as effective as any medicine—after you hear it.

I wrote you a hurried letter day before yesterday, and another yesterday, and am afraid it will be still another to day, for business is still pressing me. Yesterday from five to 7½ I mustered into the service of the Confederate States four companies. Two of infantry under Captains Scriven & Davenport, one of Artillery under Capn Sallie[,] an old man, and a company of Hussars under Lieut Manning, and this morning have been busily employed writing out orders & instructions for their movement and guidance.[22]

This evening I will go out three miles to muster in a mounted company under Captain Charles A. L. Lawson,[23] an old schoolmate of mine—and on Monday will muster in a German volunteer company. Then I will have to commence the Herculean task of straightening out the regimental and company returns.

The two companies of the guards under Captain Scriven are the finest volunteer companies I have ever seen, beyond comparison, and the only ones that up to this has made me feel as if I was looking on an array of the old regulars. They go down to Thunderbolt.

A mounted company under Lieut Manning will move to Skidaway tomorrow and on Monday another will go further south.[24] So our Georgia coast is gradually being well guarded or at least well watched.

I look forward to your moving to the hill with much anxiety, am much anxious for you to go, but still fear the movement.[25] Yet if the doctor says go, then go, but move when the sun is not overpoweringly hot—the reason why I suggested the morning was because in going out at that time even starting at 10, the sun would not be in your face whereas in the evening you could not escape it. But the doctor will advise as to the best. Give him my heart felt thanks for his kindness and tell him I will always remember it. I hope he will be the Surg^{n}Genl of the Confederate Army.

22. John Sceven, Georgia, captain, later mayor of Savannah; Archibald C. Davenport, Georgia, captain; John B. Gallie, Georgia, captain, later major; Lieutenant Manning unidentified. The Savannah Volunteer Guards was organized under Sceven's command.

23. Charles A. L. Lawson, Georgia, captain, later colonel.

24. Skidaway Island is one of several marsh islands southeast of Savannah on the Atlantic coast.

25. LM is referring to the Sand Hills, located outside of Augusta, where his brother Abram Huguenin McLaws owned a home.

I do not recollect sending you a copy of the order putting me on duty here, and accordingly inclose it now.

Major Sanderson has gone to Virginia, Genl Walker to Pensacola [Fla.].[26]

Give my love to Laura & W^{m}R and family.

Tell Willie I am thinking a great deal about him, so he must stir himself up, and make those who can, write me every day until he is up on his feet. I wish to hear that Johnny has been carrying the terrapin about. Kiss Laura once for me, if she is good. Nothing new except in the telegraph & that is not worthy of notice. Write to Hugh. Send one of the rifle musket balls to Mr Rogers the gun maker and ask him to make a mould for the gun.[27] Tell W^{m}R I have been trying to have one made ever since my arrival in Augusta, but failed. He may get Rogers to make one & can [hold] the gun until called for by Hugh. Your devoted husband L McLaws.

((( )))

[LB1]
Savannah G^{a}
June 8—1861 [Saturday]

I have just received a letter from Gen. Walker asking me to come to Pensacola & act as his Adg-General which I will decline with many thanks as this command is a much more important one with more probability of service than the Pensacola one & have more chance of being ordered in the field. Gen Lawton & Mrs Lawton have both asked me to stay at their house. She was very pressing. I did not accept this perhaps was wrong.[28]

((( )))

Savannah Geo
June 10th 1861 [Monday]

My dear darling wife
I leave tomorrow morning for Brunswick and the Georgia coasts generally, perhaps for Darien. Together with General Lawton, Comodore Tatnall, Cap-

26. S. W. Anderson, Georgia, major; William Henry Talbot Walker, Georgia, USMA 1837, brigadier general, later major general.

27. In 1860 E. H. Rodgers was a forty-seven-year-old gunsmith from New York living in Augusta. Eighth Census, 1860, entry for E. H. Rodgers, Augusta, 653, RG 29, Richmond County, Ga.

28. Alexander Robert Lawton, South Carolina, USMA 1839, brigadier general, later Confederate quartermaster general. Lawton appears to have been a friend until LM's death. Sarah Gilbert Alexander Lawton was an older sister of Edward Porter Alexander.

tain Morris[,] the last two of the Navy, Captain Echols of the Engineers and M[r] John Owen, of this place[,] aid de camp to the general, making six officers—to be gone six or seven days.[29] I am sorry that before leaving I have not received any letter from you, announcing that you had finally obtained enough letters from me to gladden your heart as much as such things can, and to tell me up to the last moment how yourself and the children are getting along as the summer advances. But it so happens that I have to leave and therefore will content myself with my presentiment that you are all well, and think of me very often. We will touch at Brunswick and inspect Colonel Semmes Regiment stationed there,[30] and if there is anything tempts us will remain there a day. And then if nothing happens will bear away for Darien, to hear what the people have to say for themselves in that section of country. The country will be then so much better known to the general commanding, that he can make his dispositions for the defence of our coast without depedendence on the thousands of different reports, all differing from each other, as to the paramount importance of that particular spot the writer is stationed.

I saw W[m] Walton and M[r] Dubose in the streets to day, both looking well. I was very glad to see the former, the latter I never saw before—also saw M[r] Sneed.[31] W[m] W proposes to go down to Fort Pulaski tomorrow, and as it is my

29. Darien is north of Brunswick on the northern bank of the Altamaha River as it flows into the Atlantic Ocean. In addition to Lawton, Tattnall, and LM, the six officers included Henry M. Morris, naval captain; William H. Echols, captain; and Jonathan "John" W. Owens, Georgia, aide-de-camp to Lawton.

30. Paul Jones Semmes, Georgia, attended the University of Virginia before becoming a banker and planter. A colonel and later brigadier general, he initially led the 2nd Georgia and became one of LM's brigade commanders. He died on July 10, 1863, as a result of a wound received at Gettysburg. The 2nd Georgia Regiment completed its organization in Brunswick on June 1, 1861, with recruits from Banks, Bibb, Burke, Jackson, Marion, Muscogee, and Stewart Counties.

31. William A. Walton, a descendant of one of the founding families of Augusta, provided the McLaws family with financial advice. He was the trustee for property owned by LM in Augusta when the 1860 census was taken. Eighth Census, 1860, entry for LM, Second Ward, Augusta, Richmond County, sheet 272, NARA M 653, RG 29. Dudley McIver Dubose, Tennessee, attended the University of Tennessee and graduated from Lebanon Law School; he moved to Augusta in 1860 and married a daughter of U.S. senator Robert Toombs. In March 1862 Dubose was an aide-de-camp to Henry Lewis Benning. He was promoted to brigadier general in November 1864 and assigned one of Kershaw's brigades after LM's departure from East Tennessee. John C. Sneed was also a resident of Augusta. Eighth Census, 1860, entry for John C. Sneed, Second Ward, Augusta, Richmond County, 777.

business to write passes for those going to those points occupied by troops, I told him he must come to my office this evening and get his permit.

The weather has been quite pleasant, to day. Last night there was quite a rain and a blow from the north east.

The harbor is believed to be blockaded, but do not be alarmed on that account as *our* boat goes along the inland passage, not even seeing the sea except on two or three occasions.

On my return from Darien to this place I will try and pay you a flying visit, try to go up Saturday morning and come down Monday. I do want to see you very much. I want to come away with fresher looking faces in my "minds eye" than I have of you all. Willies long gaunt face is continually haunting me. I must get it away by seeing him in better health, and get a look at Johnnys face stained with blackberries and Laura with her sunburnt cheeks. I am trying to write you a letter as full as possible of all things; but some one is continually asking my opinion on something that is none of my business, even now the volunteer commissary is talking to me about his accounts, which I am not listening to, but agreeing with him as he is speaking in an affirmative tone—he is gone.

I went to day and examined particularly, that is took five minutes time in examining one of the Wheeler and Wilson Machines. There are three for sale price eighty eight dollars, with the glass arrangement, and the new kind of hemmer, that is all that is new about them and the hemmer is the only thing extra. I told the man that my opinion was there were several other arrangements but he pleaded ignorance if there was— He will deliver it in Augusta for eighty eight dollars, money to be paid on delivery. Now if you say there is nothing else, that the hemmer is all you desire, send an order to "Wilmot [Wilmont] & Richmond" agents for the manufacturers, Savannah Georgia, and he will send you a machine, by express. There are some of Ladd & Webster machines and some of Groves & Backers, but you as well as myself you know prefer the Wheeler and Wilson. You will have to pay the amount for the machine, as at present I have not the money, but will have enough to send you by the end of this month to more than make up the amount. So when I return I hope to see you as happy as the day is long making up your own clothes, and those of the children and of—any one else you may desire.

It seems to me my dear wife as if it was months ago since I left you, and I am I assure you as ardently desirous of getting one of your sweet kisses as if I had been absent ever so long, and when I come on my short visit I hope that we may be well enough and happy enough to bid each other a very sweet welcome. I would like exceedingly to wander with you over those places where we once did in our honeymoon, and think of the days when I could lift you over the wet places and care not an iota for the weight—as it is now although I would like to just as much, to lift you, I fear tis not in my power.

Give my love to W^{m}R, and to Mary, and the children and tell Meta that I am very glad to hear she is giving my children such a good example of good behavior.[32] Tell Mary not to spoil the children by indulging in their whims.

I went yesterday or rather Saturday evening into three different grocery stores, trying to buy some good crackers for you but saw nothing but the soda & butter crackers. There were no other kinds in the city.

I have had no time to visit Aunt Eliza, nor can I until my return for to night[,] I must pack up—good bye take good care of yourself and of the children for me. Give them all a good kissing for me, and think of me giving you a great many. Your devoted husband.

L McLaws

If there is an opportunity, I will write you from Brunswick, but do not be disappointed if I do not, for there may not be a chance. If you do receive a letter from there take it as good luck, that is all—now again good bye.

((( )))

Petersburg, Virginia
Sunday evening
June 24? 1861 [Monday]
[Monday, LM wrote Sunday evening]

My dearly beloved Wife

I started on Friday you know, and *consiquently* instead of being in Richmond am in this place. When within three or four miles of Weldon the engine bursted a flue and the train was stopped in the middle of a vast marsh, a runner was sent on for another locomotive which came for us in an hour, more or less, but when we reached Weldon the train with which we should have connected had started for this place. After parleying with the president of the road, with the secretary, several engineers and the various outside sympathisers, we succeeded in starting about 8 P.M. in an extra train consisting of twenty freight cars and one passenger car. I have said *we,* because on arriving at Branchville, from Augusta a company of 116 Volunteers from Lowndes County G^{a} got into the train, and from that time, there was

32. Meta was approaching her sixth birthday, on July 3, 1861. Augusta, Ga., Cemetery Record for Meta Telfair McLaws.

an end to all individuality. I managed to preserve my seat entire, by piling my overcoat, pillow & carpet bag beside me. But *they* were all around me, in all the various attitudes conceivable, and dressed and undressed as suited their humor or degree of heat, artificial or natural, they had steamed up to at the time—one person, the wit of the party, said that if any body would give him a dollar he would sit in his shirt tail, and for an additional half would then pull off his shirt. Most of them pulled off their shoes, some had socks and others none and many were only partially provided. As the heat increased the *feetid* odor was tremendous—which added to the insane idea peculiar to volunteers that it was the patriotic duty of each and every one to hurrah and yell on passing through any settlement, made the time pass remarkably slow. And whenever we stopped a moment there was a general rush out in search of water, and then when the conductor shouted "get a board," various fellows would say, "I cant find a board but can get a shingle if you want one!"—all of which added to the general hilarity and made the night rather a sleepless one— When the crowd was put into the baggage cars, the noise was none the less but it was further off, so that the second night was passed more quiet. —But to day the passenger car was crowded with them again, and the odors and the singing and the patriotic yelling was truly remarkable— The Lowndes company, however are a very fine looking body of men and in fact are remarkably well behaved, and have a Captain who has them under complete control by the mere force of his personal influence, his name is Patterson and I have no doubt he will do credit to his State.[33]

I Saw Major Gatlin or rather *General* Gatlin in Wilmington N.C., he is a state officer and has charge of the coast defences of North Carolina. I did not know he was in town until it was so late I had barely time to call on him at his office and give a greeting. He walked down to the cars with me & then had to hurry off as he had been invited to tea. No Gen[l] speaks of sending for his family provided he is not called into the field as General by [Confederate] President [Jefferson] Davis— Major Holmes of old is a Brig Gen[l] I am told and in command in the neighborhood of Acquia Creek.[34]

33. LM's railroad journey covered approximately 630 miles in four days. Weldon, N.C., was a major railroad center. Branchville, S.C., was where Company I of the 12th Georgia Regiment boarded the train. The regiment, organized in June 1861, became part of H. R. Jackson's command and initially saw service in the Cheat Mountain campaign in West Virginia. Captain James W. Patterson, who was later killed in action, commanded the 12th Georgia.

34. Theophilus Hunter Holmes, North Carolina, USMA 1829, brigadier general,

There are troops at Weldon, one or two companies or more, and outside of the town there is a camp of about one thousand more or less. I Saw a line of about six or eight hundred on parade, in the distance as the cars passed on. I have not seen any one who knows any more or even as much about the condition of affairs as we did in Augusta when we left; except that the affair at Great Bethel is more magnified. The number killed is said to be two hundred on the side of the enemy and but *one* man on our side, and that man was shot because in his excitement he had climbed on a house to hurrah or to get a better shot; not known exactly which.[35]

I heard several grown men to day, about an hour since, say that there was no need of so many troops from the South as the Yankees would not fight. And one more, who appeared to be sound in the head, to judge from his looks—hoped that Jeff Davis would not stop until he overran all the North and burned the principal cities, including Boston. If such is done I may have a chance of sending you cheap thread and get a sewing machine for nothing. So you must wait.

Kiss the dear children for me especially my little daughter and write me all their doings and Sayings. —Give my love to all, with you & to Sister. I will write to you immediately after seeing how things are in Richmond. Good bye & take a thousand Kisses from Your devoted husband.

L McLaws

((( )))

Camp Near Williamsburg [Virginia]
July 2nd 1861 [Tuesday]

My dearly beloved Wife
Your letter of the 28th of June was received this evening, giving me very great pleasure I assure you. Much more than I have had at least for some time.

My duties are exceedingly onerous as my command is now over three regiments and all kinds of troops, irregularly organized.

I am in command of the forces in and around Williamsburg, including an area of country about ten miles long and three or four broad. The camp of the 10th Regiment is my head quarters and is immediately in rear of an immense redoubt now in course of erection under my control. . . . I have

---

later lieutenant general, commanded Aquia Creek, Va., and had been a member of the U.S. 7th Infantry with LM in the War with Mexico.

35. The engagement at Big Bethel, Va., took place on June 10, 1861.

an immense reponsibility and more labor to perform than I can do well, at least I am afraid so, but the hope my dear wife of giving pleasure to you will nerve me to extraordinary exertion. I have not a moment to myself from night until morning, and very often as is the case to night, I am on duty.[36]

You do not know how anxiously I have been looking for a letter from you, so much that my fears have made me imagine all kinds of possibilities. At one time I thought that possibly one of the boys had been hurt with the hatchets or possibly had been trying to ride and had fallen off, and being hurt badly, you were waiting to announce his recovery. Your letter however has cured me. There are all kinds of rumors afloat, of course, but none reliable or at least none to be relied on, for instance night before last I received notice that the enemy were re-inforcing Newport News [Va.] very largely and great activity prevailed there. And Gen[l] Magruder directed that I prepare myself for an attack on my command, and to meet the enemy with my whole force, fighting inch by inch.[37] Retreating if necessary to my interior works & sending him word and he would move to my assistance— I had examined the country and gave the necessary order for the troops at the various positions where the enemy might be expected to land, and waited the issue, which was, nothing . . . The enemy might debouch from Newport News, in boats, and coming down in force get between Magruder and myself, because there is not a gun to prevent his making such a movement, but by doing so he would make a movement so bold and so hazardous that the least reverse would ruin his command, and I therefore do not contemplate any such. However I have neglected no means to give him a prompt and warm reception, should he try it.

My command is that of a Brigadier General, and my Regiment will have to be turned over to Colonel Cumming unless some one relieves me in a few days. It is rumored that General Jackson is to come here, but I hope not, as I do not wish to be under any Malitia [militia] man, especially General Jackson—as it looks like a farce, to have such a military man with such a name.[38]

36. LM commanded the 10th Georgia Infantry, the 68th and 115th Regiments of Virginia Militia [volunteer], and the redoubt known as Fort Magruder.

37. John Bankhead Magruder, Virginia, USMA 1830, brigadier, later major general.

38. Alfred Cumming, USMA 1849, lieutenant colonel, later brigadier general, commanded the 10th Georgia when LM was promoted. On June 15, 1861, two days before LM received orders to take command of the 10th Georgia, Evan J. Prothro wrote: "We have remained here [Richmond] longer than expected because some of the companies were dissatisifed in the Regiment which was nearly formed and we had to start another

I find here in command of a Virginia Regiment, Colonel Ewell, a brother of the Captain of Dragoons (formerly), lately the professor of Mathematics in William and Mary College. Also a Mr Morrison[,] late a professor, I believe of Natural Philosophy, now a Captain [and] Qmaster, and many others who occupied high positions in the state are either officers or privates.[39] The Virginia Regts here are very sociable clever gentlemen, and I often go to their camp, and enjoy their society.

Quite a number of gentlemen have spoken to me of Hugh, and thought at first that I was him.[40] A good many have invited me to their houses but I have no time to *think* of going, even.

You do not mention that Willie is trying to ride but suppose he does not care of trying by himself.

And my little daughter, how does she get along during the whole day[?] She must not be melancholy, but laugh and sing, and learn to read.

Willie I know will write me before long so I will wait patiently, and Johnny will read the papers, and give me his views about the fight when we meet again.

Parties of the enemy are constantly making inroads into the country around Newport News and from Hampton [Hampton Roads, Va.]. Stealing negroes and all kinds of property and committing so many depredations that the inhabitants have fled leaving their homes and fields and all their wordly goods behind— Many are in this vicinity, and are really very poor now— althoug[h] but a few months or weeks ago, were rich and lived sumptuosly.

Your letter this evening and one from W^mR inclosing the letter of Dr Covey,[41] are the first and only ones I have received since leaving home. D^rC^s letter I will forward tomorrow.

The letter from W^mR will be answered in detail, at some other time. Please ask him to have me a good saddle and bridle sent on by the first express.

---

which Cummings [Alfred Cumming] of Augusta will be appointed Colonel and it is probable that Capt Mabry will receive an appointment in the same as Major." Smedlund, *Campfires,* 158. John King Jackson, Georgia, a graduate of South Carolina College, was a colonel and later a brigadier general. LM referred to Jackson of Augusta, Ga., as the militia commander.

39. Lieutenant Colonel Benjamin Stoddert Ewell, Virginia, lieutenant colonel, later colonel. He was the brother of Richard Stoddert Ewell, referred to in the letter as formerly captain of the Dragoons. Richard Ewell, Virginia, USMA 1840, brigadier later lieutenant general. Robert J. Morrison, Virginia, was a captain.

40. LM referred to his brother Abram Huguenin McLaws as Hugh or Hu.

41. Dr. Covey has not been identified.

I have a horse now sick with the distemper, which being a slight disease in this climate, I feel easy about & expect to use him in a day or two but have no saddle. Will borrow one however. Tell Laura to write me and I will answer as well as I know how, although she pretended when I wrote her before that it was entirely unexpected. Give my love to Mary and Meta & the other children— Kiss the boys & my daughter for me—write me very often and believe me your devoted husband.

L M^c^Laws

((( )))

Williamsburg V^a^
June 8th 1861 [July 8, Monday]

My dearly beloved Wife
Yesterday I received your letter of the 23^d^ written after, just after my leaving for this country—I hope that your sorrow for my departure has settled down so that you all rather look forward to my coming home than to grieve that I am absent. —I was sorry at first, sorry enough to have disgraced myself by resigning my honor^s^ and going home, but I staid for my wifes sake, and for the respect I wish my children to have for me. And I wish them to send me kind encouraging words, and to make it appear as if they were contented, although their hearts may be heavy in the effort.

But I really hope that Willie when he grows strong will be independent enough to be [able to] work out his own career of happiness and will begin to look forward to the time when if his country demands it, he too will be a soldier, and will be as brave at heart as any man, at least brave enough not to let any one see him giving away to his feelings, although at heart he may be as gentle as a child not yet weaned from its mother or as gentle as his little sister— I hope ere long to learn of his fishing in Bugs Mill and bringing home plenty of fish for everybody[.] I would be glad to hear of him & Johnny going opassum hunting, and of their learning to swim, and hunt all kinds of things. I would give Johnny a fine present if he should catch that great big terrapin at the spring, and turn him over on his back, and keep him there, and then have a fine terrapin soup for all the yard. I know he will catch him for me.

I dined the other day with a M^r^ [George Washington] Custis of this place, the Washington family Custis whom you know by reputation—or at least of that stock, and eat a good dinner, saw no one to whom I cottoned particularly, none there but old gentlemen. But the next day, Mr Custis according to an agreement of the day previous, called for me in his buggy and I went with him to hunt up Genl Magruder—hearing that he was at Youngs Mill about twenty two or three miles South, we directed our course to that point. Arrived about two oclock and found the place occupied by a Lousiana Battalion under Colonel Drew, a fine dashing young man of more than ordinary ability, fine lawyer & orator—his command was fortifying the place there, and it being the fourth of July they had had a barbacue and had delivered several 4' of July orations.[42] The Colonel had made a most exciting stirring speech himself, and all hands were in good spirits—we staid but a few minutes, as Genl Magruder had gone off to another place, known as Bartletts towards the other side of the Peninsula. We went down the road two or three miles, towards Magruders Head Quarters, when we met a soldier on picket guard who told us that Genl M^{g} had gone across the country on horseback & that the road we would have to take had been blocked up. So we turned in to a neighboring farm yard enclosure where an outlying spy company was, and obtaining a guide turned back and striking another road, went across and got to the Gen^{s} Head Quarters about sundown— I went in and had about a half hours talk with him & all on a sudden met, John your brother who came up and shook me by the hand.[43] He looked better than I ever saw him, healthier, and happier, and had a very fine looking old Colonel for his Commander' Colonel Hunt of New Orleans—[44] I staid but a few moments longer and then started on my return. Said John good bye—he said Allie was well,[45] but thought soldiering was a hard business—was determined however to stick to it. Got back to my camp about one oclock at night.

The next morning about eleven oclock, came the news that Colonel Drew[,] with whom I had had a barbacue dinner, had been killed that morning at daylight, in a skirmish with the enemy—both parties ambushed each other, and both retreated after firing a volley. The skirmish took place within two miles of where I was the day previous.[46]

42. Charles Didier Dreux, Louisiana, lieutenant colonel.

43. Four years younger than ETM, John Gibson Taylor, Kentucky, attended the USMA between 1845 and 1848, was commissioned a second lieutenant in the U.S. 8th Infantry on June 7, 1855, and resigned from the U.S. Army in June 1861. He was killed at the Battle of White Oak Swamp on June 30, 1862, at age thirty-four.

44. Theodore Gaillard Hunt, South Carolina, colonel. A lawyer as well as former U.S. congressman, he had lived in Louisiana since 1830.

45. Allie, or Ally, was Alfred E. Edwards, ETM's cousin and the younger brother of John F. Edwards. Alfred and John were sons of Frederick Geiger and Anne Pendleton Taylor Edwards. Anne was ETM's older sister from Louisville, Ky.

46. For the report of Captain S. W. Fisk, commanding officer of the Crescent Rifles, see *OR* 2:188–89. For John Bankhead Magruder's report, see *OR* 2:964–65.

I had no 4th July celebration in my camp, although some persons urged me to have—I declined because I did not wish to have anything in common with the enemy—when we achieve our independence we can have a day of our own. The principles enunciated in our declaration against Great Britain are the same we are fighting for now, according as we understand them.

I hope to day will bring me a letter from you, good bye and God bless you.

I have a great many things to write about, but have no time at present.

Give my best love to all with you[,] sister Laura & others—and my dear wife do write me often—addressing to Wms Burg, Williamsburg Virginia— I have now to go & examine a large hospital over two hundred sick, measles—mumps—diarrhea &c. Good bye.

Your devoted husband L McLaws

((( )))

Camp 10th Geo Regiment
Near Williamsburg Va
July 18th 1861 [Thursday]

My dear Wife
Your dear kind letter was received yesterday and I should have neglected all of my business in order to answer it at once, so as to relieve you of all uneasiness. The measles and mumps are prevalent to be sure, but they are of a very mild type and men have them & walk about from morning to night without caring an iota for their disagreeable appearance or thought of risk to their health.

I was awakened this morning just after three oclock, by an express from General Magruders Head Quarters directing me to order the movement of the 2nd La Regt to a point seven miles from here. To march at once without breakfast, with knapsacks, haversacks &c and also ordered two six pounder to accompany them, and two more to be sent to one of the works under my charge four miles away. —Until now 8½ my time has been occupied in carrying out the orders, and I am writing hurriedly to console my dear wife.

Last night about twelve oclock, sound of cannon were heard in the direction of a fort about nineteen miles from here. It proved to be a signal agreed upon between the officer in command at a fort where the cannon were fired, and the commanding officer of a fort, under my command at Grove's Landing seven miles southw[est] of this. The import of it was that the enemy were observed as if in movement on James River far down towards Newport News. Every commanding officer has been put on the alert, by the alertness of commanding officers tis meant, that he has taken all possible precautions to prevent the enemy from landing at any point on the coast, or approaching from a direction without his being informed beforehand in sufficient time to make the best possible use of his means of defence. I have taken all possible precautions, in *my opinion,* and *you know* that in such cases, every confidence should be placed in the condition of affairs.

I am glad that if you wish it, you have determined to move to the arsenal. I have often thought about your lonesomeness my dear wife, and was thinking at one time if it would not be more agreeable and better for you to go to some of the numerous springs in Georgia. But you want active employment to draw your mind away from distressing thoughts, and I hope and believe that housekeeping will destroy your ennui.[47]

The enemy have been extraordinarily quiet, and no doubt are in contemplation of some grand movement. I do not think he will march in this direction for the reason that it would take too much land tranportation, the means for which, it would be necessary to bring by water. However, I am in rapid preparation for his coming and if allowed another week, will be in very strong position.

I am not a General as yet, although I hear of many appointments I feel are not so worthy *in my opinion.*

The news received in relation to General Garnett is very distressing if it could be believed, but there are so many reasons for hoping it is false, that I am one of those who do *not* believe it.[48]

I will subscribe for a newspaper for you at the first opportunity—either the Richmond Dispatch or the Whig, the latter is said to be the most reliable—I do not take either, not having time to read newspapers.

My camp and whole command is a very busy one, and I have been complimented on my energy. I am certain that more has been done during my short reign than for months previous and the different departments are very much more effectively organised.

I hope my dear boys will so conduct themselves at the arsenal as to be considered good company wherever they may go, and will learn all they can about arms and accoutrements—how to make cartridges, both of cannon and small arms, and be able when I come back to learn me many things I

47. The former U.S. Arsenal in Augusta produced gunpowder and other munitions for the Confederate war effort.

48. Robert Selden Garnett, Virginia, USMA 1841, brigadier general, was the first general officer killed on either side.

never learned because I did not have an opportunity when I was a young fellow. —And very sweet little daughter she will know all about big guns, and shot and shell—but she must not become warlike like a soldier, but be gentle as a dove always, and as smart in cooking and keeping house as any woman of old time when ladies were proud to know such things.

I am really in hopes that John will arrive shortly—but there is no telling.

The mail I fear will close ere this is finished, but if it does, it will be only a delay of one day, and you will pardon that when I tell you that I have been writing this letter a little over four hours.

I think that Captain Humphreys can draw forage for my horse, and muster him for me, ask him about it or shall I write?[49] My saddle has not been recd although I hear it is in Richmond.

I will try very hard to write you again tomorrow morning and give a few items of the position of our troops here— Good bye my darling—may God bless you is my daily prayer, of your husband L McLaws.

((( )))

Camp 10th G^{a} Regiment
near W^{m}Burg V^{a}
July 21st/61 [Sunday]

My dear children
You no doubt often think of your Pa, and wonder what he can be doing at that particular time, imagining all kinds of dangers and accidents. It is my intention therefore to answer your inquiries by giving you a sort of journal of such events as will probably interest you, and let you know every day what I have been doing.

To day I went to town, and visited the General Hospital where there are about one hundred patients, with the measles, mumps, & all kinds of diseases such as soldiers have[;] every thing there is out of order, principally because of the neglect of the Department in Richmond in not furnishing supplies, and secondarily because the doctors do not know how to conduct a hospital. Thirdly because the men who are sent down as nurses do not attend to their own comrades. When a man from civil life first becomes a soldier he seems to lose his former notion of things to such an extent that he is no longer the same man in feelings. The necessaties of a soldiers life makes him selfish to such a degree that until custom makes him an adept in that way of living, he cares for no one but himself, and very often cares noth-

49. Captain Humphreys has not been identified.

ing for himself, or not enough to take care of himself. The consequence is that soldiers or volunteers will not nurse each other unless there is a strong personal friendship to urge it. To do so as a duty they owe to humanity they will not unless driven to it.

July 22nd

Busy all day. The place full of rumors about fights, but nothing known certainly about anything.

July 23rd

Went to town and found the hospital improving, put the guards under much stricter orders, and hope to have more quite every where. Had a long communication with General Magruder, who had called for my written plan of defense of this section of country. He approved it entirely and has given orders for it to be carried out, which I consider quite flattering, as the line of defense embraces quite a large extent of country.

The news from Manassas is so very glorious that I cannot believe all that is told. It seems a dream only, to think of our army meeting with such extraordinary success. While we were talking of the event as rumor brought it to us, the sound of heavy guns was heard in the direction of Yorktown, immediately the men commenced chasing all through the camp thinking it was an engagement with the enemy, but the regularity of the fire and the number fired convinced us that the troops above were firing a salute in honor of the victory of our arms. Soon another salute was heard coming from Yorktown. Telling us that the first salute was from Gloucester Point. I then ordered a salute from the guns here. Which created quite a stampede in W^msBurg, thinking that the enemy had attacked us. A very violent storm was prevailing at the time, but the whole camp nearly was out to see the guns fired. Our men are very eager for the fight.[50]

The weather cleared to day the 24th: but the country filled with pools of water. The works were considerably damaged by washing but will soon be in good repair again. Took a ride along our left flank to examine into the working on a mill dam we are building over again, in order to raise the water over a part of the country we have to fear the approach of the enemy. Found the dam nearly completed, but the water does not rise as much as I want it, or should wish it to do to answer my expectations, but if I could order

50. The Battle of First Manassas, or Bull Run, was fought on July 21, 1861, at Manassas, Va.

what I wanted, a great many obstacles to many things would be removed. For instance there would be no difficulty in my having my children around me and my wife by my side.

25th

Intended finishing this letter to be sent off this morning but was intercepted and obliged to leave, and go off about a mile to put a working party with axes to cutting down a grove of trees that obstructed the field of fire of one of the batteries, and to entangle a ravine that led up to within a few hundred yards of one of ten redoubts[.] [B]y entangling I mean, cutting down trees and making them fall across each other and in the direction the enemy is expected to come, where the wood are thick, as they generally are here; it makes it very difficult to get over them, by doing this we prevent a large number from rushing suddenly upon us, and those who attempt it are exposed a longer time to our fire.

I put twenty men to cutting and then went off to an examination of the country below towards another fortification which commands another mill dam; at a place called *Tutters* neck, found the work nearly completed. The water had risen considerably and the company of men there were comfortably placed, but doing nothing.

Went then to town and saw General Magruder who was sick in bed with gout. Had a long conversation with him, and returned home about four oclock, heartily tired of the days work— I have near four hundred negroes at work, and hope within a week to be able to present such a strong front to any advance as to make the place too strong to be attacked except by a very large force.

I will send this off tomorrow— You must not allow Ma to be jealous because of my writing you and not her, for you know that we are all one to each other.

I will talk to you about the fight at Manassas another time. At present, I do not care to write about it. One at least of my best friends has fallen. Genl Bee—and you have read all about it in the newspapers.[51] Kiss Ma for me an be good & patient and active & learn to work.

Your devoted father
L McLaws

I will keep on writing you and think you might write in return occasionally.

51. Barnard Elliott Bee, South Carolina, USMA 1845.

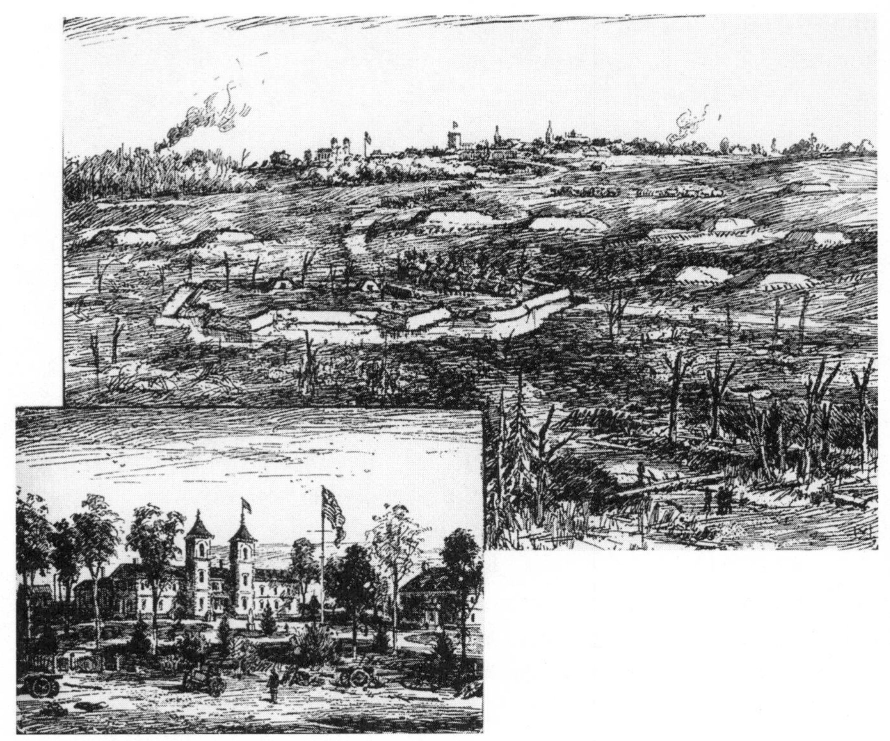

Drawing of Fort Magruder. (Robert Underwood Johnson and Clarence Clough Buel, eds., Battles and Leaders of the Civil War, *vol. 2 [New York, 1887–88])*

((( )))

[Fort Magruder, Virginia]
July 30 [1861, Tuesday]

My Dear Wife
Such a length of time has elapsed since hearing from you all that I am downright uneasy.

My busy time has not passed as yet nor do I see the end of it for some time to come. Yet I am healthy, and discontented only when I have had no news from home.

Since the glorius battle of Manassas which seemed a battle given us by the Almighty. So complete the panic and route of the enemy, everything has been quiet, not even a rumor of the advance of the enemy disturbs us. Our coast is well guarded. So that any advance would be immediately reported, and our fortifications are fast assuming proportions that will make them exceedingly formidable. The main work here called Fort Magruder, is fast approaching completion, and on the right and left redoubts of formidable strength are either already finished or will be within a week. I therefore do not believe that the enemy will advance in this direction unless he does so within a short time, and I do not have any thought of their doing so, because their army was so thoroughly disorganized it will be impossible to rally a force sufficient in number or complete enough in organization to hope for any success against forces such as we can bring, equally as well equipped, and very far superior in the morale of invincibility against Yankees that inspires our southern soldiers. It is the ardent desire of our men to get at the enemy. It seems as if they are wish to let off their pent up vengeance, which has been collecting for years past. I believe, and believe so earnestly[,] that in a fair hand to hand fight, we will defeat any northern army with anything like an equality of numbers. I hope in our next engagement there will be a fair field, and open fight.

There are but three persons talking to me now, none of them want anything particular, but they prevent me writing. I commenced this morning at 6½ and it is now nine ½.

I have several friends who are, so they say, endeavoring to have me appointed Brig Gen[l] and they say with a goodly prospect of success, but we shall see—at present there are very many prominent politicians who are seeking military promotion. Among them may be mentioned the two Cobbs and it may therefore be presumed that until their desires are gratified mine can remain in waiting.[52]

Col Cumming is certainly one of the most extraordinary young men I ever saw in the particular of having such an appreciation of his merits, as to always be thinking that he should receive more than has been given him. He thinks he should have been Colonel of the 10th G[a] Regiment, but says that I should have been Brig Genl. He is continually grumbling on his own account, and cannot imagine why it is I am satisified. I am not satisfied, but see no sense of being discontented, and therefore am very much afraid I am getting fat *again*. I am hopeful, all the time, and among other things hope to receive a letter from you this evening giving a hopeful account of your

52. Thomas Reade Rootes Cobb, Georgia, University of Georgia, a lawyer who was active in secession politics, a colonel when his brigade moved onto the Peninsula, and later promoted to brigadier general; and Howell Cobb, Georgia, University of Georgia 1824, lawyer and antebellum politician, brigadier, later major general. Although LM's concerns regarding political generals was correct for Howell Cobb, his brother Thomas was a different story. T. R. R. was one of LM's best brigadier generals; he commanded the troops in front of Marye's Heights but was mortally wounded at Fredericksburg.

housekeeping. But your long silence alarms me, I assure you. It is too late for the mail to day. So I'll write more for tomorrow.

The mail is soon to arrive, and my wishes may or not be gratified with a letter from you.

I heard yesterday from the Colonel of the 5th Lousiana Regiment with which John was on duty as Adjutant, that John, so he heard, had been made a Major of a Mississippi Regiment, and he deserves it, says the Colonel.[53]

Colonel Hunt, the Colonel of whom I speak, is an old gentleman of independent manners, and an open talker, was Member of Congress from Lousiana and has a considerable opinion of his influence, and of his ability both as a soldier and a member of society. He said that he became very much attached to John and showed it by a letter to the war Dept, recommending him in the strongest terms for a high position if a new regiment was to be formed. I sincerely hope he has been.

The weather is excessively warm and the mosquitoes very active all the day long, but I have on tar & when in bed am independent.[54]

This morning I received a tin bucket of tomatoes from a lady in W^{m}Burg who at the same time sent a basket of buttered biscuits for "The Georgians" and about two & half gallons of butter milk[,] also a bunch of flowers for Colonel McLaws. I send you a leaf or two, their roses are not so sweet as those in the south, nor have they the great variety of flowers. The ladies are exceedingly kind to the sick, giving all kinds of delicacies indiscriminately, supplying quantities of bedding of all kinds, clothing of every description and above all giving them constant *personal* attention. The attending surgeon in the hospital informing me that fifteen ladies at least were from time to time attending in person to the wants of the sick in one hospital alone. No letter for Me! So good bye my dear wife; I am exceedingly anxious and nervous because of your silence. I cannot im [. . .]

I had written the above, when my Regiment Qrmaster called out "Colonel here is a letter for you!" which made me jump and run for it, leaving the word "imagine" unfinished.[55] —I thank you very sincerely my darling wife for your very sweet letter, the sweetest to me that has been received for such a long time that I will preserve it especially.

53. John Gibson Taylor received his promotion to lieutenant colonel of the 2nd Mississippi Infantry Battalion on July 17, 1861.

54. Tar was used to ward off mosquitoes.

55. LM's regimental quartermaster was Captain Samuel T. Neal.

Aug 1"

I commence again, having been compelled up to ten oclock last night to put this letter by because of the press of visitors—General Magruder came up and visited me and remained a long time. He in going away said that it was his intention to recommend me to the appointment as Brigadier General[,] that he was convinced that it was necessary and would ask that the appointment be made. So this is an additional link in the chain. I am hopeful that I will get it, but not so much so as feel that if it is not granted, I will [be] very much discouraged or downhearted. —My determination is to do my whole duty to the extent of my ability, and rest content with that consciousness.[56]

Tell Willie that I thank him very much for his short note and for his signature. I will preserve both, and compare the handwriting with his next which he must send me shortly. Tell him to copy sentences every day, or write down what he thinks and he will soon learn to write without trouble, and I will write him in return in a plain hand, so that he can read it. Kiss my darling little daughter for me, and tell her I am glad she is such a good housekeeper, but she must learn how to read. —And M[r] Johnny[,] why does not he write me his name[?] You write it first and let him draw it, he must be a brave man now, among the guns & balls at the arsenal. Good bye & God bless you. L M[c]Laws

You did not mention sister Laura. I suppose therefore she is perfectly well. Take good care of yourself—and do not read my old letters if they make you at all sad. —Give my love to W[m]R, Mary, Meta & all. L.M.L.

((( )))

Camp 10th G[a] Regiment
[Camp near Williamsburg, Virginia]
August 18th 1861 [Sunday]

My dear Wife
This evening I received another of your sweet letters, for which take two kisses from my sweet little daughter, as you cannot take them from me. Why cannot you receive my letters? last week I wrote you two, and I believe three, and subscribed for the Richmond Whig, daily, for six months for you. My

56. In a letter of August 15, 1861, Magruder wrote: "Colonel McLaws is a most competent, experienced & energetic officer and I earnestly recommend his promotion to the grade of Brig Genl as not only one to his merit & service and as being emminently conducive to the best results of the Army." SHC-LM.

last letter I thought a very interesting one, at that time I had not received an answer from General Magruder[.] I have now the pleasure of setting his reply before you and it is as follows on a seperate piece of paper. You have no idea how, for what you would not consider any great gain after all, I have been working for promotion, and then to see others, whom I know are not activated by any but the most selfish motives, and are unworthy of the position, promoted over me, is most mortifying and ought to be to any one with proper pride. If it was not that it would be disgraceful to resign for mere personal considerations, and it was the duty of every one to do all in his power to aid his country in this her hour of peril—I would have been back home with you long ago striving for a livelihood in some other way.

But let us be done with this. Captain Morrison, of whose efforts in my behalf I wrote you last week—has returned[.] [H]e tells me that he saw Gen[l] Davis in person and presented my application to him—that the general or rather President said that he would attend to it. This is all that Captain M. has told me, but he remarked that "It would be all right." So I have to wait and will it not be better that I should soar to prize more highly that which I am contending for? and if it should be denied me—then I can do my duty still and wait—and long for the pleasure which I hope fortune still has in store for me, and that before long, of having my arms around my wife and children.

This morning I received a dispatch informing me that Colonel Marignys Regiment, the 10th L[a], would report to me for duty.[57] The regiment is a Zouave Regiment, and has the reputation of being most lawless set in existence, so far as our army is concerned, the people call the Zouaves the Zousabs—and they call themselved Zu Zus— It is said that they are nearly all Frenchmen, a great many not speaking any English. Indeed the Colonel & Adjutant who have just left my tent, speak English but indiferently well. The Adjutant did not say much. I think but two words & I do not believe he can talk in English. Colonel Marigny is a son of a celebrated Count Marigny from France, a friend of the once exiled and once King of France Louis Philippe. The peculiarity about him is, that he never laughs, never smiles—His regiment was on Jamestown Island for twelve hours & during that time,

57. Antoine James "Mandeville" DeMarigny, Louisiana. Educated at a French military school, he commanded the 10th Louisiana, whose members were from New Orleans, Bossier, and St. Landry's Parishes. The regiment was composed of many foreigners, including Greeks, Italians, and Spaniards, who wore the colorful Zouave uniforms.

tis said, eat up every living thing on the island, but the horses, and their own species.

20" Aug.

I have been doing my best to finish my letter but really I cannot with any degree of satisfaction, and therefore will only say now, that I would be very much gratified if you could go to Hughs, whenever you wish. To be sure her objection of distance from each other would very materially have an influence over me, against it, under any other circumstances— But at present nothing would gratify me more than to hear of your being pleasantly located under the proctecting shadow of Hughs hospitable house.

The officer who is ordered to the Augusta arsenal is a northerner, who was turned from his allegiance by a pretty Georgia [Alabama] lady.[58] —He is a good fellow I believe and will not interfere with you in any way if he can help it—his wife was quite pretty & seemed to be a good girl. There is quite a furor in relation to the announcement that England has acknowledged us[,] all of which I fear is premature.

Tell the boys that I have not received that letter from them as yet.

And my little daughter, if she cant write must send me the print of her foot.

Give my love to Laura, and W^m^Rs family.

Your devoted husband
L M^c^Laws
Colonel 10th G^a^

P.S. It is with great difficulty that I can sign my name without the official part attached.

((( )))

Camp Near Williamsburg V^a^
August 26th 61 [Monday]

My dearly beloved wife
I am very much obliged to you for the second letter you wrote me, the day following one previously written, which previous letter never was received. Making your second so much the more valuable.

58. The officer was Josiah Gorgas, Pennsylvania, USMA 1841, major, later brigadier general. Under Gorgas's energetic supervision, the arsenal began producing large quantities of ammunition and materiel. It soon turned out 20,000–30,000 rifle cartridge rounds and 125–150 field ammunition rounds each day.

Mr Wm Walton arrived in camp day before yesterday on his return home. He is now in my tent dressing, it being at this present time twenty minutes of seven A.M.

I wrote you a hurried letter on Saturday because it was Saturday, hoping you would receive it and be consoled more by it than by none at all, even though it was so hurried and badly written.

Mr Walton has been to Manassas nursing the sick and has some very interesting accounts to relate. He has seen a new chapter in humanity and one that can be seen no where else than in the army; it is one too that he will never forget. As I have said before to you in my letters— The being a soldier is a very severe test of character to which very many men give away under, exhibiting themselves in such unenviable characteristics that if they could see themselves, as others see them, and have not lost the instincts of decent humanity[,] [n]ot a few would feel very much like committing suicide, to escape from themselves, and the scorn and contempt of those who have come through the fiery furnance purified as by fire.

There is a rumor that the enemy have landed about three hundred horses at Fortress Munroe, and it is believed that tis their intention to attempt forays along the coast, stealing negroes and chickens, killing cattle, and burning houses, as seems to be their practice now whenever an opportunity offers.

I am very much surprised at your not receiving my letters, not so much surprised however as annoyed—because it is the common complaint of all parties. Why it should be so, is plain, because like everything else, the post office is irregularly conducted during these troublous times.

I have heard nothing from my Generalship, and from all accounts, I think the government is devoting itself to rewarding politicians to such an extent, that no one else but those kind can hope to receive other than the crumbs which fall from the political table.

My regiment has not been paid off, and I am afraid that the new Confederacy has some agents who are as desirous of making money as were some in the old U.S. army. Four weeks ago money was sent to a gentleman officer of the army to pay off the regiment, but up to this time nothing has been heard concerning him. I have reported the case strongly and stated in addition a circumstance which I would not have done except to give force to the appeal I made for payment because it is better not to allow such matters to go abroad. I told him that the officers were so badly off for money I had been compelled to order the Regimental commissary to credit the officers messes in order that they could obtain the common necessities of life, and that the private soldiers were offering ten per cent for an advance on the amount due them, all of which is shameful in the extreme.[59]

My time is up, although I commenced this three hours ago. My tent is now besieged and I must to business.

I wrote you that the idea of your domociling at Hughs would give me great pleasure providing you wished to go. I remention it for the reason that it is possible my letters have miscarried.

Give my love to my children and kiss them over and over again for me, also love to Laura and W^{ms} family[.] Give my kisses to my sweet little daughter, good bye.

Your devoted husband L M^{c}

Do not be alarmed about me, I am well and well cared for, am comfortable as can be expected. Recollect that camp life is home life for me. I intend writing a letter through the War Department to Longstreet,[60] inquiring about John. I have made numerous inquiries and cannot find his whereabouts.

Your husband
LM

((( )))

Camp Near Warwick [Virginia]
Court House, Sep. 11th/61 [Wednesday]

Your letter of Sep 3^{d} was received this evening, eight days coming.

I am glad that you met Captain Richards, and am glad that he was pleased to speak so highly of me.[61] In response to your flattery I may have to make you blush in return.

I was introduced yesterday to a Zouave Captain. He said he was delighted to make my acquaintence, that he had heard me spoken of so well by the ladies, that he had heard one say that she wished she knew you, for although I (Col McLaws) had been absent so long from you in the Rocky Mountains, I was apparently as true to you and as much attached to you as if you were my

59. LM's regimental commissary was George H. Cheever. Henderson, *Roster,* 2:2.

60. James Longstreet, South Carolina, USMA 1842, brigadier, later lieutenant general. Longstreet spent his preteen years in Augusta and was acquainted with LM; both were USMA classmates and served in Mexico and the western United States before the Civil War. In the vast majority of his letters, LM did not refer to Longstreet, his corps commander for a large part of the war. SHC-LM contains seventeen letters exchanged between the two officers after the war. The last letter, dated October 20, 1892, gives Longstreet's acknowledgment that he had wronged LM. Longstreet died in 1904.

61. Captain Richards has not been identified.

young wife. And, I may add, the young lady said, 'If he was only unmarried!' How I wish he was? Now my dear wife, I do not care much about flattery unless in flattering me the person pleases you—and I mention the above circumstances merely on that account.

I have just arrived in camp here, and of course have much to do. I am writing in a great hurry but in good humor, for my officers have recd me so cordially, I have no right to be otherwise.

I am in a responsible position, and intend to try an[d] fill it, particularly on your account. So write me and write me sweetly as before.

Write often, which will do away somewhat with the distance.

L M[c]Laws

((( )))

Camp 10 G[a] Regiment
Youngs Farm
[Young's Farm, Virginia]
Sep 29 '61 [Sunday]

My dear darling Wife

It is now Sunday, a clear night and quite cool. Day before yesterday we had the usual September gale, with plenty of rain. On that day I was on a scout down towards the enemy, to New Market Bridge. I had with me three companies of dragoons, one hundred infantry and one gun. From Bethel church down to the bridge I saw many deserted houses, many fields with all the fences down, and cattle ranging in herds over what had been fine fields of wheat and corn, and through gardens and yards once cultivated with much care and adorned with flowers & shrubs and beautiful trees. Again many of the fields were under good cultivation[,] the fences in good order. The gardens cultivated and cared for, and women & children living at their homes with an absence of care for results which appears rather extraordinary—until one finds out that those persons are under strong suspicion of being of the enemy, and have received assurances that they will not be hurt or their property damaged. As we approached New Market Bridge within a mile, none of the houses were inhabited, and the fences were generally all broken down, desolation was never before so strikingly presented to me. The day was very stormy, the wind blowing a tremendous gale and the rain, off & on, pouring in torrents, then there would be a lull & the wind & the rain would cease for a time. I was impressed with the idea that, if the enemy should advance his forces but a few miles and was extended to the fort this country would be a dark and bloody ground[,] the resort of thieves and robbers. The scene of murders & violence, long to be viewed with and remembered with a feeling of horror.

I threw my pickets out to the right and left, on all the cross roads to guard against surprises, and had left the cannon at Bethel church in the fortifications there to guard against an advance from Hampton. So I went on to New Market Bridge or rather to where it was, as it has been destroyed, within three miles of Hampton and about five from Newport News, scoured the country and returned over the same road I went. My infantry reaching camp about an hour after dark, and just before a tremendous storm of wind and rain. T*he* September gale burst over us.

Much to my surprise the enemy had no pickets, on the opposite side of Back River creek, at New Market crossing. So there was no firing between the forces.

I started to drive up some cattle but the day was so stormy I desisted.

My dear wife! I am getting very much disposed to come home. The Cobbs are coming over to the Peninsula, and I suppose their worships must be provided for before the claims of any others can be considered. Thos R. R. Cobb with his legion has already arrived, and report says that Howell is to follow & will come as a Brigadier General. I do not wish to be under any politicians, nor will I if it can be helped. Howell Cobb or any one else—I am indebted to General Magruders partiality for the honorable position I am now occupying. To his favor alone do I owe the fortune of being in command all the time since my arrival— He has recommended me strongly for promotion, but as yet nothing follows. [Letter ends here; apparently the remainder is missing.]

((( )))

[LB1]
Oct-1-1861 [Tuesday]
Camp Youngs Mills
[Young's Mill, Virginia]

The fortifications are progressing, & the men are getting dissatisfied for want of something to excite them, but I will not do so unless under orders from Genl. Magruder. I am occupying the right flank within twelve miles of New Port News having picketts in advance six miles. A large force has gone south from Fortress Monroe[:] 70 vessels of war & transports, majority steamships, 16000 infantry besides a marine force. Fear for Charleston [S.C.], Savannah, Brunswick, Pensacola & Mobile [Ala.].

((( )))

Camp Youngs Mill
[Young's Mill, Virginia]
Oct 3[d] 61 [Thursday]

My Dear Wife
I am at last a Brigadier General. So you may call me General Lafayette at last.[62]

I have been congratulated from various sources, and feel very much gratified[,] more so at that than at the promotion itself.

I do not feel any special exhultation at the promotion, except I know it will [be] a special gratification to yourself and [the] children and to my family and friends.

My appointment is dated September 25"! ultimo but was not received until yesterday.

There are a number of persons talking to me officially and otherwise and I hardly know what I am writing.

Give my love to all. I will write very soon in full.

Your devoted husband
L M[c]Laws
Brigadier General C. S.
Address Me
General L M[c]Laws
Youngs Mill
via Williamsburg, V[a]

((( )))

Camp Youngs Mill
[Young's Mill, Virginia]
October 10th 61 [Thursday]

My dear Wife
Your letter of the 1st was received last evening. Nine days in transmission. I am sorry that on the day I received my commission as Brigadier General you should have had the blues[,] the day of all others in my military history you should have [been] joyful. Let me hope however that as towards the end of the day you felt so much relieved. So it will be with us in relation to the campaign. Trouble at first but the bright is coming.

62. For the order establishing the brigade structure and the distribution of the troops and their positions, see *OR* 4:668–70.

You very properly remark that it will take me but a very short time to write daily, but the difficulty is not in the time[,] it is in the way of transmitting, and you know how prone we all are to put off. There is no regular mail and we have to seize chance opportunities to send off our letters and rely entirely upon chance to receive any. Again when the weather permits, I am in the saddle nearly all day, and when night comes my time is occupied until late with office business. Sometimes until twelve oclock, and I drop into bed thoroughly sleepy and worn. I have but one tent for myself and one for my office, both of which are full from before I get up in the morning until after bed time—I frequently going to bed with some persons talking & writing at my table, and I do not like to write to my wife when any one is about me. Although I am now doing so, with six or eight waiting on me.

It has been raining for five or six days, off and on, and for the last two, continuously. Troops are in motion nevertheless and I am compelled to be out in order to put them in position. The 2nd Florida Regiment Colonel Ward, Lieut Colonel Rodgers, are to come under my command to day, although it is pouring down rain, and the roads are in an awful condition.[63] The Lieut Colonel is now waiting for me to go off about two miles and point out the camp for the regiment. These things I have to do for there is no one else about who knows the country.

I do not anticipate any movement of a serious character; either against the enemy on our part, or of them against us. In fact the roads are nearly impassible, which of itself prevents such. I am having a map prepared and will send you a copy.

The order has been given for us to go into winter quarters here. Much to the disgust of a very great number but it cannot be helped, so there is no use of grumbling.

My dear wife, I am really tired of soldiering although there is no reason why I should be for fortune seems to have favored me, and a great many persons have congratulated me on my *deserved* promotion.

At present I have for my staff a young Lieutenant of the Confederate Army, Louis McIntosh from Savannah[,] as my Adj Genl, a son of Thomas Butler King as my aid and a son of the former professor of Wm&Mary Col-

63. George Taliaferro Ward, Kentucky, Transylvania University, colonel of the 2nd Florida; Samuel St. George Rogers, Tennessee, lawyer, lieutenant colonel, later Confederate congressman. The regiment's troops were drawn from Alachua, Columbia, Escambia, Hamilton, Jackson, Leon, Madison, Marion, Nassau, Putnam, and St. John's Counties.

lege Tucker, as another aid.[64] Several have offered their services but I have not yet finally determined as to my permanent volunteer aids. I wish Willie was old enough or could write a good hand, and I would make him one. If he desires the position however I hereby appoint him & Johnny both aid de camps, and my little daughter will be the aid de camp of Mrs Genl McLaws.

A young lady, Miss Ewell of Williamsburg whose father is professor of Mathematics in W^{m}&Mary College, and is also a Colonel of a V^{a} Regiment, wrote me the other day that she wanted the appointment, and I will send one in course of time.[65] I am living in a ridiculously plain manner principally because I cannot help or afford to do otherwise. Ham and bread and coffee is all that graces my table, very often for days. Then again some one sends me fish, or a bushel of oysters and I have a feast. Yet I am very healthy which is all I ask for and can pray for excepting for my wife and children.

I hope you have not been in any want of money as I have not sent you any as yet, although at the end of this month I hope to do so & to the amount of three hundred dollars.

I have had to buy horses, which are exhorbitantly high. A good common horse selling for two hundred and fifty dollars. Have had to buy a new saddle, bridle & equipment and new uniform, messing equipment and new cap & hat. The cap, a common one with lace around it cost me 8 dollars. The coat 43, pants 10, saddle 45. My old one, the one from G^{a} was an outrageous affair. The bridle broke in putting on the horse. I have had to go into debt in getting horses, but hope to be all straight in a short time. And can be more regular in my transmissions. Please write me particularly on that subject.

I have had to by some new socks and will have to get more underclothing. Such as drawers & flannel shirts, I am afraid. How I miss my big overcoat that Col Williams had lost for me.

Give my best love to my aid de camps, and to your sweet little one, and

64. Thomas Spalding McIntosh, Georgia, captain, later major, was appointed assistant adjutant general on October 19, 1861; in LM's reports he was consistently cited for bravery, gallantry, and coolness under fire. Henry Lord Page King, Georgia, became captain and aide-de-camp in 1861. He was the son of Thomas Butler King, a Georgia planter who served in the state legislature and the U.S. Congress and as collector of the Port of San Francisco. Tom S. B. Tucker was appointed lieutenant and aide-de-camp. Compiled Service Records of Confederate Generals and Staff Officers & Nonregimental Enlisted Men: Thomas Spalding McIntosh, Henry Lord Page King, and Tom S. B. Tucker, NARA M 331, RG 109. LM noted that since his appointment to brigadier general, both King and Tucker had served as volunteer aides-de-camp.

65. Lizzie Ewell, daughter of Benjamin Stoddert Ewell. LM carried on a correspondence with her throughout the war.

rest assured that so soon as I receive my new tents and get better fixed for the winter, you will hear of me or from me very often. Your devoted husband L McLaws

((( )))

Camp Youngs Mill
[Young's Mill, Virginia]
October 18th 1861 [Friday]

My dear Willie
To day it was reported by one of my pickets who came in looking like a scared rabbit, that the enemy had driven in the advanced pickets and were on this side of Watts Creek, distant about six miles— As I had a party of five or six out in that direction, removing a saw mill, I was rather annoyed and sent at once a cavalry force of two companies to go around and inquire into the circumstances. Sending two companies of infantry at the same time, by another route to act as a support.

The companies of cavalry returned and reported that five or six of the enemy had been at a house on the other side of the creek, opposite to the place where the picket was, but had not crossed. That the persons seen by the pickets were negroes who had been sent over on business. So much for picket reports!

The enemy, so the Yankees reported to the gentlemen who inhabited the house, say that they do not expect to attack us, but on the contrary are expecting us to attack them daily.

Occasionally a deserter comes in to us, and some remarkable stories, which no one believes. We are busily engaged in fortifying our position and getting ready for winter quarters.

I expect to live in tents, with chimneys, but have not as yet made up my mind.

General Magruder was over to my camp to day and gave me a long talk. He appears worse and sick, indeed he has a great many things to try him, and many annoyances to deal with and contend against.

I have now under my command, the 10th G^{a} Regiment 2nd & 5 & 10th L^{a} 15 & 14 V^{a}—Montagues Battalion— Four batteries of artillery, & four companies of dragoons, and have the most important positions to occupy, and yet I am ready for the enemy.

The Zouave regiment is in W^{ms}Burg, giving parties and picnics, singing and serenading. I have not visited W^{ms}Burg since my departure, although I have been very warmly invited on many occasions.

I have heard several anecdotes concerning the Zouaves. One or two of which I will relate.

A colonel of one of the regiments saw a Zouave kill a hog, caught him in the act, and asked him "how dare he kill the hog." —"Colonel" he said, "I had to do it for the hog was going to bite me." The colonel was so completely nonplussed he had nothing to do, but laugh.

The other day two of them were caught pulling plank from one of the houses. The owner made them desist and asked the name of their regiment. "Ve belongs to the first Georgy" says one. No you dont says the gentleman as you are Frenchmen— "Vera well, says the rascall. "Bon jour" & off they went with the plank. I believe I told you about the Zouave who had been watching a pig for some time, waiting for him to come in his vicinity, lying flat on the ground for the double purpose of concealing himself from the pig & from general observation, when a North Carolinian coming along, boldly shot the pig. The Zouave immediately rose up on his hands and shouted out, "Aha de Zouave is not the only one who shoots de pig, some body else is the d—d rascal besides."

Our cavalry took some twelve prisoners the other day. They did not fire a gun and appeared very much delighted at the idea of being taken. They thought at first they would be shot, but finding out their error, became very merry and communicative. One said "I think boys, we can have an honorable discharge now." They belonged to the New York Fire Zouaves, and said that all the regiment, but eighteen had been forced into service. That the authorities in his fort kept them very close for fear of their running away.

I am delighted to hear that you have been to school and are pleased with going. I am in hopes every day of receiving a letter from you. It makes me much happier to hear that my boys are learning how to be useful, rather than loafing about doing nothing but play and giving trouble to all about them.

I know you have pride enough to always act right, or at least never to do wrong, if you know it, and will teach you[r] brother and sister what is right & not allow them to do wrong if you can help it. So you see I look to you for a great many things, and feel confident you will be manly enough not to disappoint me.

I write this to you in hopes of getting one line at least in return.

Kiss my darling little daughter for me and take good care of her and Johnny. I hope to be with you this winter for a few days. In fact I hope that this horrid war will terminate before very long, and we will all be together, once more, around our own fireside, as happy as we used to be.

Give Ma plenty of kisses for me and tell Johnny that I will write him so soon as he can say his multiplication table. Kiss little sister for me, and recollect that you are my aid de camp. Johnny is the second aid, and sister is aid to Mrs. Gen[l] M[c]Laws. Kiss Aunt Laura for me, give my love to all. Remember me to Caroline & write your devoted father.

L M[c]Laws

((( )))

Camp 2nd Division
Youngs Mill
[Young's Mill, Virginia]
October 23 1861 [Wednesday]

My dearly beloved wife
I have had no letter from you since my promotion, or rather none from you of congratulations on my being General Lafayette at last. I miss that congratulation my dear wife more than any other, and every day have been more and more anxious about it, until at last I have become so disappointed and so anxious that I am very much alarmed for fear something has happened to yourself or the children to prevent your writing. Last night I dreamed that Willie was missing from home, no one knew where he was. The dream awoke me and I lay a long time thinking about it, and wondering why you were so long silent— Your last letter was from Marietta dated the 9th. I have frequently written you since, and have written also to Willie. I have been supposing that your change of residence and the wear & trouble of arranging a new house is the cause why my usual letters have not been rec[d]. But my dear wife I am tired to day and have been troubled a great deal with the arrangements of the staff departments of my division, and I am talking with a rather too lacrymose a disposition to suit either of us.

Yesterday I had over twenty seven hundred men in the field endeavoring to get a fight from the enemy, but failed. I was on the ground arranging the troops for their bivouac until long after dark, about six miles from here and then came home, through the rain & mud & gave the necessary orders for the defense of this position during my absence. To day—went to bed and dreamed of Willie being lost. Got up[,] attended to my division affairs—went to the troops in the field again and here I am back again with all my men in position as before.

The nights are getting quite cool, although it has been raining continuously for a week or two. In fact the weather is never good here, the weather or the ground are one or the other always bad, wet, muddy and disagreable.

I have never been anywhere, where it rains so much. It is cool to night, quite so, but if it should not rain tomorrow the sun will be disagreably hot. My health however thank heaven is very good. I have fine aids de camp, and three of them have been Sick, and I who am exposed twice as much as they are and do ten times the business am spared.

Our troops to day, of my command went within three miles of Newport News to day but the enemy did not make his appearance.

A few days, day before yesterday in fact, a party of our men[,] one hundred[,] had a skirmish with a considerable body of the enemy, killed one or two and took one of them prisoner. One of our men was wounded, not dangerously however. I saw the prisoner, not long after he was taken, he was crying bitterly. He belonged to the 2 N. York Regiment. I spoke but a few words to him and sent him on to General Magruder at Yorktown.

To day just before leaving for the troops in advance, I received the inclosed order from Head Quarters. On arriving I had it read in front of each regiment in turn, and they hurrahed most enthusiastically and vociferously.

The general still places great confidence in me, and I try and deserve it.

The greatest draw back is the want of proper staff officers, of men who are devoted to their duties and the cause, and devoid of utter selfishness— If I knew where John Edwards was I would have him as my division commissary or Qmaster and would be very much obliged to him if we would accept the position.

I do not wish Hugh to leave home, otherwise I would write him to come on and be my Division Quartermaster. I would apply for his appointment and think it not improbable he would get it— I wish one very much, and one too in whom I could place implicit confidence, and I know that Hugh would be the man for the place. Read this to W^{m}R and ask his opinion. If he thinks that Hugh would take the appointment and would use his influence to get it backed by my recommendation, which is generally paramount in such cases; let him write to me at once, or telegraph, which would be better & I will write for his appointment—the same with John Edwards. —I have not heard from John E. nor Alley, nor your brother John since arriving here last summer.[66]

66. John F. Edwards was recruited as LM's division commissary officer in 1862. Allie served as an aide and then ordnance officer on LM's division staff. John and Alfred continued their service with the Army of Northern Virginia after LM's departure following the 1864 court-martial. After the war, John became a merchant in Atlanta, and Alfred moved to Decatur and then Alvin, Tex., where he was an attorney.

I asked General Magruder for a leave the other day and he said, no, he would give no leaves to any one, now.

How comes our[,] my two aids de camp and your little one[?] Do they behave themselves in a military way, by being very obedient to the orders of their superior[?] I will send you a book showing the uniforms of aids, and they may wear the insignia at least. My 1st aid is the son of Thos Butler King, a very clever young fellow but quite an exquisite. I am entitled to but one by rights, but the others are volunteers. —Several more have offered their services, but I have no room for them, at least in camp. I doubt very much if circumstances will allow me to live but in tents this winter, but I am used to that you know—so do not regard it as a peculiar hardship. Good night my dearly beloved wife. Kiss my aides & your aid for me. Give my love to sister L. & all with you & believe me your devoted husband L McLaws.

Tell Sister Laura that there is a son of Governor Reid, by his second wife in the 2nd Florida Regiment under my command.[67] I have not seen him. Colonel Ward is the Colonel & Rodgers the Lieut Colonel. Good bye for the present.

((( )))

Camp Youngs Mill
[Young's Mill, Virginia]
October 27th 1861 [Sunday]

My dearly beloved Wife
Up to this date I have not recd a letter since the one dated the 9th August, the anniversary of our marriage. Such is my recollection of the date, have you any recollection of it[?]

Much to my annoyance I have seen an account in the Richmond papers of a very desperate engagement, with the enemy, in which the 10th Ga Regiment participated, and were badly cut up. Since then there was a report of my division being engaged with the enemy in front, with the prospects of a general engagement, all those reports, being false, excepting a small affair between skirmishers, which may have given rise to the second—and of

67. Robert Raymond Reid married James McLaws's sister, Ann Margaret, on April 3, 1810. Born in Beaufort, S.C., he became a lawyer and entered politics in Augusta. He was elected to the U.S. Congress in 1819 and held his seat until 1823; was a superior court judge from 1827 to 1832, when he became judge for the eastern district of Florida; and served as governor of the Territory of Florida from 1839 to 1841. His son was not identified.

which I wrote you about, are provoking in the extreme. Simply because our families and friends hear of the engagement by telegraph, are thrown into an intense state of excitement and alarm, and remain so for days before the truth can be known.

There are reports that the enemy are assembling in large bodies, at Fortress Munroe [Monroe] and NewPort News[,] for what purpose however is not known. General Wool is in command.[68]

A large body of men have gone south somewhere in small steamers, escorted by men of war of all sizes. Their destination is not known. I fear very much to hear of a descent on the coast of Georgia. We can however but wait and see, and pray that the scoundrels may be either wrecked or driven into the sea after landing, or all taken prisoners.

I write this with the expressman at the tent door—principally to let you know that I am well—and that I have not heard from you for a long time.

Kiss the children for me, give a particular one to my little daughter, and remember to write me often. Remember me to all with you.

Your devoted husband
L McLaws

((( )))

Camp Youngs Mills
[Young's Mill, Virginia]
Nov 29th 61 [Friday]

My dearly beloved Wife
The winter is coming on and I have finished the chimney to my tent, & will move in it today. But as yet the weather is so moderate, no fires are required except in the morning and evening.

I send you a letter from John Edwards not written in such fine spirits as those written formerly. In fact the tone of it is not such as I admire, it is not a high spirited letter. He is willing to war, but not to endure the hardships. I do not think that President Davis would be pleased with its perusal. But as his family are enduring so much for the war, and he must be in a very intense state of mental anxiety in regard to his parents, great allowances must be made for him, and I intend if I have time to day, to recommend him for the appointment of Commissary of my Brigade. He must feel the want of power, and position such as would enable him to aid his brothers & parents,

68. John Ellis Wool, New York, brigadier general, later Union major general.

very keenly— I have written as strongly as I could in recommendation, and petition for Hughs appointment, but have as yet heard nothing of it. But the business of the War Department must be exceedingly onerous at this time, for the crisis of our existence is now approaching. Not that we will be conquered if overcome in the battles now to take place, but we are hardly pressed with the power of the whole North at this present time, and it is reasonable to suppose that several reverses must be encountered. Yet *you* must not despond for I am exceedingly busy and sorely pressed for time. My command has been considerably extended and my responsibilities very much added to.

Write me my darling and give love to all my friends. Kiss my boys, and my sweet little daughter.

Your devoted husband
L M^c^Laws

((( )))

Camp Young Mill
[Young's Mill, Virginia]
December 8th 1861 [Sunday]

My dearly beloved Wife
Of course I cannot expect a letter from you at this time, but the deprivation is a considerable item in my wants.

I received a letter from Laura, inclosing a small scrap of *the* boys hair. The letter was so incoherently written, mixing up the hair, with Willie and Johnny & Laura and the baby, that I began to think before reading the letter through, the hair was not from *the* boys head, but from some other boys head. And in conclusion she said that "W. H. says he can do far better I think he *can* but the good news covers defects" I have no idea what is meant. So tell me, is there a baby in fact, and is it a boy with black hair? —Who said his name was Fayette? Am I so far out of the family that I am not to be consulted in the matter? Does not everyone know that I have always preferred *Peter,* to Lafayette, believing it to be a much more musical name, and one not so calculated to annoy the sensitive child? Call him Ulric Huguenin, he is or was a Count in the family, and there is some claim to it, besides there is no one else of that name. But joking aside I do really think that Ulric Huguenin is a very pretty name. Much better than Lafayette or Fayette which is an affected abreviation. But do not let us quarrel *now* about the name. Laura says that *it* is the finest boy in Augusta. Magnificent forehead, fine eyes, fine head of hair, straight legs, good fingers, fine shoulders, turn up nose, and good voice—in fact a regular General Lafayette. But I think that the boy would like better to say when asked of the reason of his being named Ulric, I am named after Count Ulric of the Huguenin family, then to assert that he was called Fayette after no one at all, but have to explain, that it is an abbreviation.

You may imagine my pleasure in receiving the inclosed letter from John Gibson, who is a Lieut Colonel of a Mississippi Regiment, and is to be stationed on the Penisula. You will probably hear from him now.

I wish Hugh would telegraph and let me know if he is coming on, and when. I want him very much.

The weather has been exceedingly warm, too much so to be agreeable. For I cannot help but think that the winter will be like the one we experienced in Georgia in 1851/2, when we were on our honeymoon trip, & you loved me so much.

Tell Willie that I wish him to write me about the baby, whether or not in his opinion it is a good looking one, or nothing uncommon. I would like to get Johnny's views on the *case,* and my little daughters ideas about it. Tell Mr Phinizy that his son is very well indeed. that I would have telegraphed as he desired, but his son did, which was all that was required.[69]

There are so many rumors about the enemy that I forbear mentioning them. I was much astonished this evening, by a young engineer officer remarking to me "General we all believe that you can get us out of any difficulty and therefore feel no uneasiness about our position."

I believe that within the next ten days, or twenty at the furthest, the enemy will put forth their greatest strength, but whenever it is done it will be done very cautiously, and with great preponderance of strength.

I must to bed, for I have a ride of thirty miles there or thereabouts to take tomorrow, as General Magruder has telegraphed that he wishes to see me. I expect to see John there, and will write you again about him.

Good night my dear wife, kiss Ulric for Me, and the other boys, and my sweet little daughter. Tell Willie to write me—love to sister Laura, to WR & Mary. —Remember me to John and the servants, take most excellent care of yourself, and write me when you can, but I forbid you positively from writing

69. John Phinizy was the father of Charles H. Phinizy, captain and commander of Company B, 10th Georgia Infantry Regiment, later colonel. John Phinizy held stock in the antebellum Bank of the State of Georgia with James, Abram Huguenin, William R., Lafayette, and Anna L. McLaws.

before the doctor gives permission. All leaves of absence have been revoked for the present, but I hope we will have the privilege again before long.

Good bye, my darling wife, a thousand kisses for [letter ends here]

((( )))

Camp Youngs Mills
[Young's Mill, Virginia]
December 20 '61 [Friday]

It is very near Christmas and we are so far separated from each other that our letters are our only means of communication. It seems fated that we are to remain yet separated, although I have been all along pleasing myself with the idea that we would be together this year.

I confess that the idea of going to see you on a short leave is repugnant to me in the extreme, especially when I may be recalled at any moment by the vanity of a commanding officer who is a sensationalist, because he is constantly afraid he will be forgotten, unless by startling paragraphs he keeps himself before the country.

The rumored hostile attitude of Great Britain towards the United States has produced great rejoicing, as it is our belief that, if we had arms, and could obtain supplies from abroad we could not only repel the Yankees from our soil but would invade them and make them feel some little of the horrors of invasion— I have certainly strong hopes that Great Britain and France both will open our ports, but it is not proper that we should allow our energies to abate one iota in a vigorous preparation and prosecution of the war.

There has been extensive preparations making for a descent somewhere along our coast, but where the scoundrels will land is yet to be ascertained. The preparations for departure were to be made in Annapolis, and then the sudden descent would go from there—I hope the south is prepared at all points to repel them— The army base, where the passing fleets can be seen is kept in a state of inquietude because of the fact being known of a large number of vessels having passed in view towards Annapolis. Every thing however remains quiet up to this hour, and it may be that this will not be the point of attack.

My dear wife I try and write daily in order that you may receive some letters, so must excuse their being short. I was in hopes to get a Christmas kiss from you, but our affairs are too unsettled to allow of my departure as yet. If I can get away I will ask to be put on duty in Georgia, as the Peninsula is not a place to long for.

Good bye my darling—keep in good spirits, and maybe it will happen before very long that I will have you in my arms and will give my opinion of the new one whose name is not agreed on.

Kiss the children for me. Remember me to all—to John & Caroline.

Your devoted husband L M^c^Laws

((( )))

Camp Youngs Mills
[Young's Mill, Virginia]
December 23rd 1861 [Monday]

My dearly beloved Wife

I incidentally heard to day that a Lieutenant by the name of *Tweedy* had a Daguerreotype and a letter for me, had had it in his possession for about a week and had forgotten to deliver it, and I have not received it yet.[70] —Tell W^m^R to recollect the name of Lieut *Tweedy* and never trust the individual again. It may happen that Lieut T may come into my way and he will very probably learn the necessity of promptness. I feel very much like twisting his neck for him.

I have received no letter from you or from W^m^R. nor any one for several days and feel therefore very anxious, as although your last letters report Willie as much better I am not at ease until he is well.

The enemy is constantly in sight with his ships, engaged at some hellish work, or preparing for it—but what it is, no one can tell— Our pickets see the enemy constantly, and occasionally some are killed on both sides, but no general movement is discernable, nor are we prepared for them in very large numbers— I am one however who does not believe that the enemy will advance on this line at present, at this season of the year. For if he should advance by water, should succeed in forcing either of our flanks and driving back our land forces[,] [t]he cold weather may close the rivers, and the snow will render the roads so bad they will be impassible. So they would risk their whole army supplies, the loss of their ships by having them frozen in the rivers, and a most disastrous retreat in case of failure.

On the other hand an advance in this direction would create a very powerful diversion against the army of the Confederacy at Manassas, would if suc-

70. Second Lieutenant, later First Lieutenant, Ephraim A. Tweedy. A daguerreotype was a process to reproduce an image on silvered copperplate. Louis Daguerra's process was first introduced in the United States in 1840. By 1844 American improvements reduced the portrait sitting time from ten to one and one-half minutes.

cessful necessitate a retreat of that army to save Richmond, or risk the loss of that city before sufficient re inforcements could be brought from the south.

The loss of Richmond would be the most disastorous of events to our cause, for not only is it our present capital, the loss of which would so much prejudice our cause in Europe where to lose the capital is the loss of empire. But Richmond contains our principal manufacture of arms, & her iron works are daily giving us the materials of war in greatest abundance, to lose which would prostrate us for months. & besides the location of the city is such, with its many advantages of roads, canals & other means of communication, that to lose that city would be to lose the State of Virginia at once, and almost oblige a disastorous retreat to the true land of Dixie, the land of cotton— So you see the importance of our positions, circling Richmond in advance towards the enemy— So far we have been successful in maintaining our lines, and the country is such we have hopes of still doing so. But we are surrounded by a class of population who although southern born and have southern inclinations are very poor, and they have not that patriotism which would lead them to sacrifice their property rather than bow to the invader. So that they are on the strongest side is the extent of their ambition. They are for us now because we are here; they think, themselves that they would still be with us if the Yankees should come but they have not yet been tempted, and I am very much afraid if the enemy advances, and the question is "Remain & take the oath of allegiance to the U.S. or lose your property" they will take the oath and give all the assistance in their power, and the most dangerous business for us is that kind of aid they can give, & that is, a knowledge of the country. We have others who are natives of the north, but who having married southern wives pretend to be with us, their sympathies are with our enemies their interests with us, if their interests should change sides, so will their persons.

I have been ordering off all suspected parties, forcing them away with their household furniture, goods & chattles, both those who are natives and Yankee born, in order to give me a front with no body but my sworn enemies or known friends.

The inhabitants who were poor before are much poorer now of course, many in very destitute circumstances, so much so that I have been compelled to issue rations to them. The lower Peninsula has become perfectly devasted[,] houses and fences burned, cattle and hogs & all living things stolen or destroyed. The enemy have adopted now the course of burning and otherwise destroying everything.

Captain Phinizy has a leave of absence to take effect the 1 P.M. 6 Jany. I will send by him three or five hundred dollars according as I may be paid[.] [M]oney is not *very* plentiful, but it comes in such large bills that we cannot make any use of it.

I am anxiously waiting for Hugh in order to install him in his business, and then I will apply for home, if everything should at the time be quiet and promise quiet. Give my best love to all with you, tell W^m^R that he owes me a letter.

Tell Willie that he owes me some writing but I do not wish him to try even, until he is *perfectly* well, and when his letter comes I will write him a long one in reply.

My dear little Johnny must *try* and write something, write from a book, if he has nothing to say.

And my little daughter who has three brothers, and whose likeness I have not yet seen because of a stupid Irishman of a Lieutenant *Tweedy*. How does she like her other brother? She too must write her name with her own hand without assistance. Many kisses to her.

And my littlest fellow, many kisses from his Pa, and a thousand for his mother from her devoted husband.

L M^c^Laws

I will write Laura in a few days, if I can, my time is more and more occupied. I wish Hugh *very* much—officially and privately.

I have not heard from my application for the appointment of John F. Edwards, do not know whether it will be no, or yes.

((( )))

Camp Youngs Mills
[Young's Mill, Virginia]
Dec 30th 61 [Monday]

My Dear Wife

Tommorrow will be the last day of the new year, and Hugh has not arrived, although I have been anxiously waiting for him. I had hopes of meeting you by the first of January but it seems that the fates have decided otherwise. Let us hope that it is all for the best, although it seems to me as if it would have been better for me to have had you with me or rather to have been with you.

Captain Phinizy will leave for Augusta tommorrow or the next day and I send by him some money as my new year gift, please acknowledge its receipt! You have often been surprised and alarmed by very startling reports from the Peninsula, because General Magruder is a sensation man, he loves excitement and wishes others to enjoy that species of intoxication with him, he therefore has occasional bulletins issued and printed for general circulation.

There is a steamer in our possession. One that was sunk by the scared enemy when they evacuated Norfolk [Va.][.] [I]t is a first class steam frigate and is called or was called the *Merrimac.*[71] She was raised by us and is receiving a plating of iron. She is without masts, and has a long heavy snout from each end (she being made so that her facility for progress is especially great running either way) whereby running against any vessel, the snout hitting under water, the vessel is irreparably injured and must soon sink, her snout is then withdrawn and the Merrimac runs after another. Her speed too is very great[.] [S]he shows but five feet out of water—and all that, and more, is covered with the heaviest iron plating. Her armament is of the heaviest caliber, the port holes have iron shutters that open with a spring as the guns are run out and close ~~like shears~~ when the gun recoils.

Well this vessel is expected from her dock in a week or two, and as her destination is to open the port, by sinking the blockading vessels, her appearance is looked for with very great anxiety.

Her shape I will try and draw and send to Willie, that is as it was drawn for me by one who had seen the vessel. But you must bear in mind that my drawing is not of the most splendid order.

My little daughters picture is before me looking so sweet, that I must beg of you to give her a present from me, something to make her remember the occasion. I am away in the woods, or I would send her something myself. She would laugh I know to see my long beard, and if the chance offers I will send her my Daguerreotype.

I have heard nothing concerning the appointment of John Edwards, but will urge it again. So soon as I can get an opportunity of sending it by a sure hand. I am afraid that situated as he is, John will find it difficult to get his bond ex[e]cuted, for such a large sum as is required—viz thirty thousand dollars; but your brother John thinks he can— I am afraid of another item which is Johns age. President Davis may think that the position should be given to an older person.

You would laugh to see my two little houses. Which are merely two wall tents each, stretched over a wooden frame, the walls being somewhat higher than my head. I have a nice chimmney, answering for both, with double fire place and have really a very pleasant looking and warm setting room &

71. CSS *Virginia,* formerly the frigate USS *Merrimack.*

sleeping room. And how does my little Johnny get on with his measles[?] I have been looking at his & Willies pictures very frequently of late and long to see them more than they can imagine. I wish they would both learn to write and would write me something as to their daily occupations— I wish you would give them some money to buy such things as they want.

I am writing a very dull letter, because my business has not that variety to interest you. And I am so tired of it when the day is over, it makes me more fatigued to think of it.

I think you told me that a uniform had been ordered for me in Augusta. —I have one for dress purposes, but would like very much to have another, and will be glad when the Augusta made one comes. At present I dress much too plain for a General, but I have been in the woods so long, there has been no chance for me to buy dresses.

There are about ten persons talking about me, making a hubbub, not at all calculated to expedite correspondence, so you must excuse errors.

Give John & the servants Christmas for me, and being sorry that I can not give you myself for my Christmas. You must take this with a great many kisses wafted by desire[,] your devoted husband. L M^c^Laws

Kiss the baby for me, and do not let us quarrel about the name, *yet* if he should be named Lafayette, he would be Lafayette M^c^Laws Junior— think of that! And I would have to sign myself L M^c^Laws *Senior,* and *then* there would be Laura M^c^Laws, Laura M^c^Laws junior! Lafayette M^c^Laws & Lafayette M^c^Laws junior, four *L M^c^Lawses.* Horrible!

1862

The Bayard of the Peninsula

Head Q^{rs} Camp Youngs Mills
[Young's Mill, Virginia]
Jany 4th/62 [Saturday]

My Dearly beloved Wife

Your Christmas presents, the shirts, drawers, socks &c have been very welcomely rec^{d}. And tell John that his cake has been pronounced magnificent. I intend reserving the cake and candy for the women and children who come sometimes to make some request of me, all ragged and tattered and destitute as some of the refugees from Hampton are. Very little Christmas have they had.

The oranges are certainly a very great treat and the sausages will be magnificent for a scout. I think of giving a ball, as there are *two* young ladies, refugees from below, living within a mile & half of this place.

Thanks to your kindness I have now a plenty of flannel and drawers & socks & hankerchiefs and gloves. My only difficulty is about shoes and boots. My boots having now one of the toes out.

Hugh is very large and heavy, but looks well and I hope will make a good QMaster. I had but a very short conversation with him as he came in night before last about 12½, and I ordered him to Richmond the next morning about ten. I rec^{d} a letter from John F. Edwards concurring his acceptance of appointment of Commisary of my brigade—and complaining of the hardships of a soldiers life—not patriotic certainly!

I have not heard from your brother, he never writes but he is within twelve miles of me in Yorktown—and I believe occupies a very prominent position.

There is a large fleet assembling below for some outrageous scheme of the scoundrels, as it is but twelve miles from my head quarters. Of course we are on the alert and General Magruder favors us with stampedes very generally—but we have become so much accustomed to his cry of wolf that it will be very difficult to arouse us from our apathy, even when the enemy does come— I have more to fear from that than from anything else.

I was sorry that Hugh did not bring me the uniform which you wrote me had been ordered, as I will be quite in want of it. I am now wearing my old

U.S. single breasted uniform. My old Georgia Majors coat has lost colour and looks very shabby.

Give Sallie my love, by the way, you have not mentioned having seen her.[1] I was in hopes you would be very cosy and intimate.

I keep my daughters picture open on the table before me all the time—have the first and the last side by side—give her several kisses for me two on her eyes.

Give the boys my best love, including the littlest, and tell them to be very kind to the youngest, and to their sister. Johnny must grow fast or he will be caught & some of these days will [be] whipped by the baby.

I inclose my "picture" of the Merrimac, not splendid but will give you an idea. Love to Laura & thank her for her very acceptable presents. Your devoted husband L McLaws

((( )))

Head Quarters Division
[near Williamsburg, Virginia]
Jany 10th 62 [Friday]
11¼ P.M.

My Dear Wife
I came back this evening after a long days ride in the rain, examining my lines, and changing the camps of my troops, and found your letter of the 31st for which receive my sincere thanks. You have no idea how a good unaffected and affectionate letter such as the one now before is, cheers and revives me. I feel like another individual, with ten times the heart and energy and I am sure it makes me twice as good a soldier. So you perceive how intimately connected your thoughts and feelings are with my happiness and usefulness. Both Hugh and myself were looking very anxiously for a letter from home as in your last letters you had mentioned that Jimmy was quite ill.[2] Hugh was very miserable and anxious, and I was so on his account and my own.

The enemy are still in our front & equally as noisy and demonstrative as before. To night at 9½ I could hear one of their bands playing Hail Columbia very loudly, although the night is very dark and rainy. But they are continually playing some bragadoci prank, and this may be one of them.

The reported capture of the Harriet Lane by the Texans at Galveston

1. Hu's wife, Sarah, was also referred to as Sallie.
2. Jimmy was Hu's son James.

served to day to enliven us a little, although J. B. Magruder stands so conspicuous for humbuggery that we always suspicion everything over his signature.[3] That he had nothing to do with the affair we all feel assured, provided it was done. But no matter who did it, it is a glorious chapter at this time in our cause.

I have written you very often indeed[,] not daily to be sure, but I think that three letters per week would not be a bold assertion. Can you lay your hand on your heart and say as much[?]

I wrote Johnny a letter by the mail of yesterday, thanking him very much for his really very clever letter, and asking him to write me frequently. I hope he will do so, as he now knows how.

Fred^s visit must have been a very pleasant surprise, and a very great gratification to the children.[4] Tell the boys that they are not yet old enough to belong to the cavalry but must listen to the stories of old soldiers in order to learn how to do when they are of the proper age.

I have been applied to several times by the Southern Illustrated News for my *picture*[.][5] [W]ill you please send me a copy of my photograph as soon as possible.

My best love to the boys, my sweet little daughter. The count & a great deal to my dear wife. Your devoted husband L McLaws.

((( )))

Head Q^rs Camp Youngs Mills
[Young's Mill, Virginia]
Jany 14th 62 [Tuesday]

My Dear Darling
Your letter of the 7th was rec^d this evening, I am very glad indeed to hear of the arrival of that letter sent by Captain Phinizy, as from your letter of the 3^d, I was afraid some accident had happened to him.

I do not blame Willie for liking the country so much better than the town and would be glad if he could be allowed to run wild for a week or two in every month, him and Johnny.

3. The USS *Harriet Lane* was captured on January 1, 1862.

4. Frederick Geiger Edward's visit.

5. The *Southern Illustrated News* was published every Saturday afternoon in Richmond, Va., by Ayres & Wade, Editors and Proprietors. The *News* of April 4, 1863, presented an article on LM with a full-page picture appearing on the cover. The article was a lengthy biographical story focusing on LM's role during the Battle of Fredericksburg.

I have been thinking how much better satisfied you all would have been, the children in particular, if you could have remained in Atlanta or rather the neighbouring Marietta, where the woods are so convenient, and corn was cheaper, and the Yankees were not so thick as in Augusta.

Concerning my visit to you, I cannot give any definite answer. I think that the crisis of our fate is now at hand, and it behooves us all to be at our post.

I have many and very anxious thoughts concerning you and the children, and my heart is yearning to embrace you hourly day & night, sleeping and waking, but my duty demands my presence and my absence might be injuriuosly commented on, until therefore the ends and aims of the enemy are disclosed.

I am, as is now often the case, writing to give you the information of my continued good health, and to relieve my heart ache by writing to you.

I often imagine how happy we would be together, but then the idea of parting again after a few days makes me so dispairing that I hesitate very much in taking the step homewards.

I have sent Willie [a] drawing of the ship and in the letter was a five dollar bill[,] all of which I hope has been rec[d]. Johnny must invent some terrible weapons with which to attack the enemy by land, when he comes off his big ships and send me a drawing of it.

Good bye. Hugh has not yet returned though he writes cheerfully from Richmond. You must be aware of the depressed state of business more than I am. The contrast between the life and activity of old times and the lethargy of this is not shown to me, as I remain in the woods. To go home and see this stagnation, would be very depressing to me as it is to all those who have been away—so much is it so, that those who have returned from leaves of absence tell me that they could not remain at home. They were forced to come back from the overpowering sense, that it was against their manhood to remain—I have no doubt but that it would be so to me—but it does not seem so now.

Give my best love to Sallie, and her children.

Tell Willie he must write me—after his eyes get well. Let him run in the country if he wishes & do not feel mortified at his preferring it—he should be encouraged to remain away from home and not be always a home sick fellow.

Kiss My litte daughter for me, and tell her to give the baby my blessing.

Tell Johnnie that I forgot to mention— The steamer has an engine on board of her, by which she can throw boiling water over any of the enemy who should dare to touch her with their hands.

Good by, my dear wife, a thousand kisses to you and kind rememberance to all, including John & Caroline.

Your devoted husband
L M^c^Laws

((( )))

Head Quarters Divison [LB1]
Camp Youngs Mills
[Young's Mill, Virginia]
Jan 24-62 [Friday]

The roads are now in such a terrible plight that locomotion with teams is difficult and dangerous, and they are daily getting worse. Rumors of advance of *enemy*. I believe that we are ready for them, a rumor that our army was falling back from Manasses [Manassas].

If the army is falling back, it be a ruse to get the enemy to come forward—I have every confidence in those who have the direction of affairs & believe everything will be for the best—another *rumor* Gen. Beauregard is to go to Columbus and take the direction of affairs in that quarter.[6]

((( )))

Camp Youngs Mills
[Young's Mill, Virginia]
February 7th, 62 [Friday]

My Dear Wife

Your letter of the 30 & 31st was received to day, handed me this morning when in bed, and I read it and wished all kinds of things, one of which was that you were somewhere about me, at least within sound of my voice. As so many persons were waiting on me I got up and dressed and have been busy ever since.

The big dinner came off yesterday evening. General Magruder was there, also Thomas R R Cobb and the Colonels of the 15 Va 2 La 5thLa.[7] Numerous other officers of various grades, and myself.

The dinner was magnificent, and would have graced a New Orleans restaurant.

6. Columbia, S.C.

7. Colonel Thomas Pearson August, Virginia, who commanded the 15th Virginia; Colonel William Mallory Levy, who commanded the 2nd Louisiana; and Colonel Henry Forno, who commanded the 5th Louisiana.

A great many toasts were given and speeches made in reply. Much to my confusion I was toasted among the regular toasts as "The Bayard of the Peninsula, Sans peur & Sans reproche[.]" [O]f course I had to respond to such tremendous flattery, and of course obtained applause.

I eat all sorts of things[,] nuts, cakes & sugar plums, and in consequence have to day something of an indigestion.

Feby 8th

General Magruder has been called to Richmond for what purpose I am unaware. What especial purpose, some think he will be sent to North Carolina to take charge of affairs in that direction. Others think it is to concert operations in connections with the steamer Merrimac which is shortly to make a trial of her skill and prowess to clear our harbor of the blockading fleet. It is understood that the famous vessel is afloat and promises to be a perfect success.

The Herald I sent you as a curiosity, but did not expect it would be paid for with letter postage. I will learn better for the future, but do not really pretend to hope of getting another.

I have received a commission for John Edwards, and sent it to John, your brother to be forwarded to him. There is required of him a bond of thirty thousand dollars, which I hope he may be able to obtain but which makes me nervous to think about, under the circumstances.

I saw a letter from Savannah, in which the writer states that fears were entertained that the enemy were about taking a position which would enable them to shell that city, without being damaged themselves. I very much fear that the man for the time is not in Savannah or its vicinity—some say that he has not yet risen to eminence.

If the occasion calls for a better one, I hope he will be forthcoming.

Good bye. Kiss the children and Sampson. Love to all.

Your devoted husband. L McLaws

((( )))

Camp Youngs Mills
[Young's Mill, Virginia]
Feby 19th 62 [Wednesday]

My dear darling wife
I recd your short letter this moment, it is not quite so lovingly written as usual, although it would be a fond letter from any other wife. Are you a little

vexed that I gave a mild rebuke? It was not intended for even a *mild* rebuke, it was an argument against complaint or repining, nothing else.

You may think that I complain when you do not grieve at my absence[.] [P]erhaps so, but I feel as much like running away from here straight to your arms, as much as any one can feel and not act up to his desires. So do not urge me or my patiotism and ambition will all give way. I will be seeking a cause of dissatisfaction and trump up some reason to leave, which my mature reason would condemn most strongly, and my children hereafter would be ashamed to mention.

John Edwards has come. Remember me to cousin Rachael! and tell her that she owes me a letter—in fact![8]

John E has not as yet executed his bond, but has gone to Richmond for that purpose— He is looking in fine health, but of course is disponding for various and sundry reasons.

Address your letters, hereafter "*Via Yorktown. V*^{a}."

Do you receive the Richmond Whig, if not I will send it again.

The news from Donelson is very provoking, but let us hope it is all for the best.[9] —I am proud to see the spirit of yourself and the children. I really wish they all had guns and could and would shoot the Yankees.

I write in haste. Kiss *Sampson* for me, and the children all, one extra kiss to my daughter; and many then is coupled for yourself.

Your devoted husband
L McLaws

((( )))

Head Quarters
Camp Youngs Mills
[Young's Mill, Virginia]
February 19th 62 [Wednesday]

My Dear Wife

This morning I wrote you a short hurried letter in order to keep my letters on the road.

This evening a telegram announced to me that it was stated in a Baltimore

8. Virginia Rachel Edwards was John F. Edwards's younger sister. Eighth Census, 1860, Louisville—Second District, Jefferson County, Ky., entry for F. G. Edwards family, sheet 106, M 653, RG 29.

9. The surrender of Fort Donelson, Tenn., took place on February 16, 1862.

paper of the 17th inst, that Fort Donelson was surrendered on the 16th[,] 15000 prisoners & Generals Buckner, Pillow and, Johnson (Brushrod) I suppose, there being a Johnson in Tennessee formerly of the Army who was President of a military school in that state, included.[10]

All the signs tend to show that the fight is to "come off" in the land of Dixie proper, away from their steamers and Navy generally. Our affairs do not wear a very brilliant hue at present in spite of our exertions. The fact is that the border States do not entertain for the Yankees that intense hatred that we have in the Southern land of cotton[,] they have not volunteerd in that spirit of devotion we have done. One half of their population are traitors, and our forces therefore and positions are always acurately known to the enemy before they advance.

If we have them committed so as to be sure of a large mass in our favor, who are in arms, it is all we can expect.

I can scarecely credit the reported loss of 15000 men, but yet, it *might* be so, because of the overwhelming force of the enemy and their great facilities by means of water transportation of bringing forward any amount of re-inforcements.

I am not disheartened by the news as bad even as it comes to me. The enemy are only on our threshhold, when he get in among the people whose every man woman & child are his enemies, he can begin to realise the nature of the war.

I am exceedingly sorry that the beautiful city of Nashville should be under the sway of the coarse Yankee. —But force must sometimes prevail.

The weather is so mild that no fires are necessary, although it is a continual and everlasting rain, the whole country is flooded, the water stands in large lakes over this flat country, and there is no bottom to the roads.

Give my regards to Fred the unlucky, and tell him to learn my boys how to be manly.

You never told me what was the matter with Willie—if he is unhealthy take him away from school, and send him into the country, board him with

10. Simon Bolivar Buckner, Kentucky, USMA 1844, brigadier, later lieutenant general; Gideon Johnson Pillow, Tennessee, University of Nashville, lawyer and brigadier general; and Bushrod Rust Johnson, Ohio, USMA 1840, brigadier. Buckner surrendered the fort; he later became president of LM's court-martial board and clearly showed his conflict of interest in working with Longstreet to impede the trial's progress. Johnson was promoted to major general only to have his commission revoked.

Cocoa nut dipper. (Courtesy of the Georgia Historical Society)

Mr. Greenwood and let him turn farmer—better health than books, let him run after opossums, rabits or whatever he chooses so he has health.[11]

Your brother John is well. Hugh is so fat that he has had to cut open his pants for five or six inches in the back. I believe he is getting alarmed. I heard some one say the other day that Hugh was as fat as a woman. I do not know what was meant. I thought he was myself, however.

11 P.M.

I have had a fine silver mounted dipper of cocoa nut presented to me by Capn Taylor of my staff. If an opportunity offers I will send it to you, which

11. Mr. Greenwood has not been identified.

you can in turn give to any of the children from *Sampson* up to Willie, of the boys, or to my Sweet little daughter.[12]

It rains here all the time; it has been raining with very little intermission for forty eight hours, and looks as if we would have another extension for the same time, in consequence thereof, every part of the country is so flooded, that to travel is nearly an impossibility. I have however such a complete knowledge of all the by-ways that I never travel the roads, but keep the woods.

This war is tiresome to me, although I consider it a duty to my country, to my family and to humanity itself to use my utmost endeavor[s] to free the South from the dominion of the North. Yet it is tiresome and tis so because I am away from my dear wife and my children. The comfort that one kiss from you would give me is past conceptions, and still I am here, and cannot leave to get it. You might send me your daguerreotype, taken just as you are every day, without any dressing up or attempt at fine appearance, just as if you were sitting by me with nothing to disturb your equanimity. Please send it to me! and with it the boys. My little daughters likeness is on my table before me all the time. What a very fine looking manly boy, Jimmy is, I declare he is remarkable.

Give my love to Sallie & her children. Kiss all of ours, Sampson included, & write me very often— I must now to bed, to wish and hope and to pray that my wife be once again granted to me. Good night.

Feby. 21

All well.

I will write you from Yorktown where I am now bound.

((( )))

Camp Custis, farm [LB1]
[Custis Farm, Virginia]
March 26/62 [Wednesday]

My dear Willy,

[Virginia McLaws's transcription] Some left out just directing him about writing. The enemy are reported in great force just below us at Newport News & Old Point. There is no doubt their ambition is to attack & take Norfolk & then Richmond. It may be however that they are ready, if foiled or

12. Henry Taylor, Kentucky, captain and aide-de-camp from 1861 to December 1863. The dipper can be seen at GHS-LM.

defeated in their attempt on N [Norfolk], to try their fortune in the direction of Richmond. The Merrimac is ready so they say for another trial of her prowess, but, as yet, she has not made her reappearance. She may be delayed in order that, if the enemy attempt to attack N [Norfolk] her full powers can be employed to defeat that effort. The papers say that the Yankees intend taking the negroes & put them to work on plantations where their armies are to raise cotton.

Addressed Mrs. Emily A M^c^Laws
Care W^m^R. M^c^Laws Augusta Ga.

((( )))

Head Quarters, Curtis Farm
[Custis Farm, Virginia]
March 31/62 [Monday]

My dearly beloved Wife
The country here appears quiet and the enemy have retired again into their strong holds, but they are evidently bent on mischief somewhere. Their demonstration the other day may have been intended as a feint to draw troops from some other quarter where they intend making an attack, or it may have [been] a strong reconnaisance preliminary to an advance in this direction, since the movement in retreat of General Johnston appears to have disconcerted them in their advance on Manassas.[13]

This Peninsula presents a very unfavorable field for the operations of a large force, it is bounded as you know, on one side by the York and on the other by James River. York river as far up as West Point is more properly an arm of the sea, than a river, is straight in its course and very deep, as far up as West Point, where the *river* in fact empties in the sea. Far below that point the water is always salt as sea water. If the enemy should occupy West Point they would be within forty miles of Richmond, and be on a line of rail road which runs from that point to Richmond. To get there however it is necessary to pass Yorktown, by water. At Yorktown the river narrows so, that the passage is easily defended by the batteries placed on the bluffs there and at Gloucester point on the other side.[14] Yorktown is very completely fortified, to resist both an attack by land and by water.

To pass up James River it would be necessary to get by the batteries at Hardees Bluff and Mulberry Point. Hardees Bluff has a battery of thirteen

13. Joseph Eggleston Johnston, Virginia, USMA 1829, general.
14. Gloucester is pronounced Gloster.

guns, all large calibre. Mulberry Point is to have fifteen, all of large size but the barbette battery is not completed nor will it be in three or four weeks.[15] The battery is protected from a land attack by a heavy work around an elevated point, about a half mile distant—when everything is completed, the place will be stronger than Yorktown. So our two flanks may be considered secure or will be made So if time is allowed— When all that is done, we will have to resist an advance from the direct front only, having no fear of the enemy gaining our rear.

There is another arm of the sea called Warwick river, which penetrates deeply into the Peninsula, the tide water reaching up to within six miles of York river and the fresh water part comes from a source within a half mile of York river. We have dammed up that river at various points so that now the country is flooded, from a point under the guns of Yorktown, to the head of tide water of James River. So that when the works defending the dams are completed, our direct front will be very strong. Along the line of this water course from Yorktown there are two mill ponds, viz Wynnes & Lees, with grist mills. From Lees Mill to James river along Warwick river is ten miles, at the mouth on the right bank is a projecting point called Lands End where we have a strong picket to watch James River and give information of any approach by water. The enemy might land there or along the bank of Warwick river and march up the Peninsula to attack us in flank. To prevent that we are constructing some works across from Lees Mill to ~~a~~ another arm of the sea projecting inland a considerable distance, called *Skiff Creek.* From Lees Mill to Skiff Creek is nearly a mile, so our line of defense will be from Yorktown down Warwick River, with its dams, to Lees Mill & thence across to Skiff Creek.[16] Our troops being concentrated behind that line, any part can re-inforce any other, and the officers and men can be made well acquainted with the country they will have to defend, which was not the case formerly.

I have endeavored my dear wife to give you a hasty sketch of our position here, in order to make you feel a little more confident of our ability to defend ourselves although we should be attacked by a superior force. The country is so much cut up by these arms of the sea, called rivers, with their

15. Harden's Bluff, or Fort Huger, was located across the James River from Mulberry Point. A barbette was a raised wooden platform on which the artilley piece was placed and fired from behind the protection of a wall or parapet.

16. The dams were a key part of the defensive strategy. The constant rain caused concern for their stability. Howell Cobb wrote, "If there is no more rain I believe Dams 1 & 2 are safe—but I fear both will go if much more rain falls." Howell Cobb to LM, April 9, 1862, SHC-LM.

accompanying marshes and boggy fresh water tributaries that it is impossible to move through it except along the main roads. Thus it is impossible to make use of a very large force—and the tremendous odds against us can not be so formidable as elsewhere in a more open country, and a defeat on their part would be disastorous in the extreme.

Good night my darling wife—I send you a hundred kisses. Tell the boys to take care of you & their sister & the baby. —Love to all & remember me to the servants. I have been riding all day & it is now twelve o'clock at night. Your devoted husband.

L M[c]Laws

I now command thirteen regiments and of course am busy all the time day & night. So excuse my hasty letters.

(((   )))

Head Quarters 2 Division
[The Peninsula, Virginia]
Right Flank . April 23/62 [Wednesday]

My dear darling Wife

The enemy are immediately in our front and daily skirmishing takes place between our advanced parties. They have made no decided attack since that made the other day when they were repulsed. But we are in daily expectation of an attack along our whole front.

My command is now a very extensive one[,] much more so than any other officer in the Peninsula, excepting General Magruder, and I have the greater part of his as I now have four Brigadier Generals, and five Brigades under me, and an extent of country to guard equal to all the rest combined, so you will perceive my dear wife my time is anxiously occupied and constantly so.

Our troops are in good spirits and it is the wish of all, officers and men, that a grand battle should be fought in the Peninsula, as it is our conviction it would result gloriously to our arms. —The Confederacy never had a better nor a larger army concentrated than the one we now have, and the country is of such character that our force is as formidable as the greatest number the enemy can bring to bear against us.

So be of good cheer my dear wife and let us hope and pray for our own country and our cause and that we may meet again soon, to live in peace and quiet under our own flag, free from the malacious influence of Yankeedom.

I rec[d] the letters of Johnny & Willie with which I am much pleased, and will answer them in a day or two. I showed them to their uncle Hugh and have sent them to John Gibson, who is at Yorktown. Tell Johnny that his uncle John charged the enemy the first day they appeared before his position, at the head of his Regiment, leading them all in a full run full fifty yards, and drove the scoundrels like a parcel of sheep from their position. The charge was gallantly and beautifully made and is spoken of in terms of the highest praise by every one.

Good bye for the present. When I do not write, I ask Hugh to mention me in his letters to Sallie.

Every one is well. I saw Tom Taylor yesterday looking very hearty, he is Colonel of the 1st Kentucky Regiment—Alley is in his regiment.[17]

My love and rememberances to all with you, kiss my little daughter and the baby and ten thousand for yourself.

Your devoted husband
L McLaws

((( )))

Head Quarters 2 Division
[The Peninsula, Virginia]
Right Flank . April 25/62 [Friday]

My Dear Wife
Up to this hour 9. A.M. the enemy have made no other decided attack anywhere along the front of our position. We have skirmishing all along the line all the time, with casualties on both sides[:] a few killed[,] a few wounded. The service of the troops is very severe and we have many sick. My health and that of my military family continues good thanks be to Him who disposeth of good and evil.

The designs of the enemy are wrapped in mystery, as are the designs of our Commander in Chief General Johnston, who is a very quiet stern man, telling his plans to no one.

There is a very great contrast between the two commanders, General Magruder & General Johnston.

General Magruder is fond of dress and parade and of company. Conceals nothing, and delights to have a crowd about him, to whom he converses freely upon any and all subjects. He never moves from his head quarters without having five or six aides & a dozen or more orderlies.

General Johnston will never speak on official matters to but the person

17. Thomas H. Taylor, Kentucky, Kenyon College in Ohio and Centre College in Kentucky, lieutenant colonel, later brigadier general which was not confirmed. In May 1863 Alfred Cumming was sent to Vicksburg to replace Taylor as brigade commander.

interested, dislikes to have a crowd about him, never mentions military matters when away from his office. Often rides off alone, never will have more than two with him. Has not much to say to even his best friends, and does not appear to care about dress, although he always dresses neatly & in a uniform coat—if you have business with him it is yes or no, without talking more than to a proper understanding of the subject.

General Magruder can talk twenty four hours incessantly.

General G. W. Smith who commands the reserves, is most decidedly a reserved man on all military matters—although away from that topic he is as free as a boy[.] [H]e is a classmate of mine, and has always been distinguished for his talents and sound judgement. It is supposed that he has considerable influence over General Johnston and the only one that has.

General Longstreet of whom you have heard, if you do not know, stands high as a very gallant soldier, he commands the centre— General Hill who commands Yorktown is a very determined officer, and stands high as a gentleman of pure character and great honesty of purpose.[18]

Smith, Longstreet, & Hill, are all old friends of mine, and graduates of the same class at West Point.

George M. Lay[,] my old room mate at West Point, formerly Private Secretary to Gen[l] Scott, [is] here on duty as Inspector General of General Johnston.[19]

Col Rhett[,] an old friend[,] is Gen[l] Johnston, AdjtGeneral.[20]

Many other old friends I find in the army here in high Command.

On the other side we hear of Gen[l] Brooks who is an old friend of mine & who was the Adjt Gen[l] of Gen[l] Twiggs in the Mexican War.[21]

Gen Fitz John Porter, who was Gen[l] Johnstons AdjGen[l] in Utah, [is] an old friend of mine.[22]

Gen Davidson, an acquaintance of mine & General W. S. Smith who was

18. Daniel Harvey Hill, South Carolina, USMA 1842, major, later appointed lieutenant general but not confirmed.

19. George William Lay, Virginia, USMA 1842, colonel; General Winfield Scott.

20. Thomas Smith Rhett, South Carolina, USMA 1842, colonel.

21. William Thomas Harbough Brooks, Ohio, USMA 1841, brigadier, later Union major general; David Emanuel Twiggs, from Richmond County, Ga., the oldest- and highest-ranking officer to resign the U.S. Army. Twiggs was commander of the Department of Texas when he surrendered it to Colonel Ben McCulloch, commander of the Texas troops, on February 18, 1861.

22. Fitz John Porter, New Hampshire, USMA 1845, brigadier, later Union major general.

a particular friend of many of the officers here, & lastly, Genl McClelland was a friend of mine.[23]

A sortie will be made to day by General Picket of General Longstreet's division, and the results may be important.

I have been trying to draw you a map more comprehensive than any you can find, but my topographic talent is very bad, hardly comprehensive to any but myself.

I have arranged with Hugh to mention me in his letters, just as if we were not brothers. I did this to relieve WmR, apprehensions.

All quiet up to this hour, no cannon firing [letter has been burned] from any quarter, but the sharp shooters are busy all around every position and along all our lines.

April 26th 62, [Saturday]

12 M.

I send five dollars to the children, to the two boys for writing me and for my daughter for wishing to do it. Ask Johnny how he spells "wrought iron."

The enemy waked us up at daylight this morning with a fierce fire of artillery, along Dam No 1, but with what damage is not known.

I will send a map by this mail of our situation, not accurate to be sure but will give you and the boys an idea of our situation.

Did Johnny really write by himself with no one to help him? if he did he has done very well indeed. Willie has improved considerably and really hope he will "try again" as he promised.

I saw Ally this morning looking very well indeed, says he has not been sick a day since in the service—he has a fine beard, and looks considerably more manly. John E always calls you "Emmy" although I have informed him once or twice that you were Mrs McLaws. Ally calls you "Aunt Emmy."

Good bye until I have time to write again which I hope may be tomorrow—love to all & many kisses from the kissable gentleman of the family and for my daughter & Ulric, & many to my wife from

Her devoted husband
L McLaws

23. John Wynn Davidson, Virginia, USMA 1845, brigadier, later Union brevet major general, U.S. volunteers; William Farrar Smith, Vermont, USMA 1845, brigadier, later Union major general although he was never confirmed; George Brinton McClellan, Pennsylvania, USMA 1846, Union major general.

((( )))

Head Quarters 2 Division
[The Peninsula, Virginia]
Right Flank, Army of Peninsula
May 1, 62 [Thursday]

My dearly beloved wife
I have not received a letter from you for many days and would be exceedingly anxious if it were not for a letter which Hugh received yesterday from his wife, of late date, I think the 25th April announcing that all were well.

I have written you very frequently, and sent the letters per special express ~~from~~ to Richmond.

The enemy are engaged in active preparations for the bombardment of Yorktown. They now throw a great number of enormous shells in the place, day and night, but that is nothing to what will be done, when their batteries are completed. There is not much firing along the lines, except by sharpshooters, and our men are as a mass much better at that game than the mass of the enemy.

They have a regiment or two of sharpshooters which were located in most of the convenient hiding places along our lines, for annoying us—and really did annoy exceedingly for some time. But our men soon drove them away—at first they were very daring as the men opposed to them had nothing but the smoothbore musket. When our rifles came in play, the enemy retired.

The news of the occupation of New Orleans as it was first announced by telegraph, produced a very profound sensation among all parties—especially with the Louisianians of French extraction. You know how excessively open the French are in showing their sensations. They do not feel as strongly as we phlegmatics do, at least grief does not seem so lasting in them, as it comes violently and goes off quickly. One or two men of rank in one of the regiments came to me imploring leaves of absence as the enemy were in New Orleans and their "wives and children would be houseless wanderers on the face of the earth." This remark was made to me by a Lieut Colonel whose family (mother & father in law) according to his own statement made fifteen hundred hogsheads of sugar this year (finished bailing in March last). It was therefore ridiculous to say that his family would be houseless & wanderers on the face of the earth. —I suppose that in a day or two he will be as lively as a Frenchman usually is.[24]

24. The siege of Forts Jackson and St. Philip led to the occupation of New Orleans on April 25, 1862. "The hogsheads, large wooden barrels made by the slaves, each held

I do not take the desponding view of affairs as some do. The occupation of our seaports, and other places along the rivers where gunboats can ascend will lead to the concentration of our armies, and then there will be no doubt of the results.

Good day for to day. I will try and write you tomorrow again. Give my love to all, and a great deal to my children, and very much to my dear wife.

Your devoted husband
L M^c^Laws

((( )))

Camp eight Miles above New Kent C H
[New Kent Courthouse, Virginia]
May 13th/62 [Tuesday]

My dearly beloved wife!
Our army is at a stand in and about this place, recuperating from the effects of our fall back from the Peninsula, and waiting to see what will be the next move of General M^c^Clelland. Various rumors are afloat concerning his intentions. One is that he is falling back, another that he will cross over James River and make Norfolk his base of operations, and endeavor to unite with Burnside coming from North Carolina. If he does that our army I should think will move rapidly and operate against General M^c^Dowell at Fredricksburg and crush him, and then return to deal blows against M^c^Clelland and Burnside who will then be far removed from their gun boats, and there can be no doubt of the result.[25]

Our government has now committed itself to the policy of concentration, and in doing it will most undoubtedly be assailed by hordes of the discontented who will seek this opportunity to vent their disappointment.

The venture is vast and promises the most ample return^s^, and therefore before judging we must await results.

If our armies can be fed, there is every reason to believe that victory will once more crown our efforts, and our efforts be sooner achieved than it would have been by the policy we have heretofore pursued.

Did you ever get the dipper? I write to inform you that all are well, John Gibson, John Edwards[,] Hugh & myself.

---

a thousand pounds of sugar or seventy gallons of molasses. Once filled and sealed, they stood ready for shipment to market in New Orleans." Thorpe, "Sugar," 758.

25. Ambrose Everett Burnside, Indiana, USMA 1847, Union major general; Irvin McDowell, Ohio, USMA 1838, Union major general.

My warmest love to all, and especially my whole heart to my dear wife.

Your devoted husband
L M^c^Laws
Brig Genl

((( )))

Glenwood [Mr Stubbs House] near Richmond [Virginia]
May 20th 1862 [Tuesday]

My Dear wife

Your letter of the 16th inst was received yesterday. By directing to Richmond our communication with each other is rapid and more sure than formerly. I am afraid that some of your letters have fallen into the hands of the Yankees and you will be gratified by perusing some of your epistles in some of the Northern papers.

The enemy is approaching us in various directions[:]

1st comes M Clelland from the Peninsula
2. Burneside from the coast of North Carolina
3. M^c^Dowell and Banks from the Potomac[26]

But I have no doubt but that our army will circumvent all their designs.

You can have no idea how our presence has given confidence to the people in Richmond. Before our arrival there was a panic among all classes. The tradesmen refused to open their wares, and one or two of them failed to swindle their customers, showing in this last a forgetfullness of their usual habits and instincts, which proved how totally prostrating is the feeling of fear. One shoe merchant actually sold a pair of boots for twenty five dollars, when the usual price is thirty.

I still have my command of eighteen regiments, although my rank does not entitle me to it. In the movements now about to take place I suppose there will be a reorganization and my command will be, of course, reduced.

What our next step will be, remains to be seen when it takes place, and then only, as General Johnston is not one to tell what his plans will be.

I have not seen the President, nor do I expect to as my command constantly requires my presence, and the enemy is within five miles and I am ordered to support the advance, should they require assistance.

It is about time for Willie and Johnny to be writing me again, and longer

26. Nathaniel Prentiss Banks, Massachusetts, politician and major general of U.S. volunteers.

letters than before. And my little daughter should be making her mark to me, at least.

Write me, addressing your letter to this place, John G.[,] John E.[,] Hugh and all are very well.

Hugh I believe writes all the news, a faculty I am either wanting in or am too indifferent in disposition to do so.

Give my love to Laura and give a thousand thanks for the socks she sent me. I am now commencing to wear cotton socks and will find them very comfortable, and coming in good time.

Colonel Bryan wrote to Hugh the other day,[27] saying that he had received a letter from his wife, who wrote that she had just returned from a visit to you, and that the baby was one of the prettiest & finest children she had ever seen.

Good day, and God bless you is the prayer of your devoted husband.

I send you a rough draft of my report of the engagement in front of W^ms^Burg on Sunday.[28]

L M^c^Laws

((( )))

Camp on Chickahominy
[Chickahominy River, Virginia]
June 10th? 62 [Tuesday]

My dearly beloved Wife
Colonel Clay Taylor is on a visit to this place for the benefit of his health, he is on the staff of General Price.[29] He can give you the latest news from Saint Louis.

Les Walker is here from Charleston, on the staff of General Ripley. I have not seen him however, his camp being seven or eight miles distant, more or less.[30]

27. Goode Bryan, Georgia, USMA 1834, colonel later brigadier general, succeeded Paul Semmes as brigade commander when Semmes was mortally wounded at Gettysburg. Bryan was from Augusta and also Hancock County, Ga.

28. LM is referring to the engagement that took place on Sunday, May 4, 1862, on the outskirts of Williamsburg. For LM's report, see *OR* 11:441–42. It was this engagement that led General Joseph E. Johnston to recommend LM for promotion to major general.

29. H. Clay Taylor, Kentucky, lieutenant colonel, chief of artillery and chief of ordnance for Major General Sterling Price.

30. Les D. Walker, captain, assistant adjutant general to General Ripley from No-

Alley is still here out of position— I recommended him for an appointment in the Provisional Army, but no answer has as yet been given to the application.

John Edwards is well and doing well, is regarded as the most efficient Commisary in this command.

John Gibson had two balls through his clothes in the late fight, but was not touched in the flesh, escaped entirely unhurt although the ball holes looked as if ~~they~~ the balls must have gone through his leg, to have made the holes they did.

Hugh is very active and busy. —All of us are well.

Clay Taylor is anxious, first for me to write a letter to the President or to the Secretary of State, recommending Bernard Pratt for some civil appointment,[31] among other things to state—that he was editor of a secession paper in Saint Louis, is a man of fine talents, a lawyer of consideration—speaks three languages & c&c. —I told him that if the Secretary of State wished to employ a gentleman of Mr Pratts acquirements, I would be very happy to give my recommendation, to the extent of my knowledge of Mr Pratts character & attainments. That I did [not] know as to his standing at the bar, nor as to his proficiency in the languages, but believed him to be a well informed and well educated gentleman, who would give satisfaction in any department he would undertake to do duty in—and it would be a pleasure for me to write to any one, either the President or Sec of State, giving such recommendation. But I declined asking for him any appointment in particular.

Secondly—Clay wished me to recommend him for an ordnance officer of General Prices Command, which I declined doing, as I would not interfere with General Prices appointments.

The fact is Clay wished to be my ordnance officer, and probably would make a good one—but I have no reason to be particularly grateful to Mr Pratt or Clay Taylor for their kind treatment to me or my family when in

---

vember 24, 1861, through 1862; Roswell Sabine Ripley, Ohio, USMA 1843, Confederate brigadier general.

31. Bernard Pratte. Elizabeth Geiger Edwards married his son, Bernard A. Pratte Jr. The sister of John F. and Alley Edwards, she lived with Alley and Carrie V. Edwards in Alvin, Tex., after the war. Ninth Census, 1870, Fourth Ward, Atlanta, Fulton County, Ga., entry for Frederick Geiger Edwards family, p. 291; Deed assumed by Fred G. and Alfred Edwards [sons of Alley and Carrie V. Edwards], April 28, 1918, County Clerk, Brazoria County, Tex.

Saint Louis, and I therefore will not give them favors now, even if I had it in my power to do so.

Clay Seems to be a clever sort of man, but of no very great force, he has however been sick and looks badly.

The news that comes to us of the successive victories gained by Jackson over our enemies has over and over again electrified us and inspired new hopes for our cause.[32] —General McClelland in the mean while keeps his army inactive before us. throwing up intrenchments just beyond our lines, we in turn are throwing up slight works, and keeping ourselves ready to meet any advance he may make.

The Northern papers are so full of lying reports, as they are afraid to tell the truth to their own people or allow it to be known to Europe—that to read their accounts of our operations would be amusing, except for the fact we know they injure us in the estimation of those whose good opinions we value. —Their statements of the fights about Richmond are rediculously false, for in no instance have we been worsted, on the contrary, whenever we have met the enemy they have been easily driven before us. —Judging their reports of operations here are as true as of our & theirs elsewhere, for instance at Corinth [Miss.], we have every reason to believe that the disasters they report as having occured against us are all false, and that Beauregard, whatever his designs may be has executed them successfully.

If we could have his army here now, so that a large force could be thrown North the results would be exceedingly favorable to our cause, and would learn the scoundrels who have invaded us, how unpleasant it is to be invaded.

My dear wife I long very much to have you once more in my arms, and regret my promotion for the reason that as I advance it makes me more of a public character, who is expected to be devoid of all considerations of personal prediliction while my longings are the same as an individual or a husband and father. They are expected to [be] suppressed more than ever, because I am a Major General, whereas I am longing more to be with my wife & children since I have been made one, than I was ever before.

Our forces and those of the enemy cannot be long kept apart, one or the other must be attacked— It is not improbable that we will be the attacking party as the resources of the enemy are much superior to our own, and they can afford to wait longer.

32. Thomas Jonathan Jackson, Virginia, USMA 1846, major, later lieutenant general. LM is referring to Jackson's Shenandoah Valley campaign in May and June 1862.

W^m^R, from whom I rec^d^ a letter today, mentions that Willie was complaining of rhumatism, rather early is it not for one so young to be complaining of that disease.

W. mentions that you have a fine garden which is certainly a great blessing—as it is a desi [remainer of word obliterated—might be desideration] of life to have vegetables. I begin to think so, for bacon and bread and occasionally rice are our staples of diet. Occasionally we get onions, and once or twice we have had asparagus.

Mutton is fifty cents per pound—sugar is difficult to obtain and all things are so exceedingly high that the mass of people must be content to live only, without hope of luxury of any kind.

Have you any fear of Augusta being taken by the Yankees? I ask because WmR writes that the people have been appointing committees to devise means of obstructing the river from Savannah— If the people are true to themselves and will line the banks of the river with sharp shooters, there need "never be any fear of steamers ascending the Savannah, even to return again. Let them come up & then cut obstructions behind them[,] [s]hould be the Spirit. Give my love to all with you & write often to your devoted husband L M^c^Laws.

I send you inclosed One hundred dollars.

Willie and Johnny have stopped writing me—can you not start them again —and my little daughter might write her name. Kiss her & Ulric for me. — Remember me to the servants.

This letter was Mislaid and Not Mailed—I however Send it July 7/62. L M^c^L

((( )))

[The Peninsula, Virginia]
Camp June 28th/62 [Saturday][33]
8½ A.M.

My Dear Wife
Yesterday our troops were engaged all day, with brilliant results, having driven the enemy in all directions, from his strongest fortifications. But the battle is not yet won, as our enemies are powerful and well provided. It is however the opinion that if we would now allow them to run they would run, but we are surrounding them, that is we are in force in the direction of their

33. LM started the letter three days into the Seven Days Battle that took place from June 25 to July 1, 1862.

line of retreat along the York River Rail Road, and some desperate fighting is yet to be done before we can proclaim our independence.

The fighting has been carried on along the opposite banks of the Chickahominy. And although in sight of many persons on this side, there was so much dust and smoke that the accounts vary in the most curious manner. It is conceded however that we have [been] successful along our whole front and that the position of McClellands army is not an enviable one.

I have not written you my dear wife because my humor has not been for writing—I have contented myself in getting Hugh to write about me and although that kind of writing cannot be satisfactory to you, I hope you will make allowances.

My command has only been engaged in skirmishing with inconsiderable loss.

General Lee is rapidly regaining, if he has not already regained entirely, the confidence of the army and the people as a skillful and even a dashing officer. The criterion in military matters is success and up to this hour the combinations of General Lee have been of the most marked, decided, and successful.[34]

You cannot imagine how gratifying is the feeling to soldiers, to know that their chief is competent to all positions.

I received Willies letter and your short one, and was much pleased and exceedingly grateful for both— Tell Willie that I will try and write him before long. —When the battle is over, and the confusion and annoyance ceases, I will gain time very probably to give some interesting items not to be seen in the newspapers. As for that powder W^s^ [Willie] wants, what will he do with it during the summer months as there is nothing to shoot? Summer is the time to fish and to plant and to sit in the shade, and to enjoy the summer nights. All things living take the summer time to grow, so he must read and write and improve his mind and think what he could do best in life, and then he could improve his mind towards that end, and get strong and hearty and grow up to take care of his Pa & Ma when they get too old to take care of him. —There is a heap to do in the summer time. So he must not care particularly about powder at this season of the year. When the fall comes on, I

34. Robert Edward Lee, Virginia, USMA 1829, general, later commander of all Confederate armies. Lee commanded both respect and admiration from his officers and men after he took command of the Army of Northern Virginia in May 1862. LM never criticized Lee in his letters home, even after he was separated from his division in May 1864.

hope we will have plenty from France & England, with good guns, and that I will with you all to learn you.

I wrote to John in a letter to W^{m}R, in regard to his drinking, wrote him a friendly letter, which I hope will be beneficial, although in your last letter you said he was behaving much better—at which I was very much gratified. I wish you would tell him for me that I left him behind because I wished him to take care of those for whom I care ~~for~~ more for than for myself, and thought and believed he could be trusted to do so—not as a servant of other people but as one in whom I had confidence, which had been tried under every conceivable circumstance.

I hope Johnny will not only grow tall but grow smarter every day—although I know he is now a very smart fellow.

12 & 20 minutes

Continued accounts come in announcing continued successes[,] the enemy being in full retreat, losing prisoners, guns, ammunition & stores of all kinds. At the last accounts we had forty five hundred prisoners from the fight of yesterday, twenty eight cannon, & innumerable small arms.

I have my little daughters daguerreotype before me, looking as sweet as possible. I look at her constantly and wonder how long it will be before I see her.

Give Ulrick[,] whom Dr Steiner says is a very sweet and handsome boy, with a fine temper, give him my warmest opinion of his merits, two kisses.[35]

And for yourself my dear wife you can just imagine what you would wish of me & tis yours.

Your devoted Husband
L McLaws

((( )))

Head Quarters Division
[The Peninsula, Virginia]
July 28th/62 [Monday]

My Dear Willie
As you complain that I owe you a letter in reply to the last you wrote me, it is but fair your request for an answer should be granted.

I have caused two of the Richmond papers to be sent to Ma, one the

35. H. H. Steiner's medical practice appeared to be in Augusta; however, there are no records to identify him.

Richmond Whig[,] the other the Richmond Enquirer[,] both very reliable papers, especially the Enquirer. There are two others published in Richmond[,] viz. the "Richmond Dispatch" and the "Richmond Examiner"— The Dispatch is a very good paper, but the print is so very bad it is difficult to read, and the Examiner although edited by a good writer, is so abusive in its articles to every government measure, and so partisan or partial to everything Virginian that it is unpleasant reading. Besides it does all in its power to disclose the plans of the authorities, merely to exercise what the editor calls the Freedom of the Press. That paper has done as much harm to the South as any traitor in it, but President Davis allows it to go on, to show the world is independence of mindacity and audacity— Since the paper is known however, it has lost its influence. So much for newspapers. I would not have noticed the Examiner to such an extent but for the reason that the editor has lately written a book called "The first year of the war" which is entirely unreliable, being so partial in its statements and in its distribution of praises and fault findings that the intention of the editor in writing it, is apparent to all who are acquainted with the facts, the man attempts to deal with, and that object is to gratify his prejudices; he praises not because it [is] a pleasure for him to give credit but solely because he thinks that in doing so to one party, he annoys some others against whom he entertains malice. The editor is a strange compound and the book that is given by him to the world as a history pourtrays a character that would be base, if it were not that the individual does not appear to know but that he is actuated by the best of motives, when in fact he is not swayed by any other than to gratify some petty malignity and a desire to bolster up some unworthy favorite. But such productions will soon run their course and be succeeded by more reliable works.

I am writing you, just as if you were a young gentleman who thinks for himself, and will answer my letter with his own ideas about whatever subject he may entertain.

The enemy are still on the James River, doing we know not what. Some say that he is daily in receipt of re-inforcements. Others think otherwise. Some think that before very long, he will make an advance, others suppose that he cannot do it within two months, as it will require that length of time to recruit his troops in numbers, and to enable the remains of the old army to recover from the demoralizing effects of their late defeat. But after every great battle there is always a long silence. Both parties are in a great measure exhausted and retire to recuperate their strength. Our army was very much worn out by the week of continued exertion against the enemy, but we had been victorious and therefore were only fatigued, we only required rest. But the enemys army were not only equally as fatigued as ours, but they were defeated, were broken spirited besides broken down— If you were to fight a boy about your size and whip him, you would be ready to fight him again at any time. But if he should whip you, then you would not care about fighting him again until you got not only rest but stronger, or he had become weaker. And that is just the way it is now with McClellan and Gen[l] Lee. Gen[l] Lee whipped McClellan and is ready to fight him again at any time, but McClellan being whipped does not wish to fight until he gets not only rest but has more troops to make him stronger than Lee. When he thinks that such is the case I have no doubt but that he will make another move, and then so soon as he does, he will be whipped again.

Aunt Laura wrote very encouraging letters about you, but I wish you to write and show *me* that you *are* smart. And make Johnny write a little but to show that he is improving some. Ma says that Johnny is growing, but I hope tis not like the cows tail. You should show him how to go to bed in the dark, like a man, and shame him out of the idea of wanting a light always.

I wish it could so happen that I could be with you, to eat some of the watermellons of which Ma speaks so temptingly about. And then the peaches that are to come? I think of running away and turning farmer, if you think we could make a living by working in the fields. If it could be done I know it would be more pleasant for me then to be soldiering away from Ma and you children.

Kiss Sister for me three times, and tell her that every one says that she is a sweet little girl. Take good care of her always.

Give my love to Ulric, and your mother. Also to Aunt Laura, and your uncle W[m] & family. Remember me to John & Caroline. And write a long letter in reply to this.

Your devoted father
L M[c]Laws

((( )))

Head quarters Division [LB1]
[En route to Hanover Junction, Virginia]
Aug-21-62 [Thursday]

I am now moving my division northward to join the army of Gen. Lee. My station will be Hanover Junction, which is the junction of the Fredricksburg & that to Gordonsville or Staunton.

I have just returned from stray below and found that McClellan has entirely deserted his works there,[36] going off with his whole force towards his original base at the White ~~mountain~~ House [at] the head of York River, thus acknowleding that his change of base from the Chickahominy was an entire & total defeat.

((( )))

Head Quarters Rapidan Station
[On the Rapidan River, Virginia]
Aug 29/62 [Friday]

Your letter by Hugh was received last night. Although H arrived the night previous—his arrival was very opportune—as the troops were on the march and the work to be performed was more than John Edwards could well perform although he worked faithfully and energetically.

You spoke to me some time since about purchasing a nurse for you in Virginia. I really have not been pleased with Virginia negroes. Even if I should wish to buy, but strange I have not seen any for sale, nor any one who wished to sell.

You mention that Caroline could not much longer be the nurse, but gave no reason for it. What is the matter? Hugh spoke of her as a very nice looking smart girl.

My destination is not known to me. I am with General Hills division and he ranks me & is therefore in command of his own & my Division. We are moving however Northward to join the Army of the Rhappahannock. The camp this evening will be on the Rapidan. But tomorrow the march will be resumed northward. There are so many rumors concerning the movements and operations of our army that I forbear mentioning them. Your newspapers will give you all the reliable data from time to time, in a much more readable and authentic shape than I can pretend to vouch for.

Hugh told me that you had determined not to buy in Madison [Ga.]. I would advise you always to look for yourself. And if satisfied act according to your own judgement.

Hugh says that Laura is a bright eyed rosy cheeked little lady. Willie a fine large healthy boy and Johnny very talky and sociable. As for Ulric or the Count as he calls him, he says he is a very remarkably fine baby, and is continually crowing. He says you are looking well and healthy. His own family he thinks are sickly.

Enclosed is a appointment for W[m]R as A D C for myself. I offer it because

36. LM used the term "stray" to mean reconnaissance.

it perhaps may save him from the Conscription—[37] I will write him now and then to perform various duties, should he accept the appointment.

Our troops this winter will suffer very much for the want of clothing. Blankets and shoes will be the great desideratum, and unless combinations are entered into to supply them from home, there will be positive deficiencies, which will paralyse the army. —I proposed to a Member of Congress that the money voted by Congress to each soldier for the purpose of supplying him with clothing, be given to the states. That no particularly named amount be specified in the law, but that the clothing be obtained & whatever it cost, let the bill be paid by the government. —I believe that it would be beneficial to the whole southern confederacy if our army was supplied, the troops from each state, by the state from which they came. It would encourage manufactories throughout the south and would go a great way towards breaking down the monopolies which are now fattening on us about Richmond, and by distributing them render us more independent of sudden incursions of the enemy. I believe that the State of Georgia can supply her own troops with all the essentials for their comfort and so can all the cotton states, in fact so can every southern state, and it would be their pride, the pride of the people, to see that the authorities do furnish the troops plentifully and substantially— WR could make it his business to obtain clothing for my command, the Georgians in it—according as I may call for it— There are various absenties from regiments who should be collected or inquired after, if not sick should be made to join their commands, if dead to be reported so, &c &c &c.

Alley E is doing very well indeed, being very attentive and energetic. I have recommended that he be promoted to a captaincy.

As regards the boots; I wish you to inquire as to the price and time of making them. Those you sent me are very good, but are very large.

Hugh has not received his trunk as yet, and therefore your various gifts have not been received. I will however thank you for them now, and beg you to thank all those engaged in drying the ochre & sassafras. John Edwards is getting fat. Although he is still small. He is thought very highly of. Considered to be the best Commissary in the army, and is always in good humor.

I have a months pay to send you but really do not know how to do it at present, but will try and find out in a day or two.

Tell Willie I am sorry he did not write me, he should not give up anything

37. On April 16, 1862, the Confederacy passed the first of three conscription acts applying to men between the ages of eighteen and thirty-five.

he attempts merely because it is difficult, but keep at it because it is difficult. And Mr Johnny, Hugh says he talks too fast, & yet he will not write, he talks but will not do anything. Neither will my little daughter. —Ulric will do better I know when he gets as old as either of them. Good day my dear wife. I am writing in the house of a Mr Taylor, a cousin of yours, have not seen him as he is away with his family, but the house and conveniences are very fine indeed. He must be a very rich man, write to Richmond as usual, or to "*Head Quarters Department Northern Virginia.*"[38]

Upon reflection, you had better write me to, "Head Quarters Army Northern V^a." My dear darling wife I must now very unwillingly say God bless you and close for to day.

Your devoted husband
L McLaws

((( )))

Leesburg [Virginia]
Sep. 4th/62 [Thursday]

My dearly beloved wife
We arrived here yesterday after very fatiguing marching.

The enemy are not here, although the day previous to our arrival their cavalry had been driven from the town by a small force of our own.

The inhabitants were very enthusiastic in their reception of us. The ladies in particular were demonstrative. But I am very suspicious of people who live on the border, and whose property has been carefully preserved. Their loyalty to us may be questioned. I have no doubt the large majority sympathise with us. But they would rather not lose their property for an expression of it, and therefore although cordial to us they are not unkind to our enemy. I have seen the northern papers of the date of yesterday. Their repeated defeats have not been acknowledged in so many words, but their alarm of an invasion is apparent.

What our next move will be, remains to be seen.

Many of our men are without shoes, and all of them are very ragged, in addition we have been marching for the last three days with nothing to eat but fresh meat and green corn. One day with nothing but corn and that not in abundance. One day there was nothing to eat. And now we are hauling rations one hundred and fifty seven miles from Richmond. Ninety two by

38. The home of R. Taylor, located within three miles of Raccoon Ford and north and east of Rapidan Station.

r. road sixty five by land. So you may be sure that our subsistence is very precarious. But our men do not grumble, they only straggle. Riding off the road anywhere you can see parties of two & three & more settled in fence corners with green corn piled around & perhaps evidence of a meal from a stray hog or chicken. These men say they intend to join their regiment so soon as they become rested a little. They do not belong to any particular Corps but to all Corps and divisions. We meet those of Longstreet, Jackson & others ahead, those troops coming behind will meet men of my division and so we go from here to Richmond. I passed over the battle field of Saturday [where] a ghastly spectacle was presented by the hundreds of Yankees still unburied.[39]

I send you three hundred and seventy three dollars of which I spoke to you in my last letter.

Remember my dear wife to write me constantly, for the opportunities of receiving letters are very few and if one is missed I may not hear from you for a longtime.

The weather is getting quite cold, as we are not very far from the mountains. But the country is beautiful, and the air bracing, my health is excellent. And my time very much employed.

Tell the boys to write me, as they owe me a letter each. My darling daughter should write a little and Ulric must be accepted by proxy. Good day to my dear wife, and children. I wish you could make me a large thick comforter for the winter, make it quite large so I can wrap in it—my blankets are getting thin so that I need more covering.

Your devoted husband L M^c^Laws
Maj Genl.

((( )))

7 miles from Winchester [Virginia] [LB1]
Head Quarters Division
Oct. 4-'62 [Saturday]

Went to Winchester to see the sick & wounded and saw Mrs. Dandridge & Mrs. Bliss.[40] Went back to camp & ordered his brigade surgeons to look up sick & wounded & have straw hauled for them to lie on. (Speaks of Genl. Fitzjohn Porter & old friend.) It is now generally believed that we actually whipped the Yankees at Sharpsburg very badly & that they were on their re-

39. The Battle of Second Manassas took place on August 29–30, 1862.

40. Mrs. Dandridge and Mrs. Bliss have not been identified.

treat at the same time we were retiring from the Potomac. We did not have ⅓ of their forces, ours were exhausted from hunge[r], fatigue & exposure & were often without ammunition. I do really look upon our success both at Harpers Ferry & else[where] as direct interposition of Divine Providence. We fought the Yankees at Sharpsburg with less than thirty thousand men & they had one hundred & twenty thousand so *they* say.

((( )))

Head Quarters Division
[Culpeper Court-House, Virginia]
November 10th 62 [Monday]

My dear darling wife
I wrote you a long and very interesting letter last night, principally concerning myself, my mode of thinking, political principles, and thoughts on the war—which you will receive undoubtedly, if you do not, please write me, and it will be renewed.

The snow has disappeared from the earth and the weather is clear and cold day & night.

The enemy are within ten or twelve miles of us, and there is daily skirmishing with the cavalry of the two armies. To day there was such a determined fire between the artillery of our cavalry or that of the enemy, that the troops were ordered under arms. But the enemy gave way before us, and were driven six miles. So we are again in camp.

I wrote a page to Margaret to day asking her to make her way south, if she could and join you in Georgia. I did not indicate a route, for many reasons—I wrote in a letter which John Edwards had written to his mother. It was sent off to day via Baltimore. If you desire a letter to be sent I will forward it, or get some one to do it. The difficulty is in getting an answer, but I suppose that too can be over come.

If Margaret should come,[41] I intend proposing that you take a house in Sparta [Ga.] or board as you find most convenient and economical— I can hardly imagine however, how Margaret can come, unless she does under a flag of truce, via Baltimore & Richmond, unless indeed your brother Rich, who is said to be an officer in the Federal army, will use his influence to get her a permit, to travel by R. R. along the Richmond route south.

41. Margaret Lewis Taylor, ETM's younger sister.

Mary Jouett, or rather Mrs Dudley has a baby, it sounds curious! I would like very much to see her, practicing her matronly duties.[42]

I have never heard of Captain Potter since the war, unless the Major J H Potter who spent some time in the Richmond cotton bus as a prisoner, was the same person. I hope he was.

I think I mentioned that Major G R Paul had joined the Federals and was a Brigadier General in their army, in fact is now in front of us, along the Rapahannock.[43]

Captain Hayman is Colonel of a P^{a} Regt. I have never heard of Saint Plympton. Lawrence Williams has disappeared from view. Some say he was killed, others assert, he was arrested as a spy, & is in Fort Deleware.[44]

Van Dorn besides getting his army well whipped by a classmate, Rosecrans, has some very hard stories against him, he is said to be a great libertine and drinks very freely.[45]

Major Whiting is I suppose laid on the shelf. Colonel Pitcairn has not appeared in the war. Captain Little was killed as you saw, the day previous to Vandorns battle.[46]

42. Mary Jouett Dudley was the daughter of ETM's older sister, Sarah Strother "Sallie" Taylor Jouett. Sallie married Colonel William R. Jouett. GHS-VM Taylor Children, 1. In 1860 ETM and Margaret Lewis Taylor lived with Frederick Geiger and Anne Pendleton Edwards. Eighth Census, 1860, Louisville—Second District, Jefferson County, Ky., entry for F. G. Edwards family, 106, NARA M 653, RG 29.

43. Joseph Hayden Potter (previous paragraph), New Hampshire, USMA 1843, a former captain of the 7th Infantry, was captured on July 27, 1861, at St. Augustine, Tex. He was exchanged a year later and promoted to colonel; he retired in 1886 as a brigadier general. Gabriel René Paul, Missouri, USMA 1834, was a major in the 8th Infantry and the acting inspector general of New Mexico until commissioned colonel, 4th New Mexico, in December 1861. Promoted to brigadier general, U.S. volunteers, in September 1862, he lost his sight by a rifle wound at Gettysburg and retired as a colonel in 1866.

44. Samuel Brinckle Hayman, Pennsylvania, a former U.S. Army captain, was a Union colonel and future brigadier general of volunteers. Peter William Livingston Plympton, Missouri, was a first lieutenant in 1855, later a major. Lawrence Albert Williams was a former second lieutenant in the U.S. 7th Infantry in 1852. A major at the time of the letter, Williams was dismissed from the service in March 1863. Fort Delaware, built on Pea Patch Island in the Delaware River, was a Federal prison.

45. Earl Van Dorn, Mississippi, USMA 1842, Confederate major general; William Starke Rosecrans, Ohio, USMA 1842, major general of U.S. volunteers.

46. Pitcairn Morrison, New York, a lieutenant colonel in the 7th Infantry in 1853, retired from the Union army in October 1863. Lewis Henry Little, Maryland, a first

I have heard nothing of Plympton or Amory or Garland or Stevenson nor of any others of your old acquaintances.[47]

The Democratic victories in New York and Pennsylvania, Ohio &c will no doubt open the press, which has been so long muzzled in the North, and we will soon learn the true Northern sentiment in regard to the war. Whether for continuance or for peace. If for the war we have reason to hope it will be done in a more Christian spirit than has been displayed by the Republicans. If for peace I am afraid they will base their hopes on a reorganization of the union, which can never be. We might unite once more if it were not for the New England states, but with them never more!

I am having a new coat made in Richmond out of some cloth which I obtained near Winchester [Va.], it is of much darker color than the one I now have and will be therefore, I hope more serviceable.

I have eight yards of a light grey, now on hand, which I will probably send you for the children.

Huguenin is in Richmond attending to blankets & shoes & clothing generally for the division. And I hope confidently he will succeed in getting something. I intend to try and make some shoes out of raw hide for the men, to show them how it can be done. I wish the pair of Navaho shoes was here for a pattern.

You cannot complain of not hearing from me, this week. And you must not think anymore that I do not desire to see you and the children—it is not pleasant for me to tell anyone how soft hearted I am when thinking of my wife & her little ones, far away, longing to see me, and yet constantly disappointed— How lonesome I feel always being away from them, how much more contented I am when I hear of their happiness and how miserable when there is any sign even of discontent & unhappiness, and yet these things must be, & I try and be content, or at least appear so, although my friends say I am much more cross & unsociable than formerly— I suppose I am older & have seen life in more varied forms than formerly & am therefore not so trusting. I have heard that my division will be ordered south, but do not believe One word of it—the report has been put forth by some

---

lieutenant in the 7th Infantry in 1845, was killed at Iuka in September 1862 as a Confederate brigadier general.

47. No information was found on Thomas J. Armory. Robert R. Garland, Virginia, a second lieutenant in the 7th Infantry in 1847, served as regimental quartermaster for the unit between 1858 and 1860. Garland was a colonel in the 6th Texas volunteers. Carter Littlepage Stephenson, Virginia, USMA 1838, Confederate brigadier, later major general, like LM, would fight his last battle in Bentonville, N.C.

one or many in my Division who desire it should be so. I would prefer going there for one reason & that is to be near my wife & children & for no other.

You will have to put up with my changing humors, but must try and write me cheerful letters.

Hugh may go to Georgia to look after clothing.

Give much love to the children from me. Tell Caroline I did not expect to hear of her following in the footsteps of her mistress— Remember me to John [letter ends here]

((( )))

Head Quarters Division
[Culpeper Court-House, Virginia]
Nov. 16th/62 [Sunday]

My dearly beloved wife
No letter for me to night! And this is the sixth letter I have written in seven days—must I again exclaim, without any responses, on the other side. "What an affectionate husband I am, and what an affectionate wife I deserve to have!" Of course you have written but the mail has failed—but I would rather have it written by yourself, "Dear husband you are indeed a good and affectionate one" than to be forced to write it myself, it would be much more consoling. So you see the necessity of writing often.

There is no news of the enemy advancing in our front, although the order has been given for us to be all ready for battle. To have our transportation, ammunition & c & c all ready what it means I do not know. But I have confidence in our cause and in our troops, and in our generals—the north is congregating its hosts to make a final and desparate attempt to conquer us, and in the event of our being overun what a poor despised race we will be. But let us all trust in the Lord of truth and right and mercy, surely if we are so much in error as the north say that we are, our hearts are not so hardened, but that we can be induced by arguements to see our situation in the true light and reform, without ourselves going through the ordeal of slavery, worse than that of the meanest negro. —The trials that we have to undergo are sent us for a good purpose, and we must think so, and learn to bear up with them in that spirit. Never despond but be cheerful as possible under all suffering—and bless our good fortune, and be thankful that we are spared worse evils. As it is now we have won the respect of all the outside world by our valor, our patience[,] our endurance, and our trust in the final success of our cause. This we have gained when at first the opinion of the world was against us—the north had pursued a systematic course of vituperation and villification, detracting from us in all things—but now even those who were our bitterest enemies grant us the possession of the most noble qualities, and the Yankees themselves acknowledge our superiority of courage and spirit to themselves. They wonder how it is that our half clad, half starved soldiers can fight so well. The idea of any one fighting for principle has never for once entered their understanding.

My dear wife night after night I pine for your presence—your kind voice and caring looks—for the innocent prattle of our children, but I feel that I am entrusted with an important command among the thousands who are fighting for home and country and the dearest priviledges of life, against the meanest of mankind, the vilest of foes. and the more I love you, the more sacred do I think, is my duty to devote my time and energies to defend you. So you must strive to bear up, for my absence and by your example and cheerful submitting to it, do your part towards influencing the thousands of others who are also daily and nightly praying for the safety of their loved ones, who are in ten times the danger and have to endure a thousand times the hardships, exposure & suffering that I do, & without the honor—

When we do meet again[,] which I hope will not be very long[,] [y]our kisses will be ten times as sweet and your voice sound ten times sweeter, than if I had not been separated and there had not been so much danger & suffering undergone. —Of suffering however I can thank heaven that I have been spared—nothing troubles outside of my profession but my absence from my wife and children, and their unhappiness resulting from it—when I find you happy I am so, when you are discontented, so am I. —So you are my thermometer & must be careful, as to the variations of your temperature.

Hu has not yet returned from Richmond, but is daily expected—our barefooted and blanketless men are nearly all provided, and we are gradually becoming in a better condition for all contigencies than we have been for a long time.

It is now raining a fine drizzling cold rain, which I suppose will be snow before morning—my feet are cold and I think of, to bed.

Give the children much love and many kisses—the kisses expecially to my daughter and the count—my best love to sister, WR & family—remember me to the servants.

John Edwards was telling me the ring puzzles, to night which I give to Willie.

A number of persons sitting around a room—Willie goes out of the room. Those inside are numbered from 1 to say five, six or any number—a ring is passed around, & one of the persons puts the ring on a certain finger &

a certain joint or below a certain joint—the question is to find out, which person has the ring & on what finger & what joint it is[:]

Double the number of the person, Say it is the 13th   Add n° of joint
Add 5   Say it is the 2nd
Multiply by 5   2
Add the No of finger Say it is the 4th   *take away* ~~250~~
Multiply by 5   ~~452~~[48]

[letter ends here]

((( )))

Head 2nd Division
[Culpeper Court-House, Virginia]
Nov. 17/62 [Monday]

My dearly beloved Emily
I am under orders to march with my division tomorrow morning at daylight to Racoon [Raccoon] Ford on the Rapidan, further orders will be given me on the march. What I am to do or where to go, I know not, so it turns out that the order to get ready for battle was merely an order to get ready for march.

Address your letters until you hear from me again to Head Quarters Gen Longstreets Corps, Army Northern Va.

My orders to move tomorrow were not received until some time after dark, so I must to bed. Many thousand kisses and much love to my sweet wife and children.

Your devoted husband
L McL

((( )))

Head Quarters Division
[Fredericksburg, Virginia]
November 22 1862 [Sunday]

My Dear Sweetheart
You will perhaps be astonished in seeing my address Fredricksburg Va—my division was ordered in advance from Culpeper C. H. and after a very disagreeable march arrived here on the morning of the third day and found

48. LM smeared over the numbers, apparently because he could not remember the precise mathematical steps needed to resolve the game.

that—the opposite side of the river, the Rapahannock was lined with the camps of the enemy.

They had well calculated on our humanity, for their batteries were planted immediately above the town on an eminence which enabled them to command it—their trains were ostentatiously moving under our guns, their batteries manouvered within easy reach of our shot, their troops strutted along the opposite bank, some with arms and some without—everything was done as it were to provoke a fire from our side, they even fired upon the trains, coming in & going out—but we did not return a shot, did not fire upon their trains, their troops, or their numerous cavalry. For we all divined that this ostentatious display was made in order to provoke a fire from us, ~~in order~~ so as to give them an excuse to fire upon the town, filled with the sick & infirm, the aged, the wounded & the women & children—we knew too well the treacherous, fiendish, Yankee character to give them any such excuse for the exercise of their natural brutality—and the result showed but too well that opinion of their design was correct.

Yesterday evening a communication was sent through the military authorities to the mayor and common council of the city, saying that—as their troops on the opposite bank had been fired on from the city—the mills and manufactories of the place were furnishing food and clothing to troops in rebellion against the government of the U.S.—the rail roads and other means of conveyance were engaged in carrying stores to our depots—such a state of affairs could not be allowed to exist any longer, and therefore the city must be surrendered to the federal authorities failing in which, Sixteen hours would be given from 5 oclock P.M. for the removal of the sick and wounded[,] the women & children and the aged—and at the end of that time the town would be shelled.

I was at Genl Lees at the time with Genl Longstreet and he told me to go with Genl Longstreet and inform the mayor that he would consent that the state of affairs complained of, as existing in the city, should no longer exist so far as the army was concerned, that his troops should no longer occupy the city but he would not allow that the enemy should either. That it was impossible to remove the sick &c, because they themselves had driven off the trains and had taken away most of the other means of transportation—besides they must well know that of the time allowed them, not more than two or three hours would be in daylight, and the weather was temputuous & the night very dark.

Thus their second trick failed. They based their desire to shell the town upon certain grievances, some of which did & some did not exist—and the authorities assured them that those causes of complaint should exist no longer—they then said that they would not fire on the town at the time specified—but had another conference and finally it was agreed that they would send another answer and state definitely when all operations would cease & no further movement allowed on our part.

But now the whole of Longstreets Corps has arrived and circle the hills all around on this side—and our camp fires shine up & light the air as far and wide as those of the enemy—and we no longer care for any attempts they may make to cross the river.

But the effect of their threats is painfully visible in the numerous. "Women & children, sick and infirm, and aged" who are flying from the threatened bombardment—our ambulances have been running all day, and one now going back & forth, carrying out the families, who have determined to desert their homes, and property, rather than risk the chances of the threatened "shelling."

There is not even a shadow of an excuse for such an outrage upon humanity, for there is no ford about the town practicable for either infantry or artillery. But there are good fords some distance up the river—from three to eight miles—practicable for all arms, but the scoundrels wish to gratify their cruel, beastly instincts only, thinking that to frighten women and children is adding glory to their cause, and will cause a shout of exultation through the north.

Up to this evening they have done nothing but open fire upon two trains leaving the city, crowded with women & children, not doing any damage however. —The commanding officer Gen[l] Sumner I understand says it was a mistake.[49] But it was not—it was merely an exercise of cowardly malice which could not be restrained.

Hugh showed me a letter received this evening on his return from Richmond, announcing the death of another one of his children. He is very much affected, but says nothing.

You spoke about Sally coming to live with you. Of course any arrangement you make will be agreeable to me, if you are satisfied, but what will you do with the sixteen small negroes which Hugh says he has[?] —He wishes Sally to hire another place, says that Captain Thomas will do it for her.[50]

49. Edwin Vose Sumner, Massachusetts, major general.
50. Captain Jefferson Thomas was a planter from Augusta.

You will of course be anxious concerning us for some time to come, but I will write you as often as possible, and you must take it for granted that I will and have done so, but the mails have failed, should you not receive letters.

My best love to the children and a thousand kisses and good wishes to my dearly beloved wife from her devoted husband.

General Burnside is in command of the whole army of the Potomac, as you have seen, and has with him, Gen[l] Hooker, General Sumner, & some say Genl Siegel.[51]

Good night again and many blessings & kisses for you & the children.

Remember me to the servants and to Laura give my best love. My best regards to W[m]R & family—good night. I am to bed; address me, Head Quarters Gen Longstreets Corps, Fredricksburg V[a].

Your devoted husband
L M[c]L

((( )))

Head Quarters Division
Near Fredricksburg V[a]
Dec 3rd 1862 [Wednesday]

My Dear Wife
I received this evening your very kind sweet letter of the 18th and it is one that makes me long very much to kiss you, but those longings at present must be suppressed. have to be, although it is hard not to be pining after that which would make me very happy—

The enemy are still opposite us although the indications are that they are moving elsewhere. Where to tis not known to me, but whereever it is, their intention is still the same. As "On to Richmond" continues to be their war cry.

This is the third day of December however and the weather will probably render operations impossible in a very few days. The clouds have been collecting & dispersing for several days, just as the[y] have been threatening & drawing back, putting off the great catastrophe. Let us hope that some intervention may put off the the battle, and lead to peace, that the Yankees are or can be influenced but by fears or love of money, no one now believes. M[r] Beutwick[,] Member of Parliment[,] in a speech published in the Enquirer

51. Joseph Hooker, Massachusetts, USMA 1837, Union brigadier general in the regular army; Franz Sigel, Germany and Missouri, major general of U.S. volunteers.

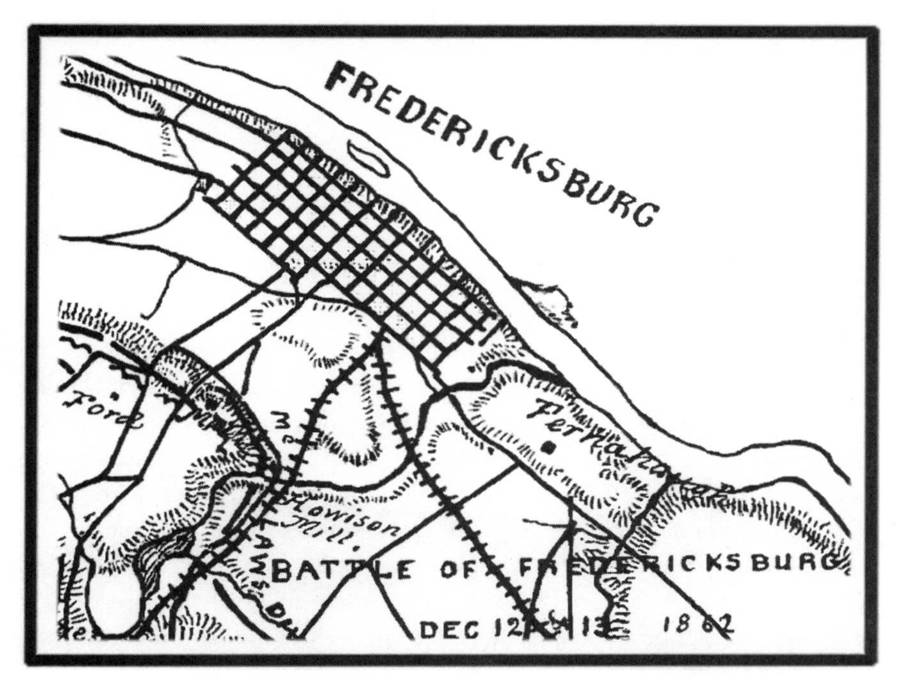

Lafayette McLaws's map noting his positions at Fredericksburg, Virginia, on December 12 and 13, 1862. (Courtesy of the Southern Historical Collection, University of North Carolina at Chapel Hill)

of the 3d inst[,] declares that the U.S. by avowing & doing what is now being done, ceases to rank among civilized nations.[52]

Our pickets and those of the enemy are within speaking distance, and daily listen in silent contempt to the vulgarities of the Yankee soldiery—the citizens here, some of whom before the war, before they were brought in contact with the Yankee crowd, had rather sympathized with the north; now tell me that their feelings have changed to utter loathing for the depraved wretches, totally devoid as they are of all delicacy and decency and refinement—they did not conceive that human nature could by any process become so brutal.

I like to read about the children, their sayings and actions. My little daughter I know is very sweet and good, doing all in her power to please her mother; give her many kisses for me.

52. Mr. Beutwick has not been identified.

Because I do not mention the others it is for the reason that Willie & Johnny will not either send me or write me anything about themselves—when I was a very small boy, smaller than either of them, I used to write home once a week. I was then at Sparta away from home. But it was not then war times, and more attention could be paid to the arts of peace. I hope both of the boys will try and write me during the long winter evenings.

I am very busy as you may suppose, day & night, doing all in my power to circumvent the enemy—watching their developments and working to counteract them. It was rumored to day, from the other side[,] that King Abe himself was with the army on the other side and that he was urging an advance—but some how or other Genl Lee seems to find out or divine the intentions of the scoundrels and disposes his troops to check any movement.

The two armies must meet some day however and the shock will be tremendous. If however the winter storms should set in, the advance of the Yankees must of necessity be checked, as the roads soon become nearly impassible. Let us all put our faith in him who is always just, and hope that he will confound our enemies so that their advance will be checked, by either confusion in council, the valor of our troops or the impossibility to move. We owe it however to ourselves to use every means God has given us to help ourselves, & do all in our power to arrest the Yankees, and this requires all our time & all our thoughts but in spite of danger and weather and business of all kinds. I have to give very many thoughts to my dear sweet wife & children, knowing how much they are attached to me & how happy we could be together. Give the count my best love & respects, & my best love & wishes to all.

Good night and a world of love and good wishes to you my darling[;] remember me to John & Caroline.

Your devoted husband
L M^c^Laws

((( )))

Head Quarters Division [LB1]
[Fredericksburg, Virginia]
Dec-9-62 [Tuesday]

My dearly beloved wife
The air is misty from the gradual melting of snow & it is impossible to see the enemies movements, tho their drums were beating along their lines as if something was in contemplation. There are rumors of large fleets of transports having been seen below, it is probable that the enemy are embarking

their army for other plans. The weather is extremely cold, it threatens to block the river which make it precarious for a large army to get supplies & it would place their gun boats & transports at our mercy.

I have a Sibley tent with a stove in the middle which makes it very comfortable when the fire burns.[53] Tell John that most of my old friends in the Army have been laid on the shelf by Lincoln, the reason being, I suppose, because they are gentlemen. Captain Sykes, though, has been made a general.[54] One of the returned officers, who was captured, states that he saw Hancock Taylor who expressed the opinion that we would soon be conquered. He inquired about his relations in our army & about myself.

53. The Sibley tent, designed in 1856 by U.S. Major Henry Hopkins Sibley of the First Dragoons, was a conical tent made of canvass that could sleep twenty men. A stove or fireplace could be built inside the tent, which was raised using an iron centerpole.

54. George Sykes, Delaware, USMA 1842, major general of U.S. volunteers and later major general of the army.

1863

I Consider Him a Humbug

Head Quarters Division
[Fredericksburg, Virginia]
February 2nd 1863 [Monday]

My dearly beloved Wife
No letter came for me to day nor any yesterday. I wrote Willie one yesterday morning, but I have no doubt the mails are very irregular if they have not ceased entirely for the present because of the military occupation of the roads and the bad weather combined.

The telegram gives us glorious news from Charleston, but of a nature which excites us to hear more from the same quarter.[1]

The news from the neighborhood of Suffolk is also very cheering but at the same time excites our apprehensions, as the repulse was not of that decided nature to make us quite sure the enemy made a real attack.

The accounts from Vicksburg also are of an exciting nature—gentlemen who have plantations in that direction assert that the canal will be a failure because the water wastes itself, will not run in any particular channel on the lower side of the head, where the Yankees are cutting their canal. But the demonstrations there are formidable, and the public mind will be in anxious state of suspense until that attack is made & is over.

The same with the army at Muffresboro. With the threatened attack at Savannah, and the operations in Arkansas were so horribly mismanaged, that we can but expect a train of disasters to follow the fall of Arkansas post.[2]

And then the papers say that the Army of the Potomac is again to try its luck, in an advance to Richmond.

1. On January 31, 1863, two Confederate gunboats raided the Federal blockaders outside the harbor, temporarily lifting the blockade.

2. Federal troops dug a canal at Duckport, outside Vicksburg, Miss., which was abandoned on April 29–30, 1863. There was skirmishing at Carthage, and on January 27, 1863, Federal naval forces attacked Fort McAllister south of Savannah and withdrew at the end of the engagement. On January 11, 1863, Federal gunboats had fired on Fort Hindman, Ark., and Confederate forces surrendered after several hours.

So you perceive there is a great deal to occupy our minds, and cause us anxious thoughts for the future.

That either side will be successful some where, will undoubtedly happen. Let us hope and pray that at the most vital points we will succeed & the successes of the enemy, if they have any, be confined to the unimportant, secondary places.

In the mean while prices must go on advancing, and the bloodsuckers of society must be drawing from their fellow beings— These are the Phinizies, Jacksons, & the men of wealth all engaged in this business, doing nothing for their country but all, to gorge their purses off the wants of others— Augusta abounds with them, and they are honored above the most patriotic. So it is perhaps in all cities, where the spirit of speculation is rife. —I have been inquiring and find out that the town of Sparta, which is off from the rail road and telegraph I suppose, is remarkably free from this vulture principle—has *six* good schools—is very healthy—fine water—good living and good society. In the language of a gentleman who lives there. The people do not know there is a war except from the newspapers—although there are two mails per day. —There are several good hotels, with board at moderate price &c &c &c. You all might take a trip to Sparta and examine for yourselves, as to marketing, schooling, boarding, health, play grounds &c &c.

I applied for leave as I informed you in my last, but may consider that it has been refused as it has not been heard from and Genl Longstreet informed me that he could not recommend it.

Congratulate Caroline for her safe escape from the awful catastrophe, the baby must be smart and I suppose is handsome, I hope she will name it after me. As you say tis Ulrics maid and he should have had my name— I will send the young maid and mother a present by the first opportunity— I hope Caroline is doing as well as could be expected.

I am in hopes of getting a leave some of these days, before Spring comes on so that you can make a choice for your summer residence in my company. I have a very great longing to quit the army & live in a quiet secluded place, and while we will be busy enough to get a living, we can I hope, have time enough to educate our children and teach them a home feeling, which they must be strangers to now— I really do not know what would suit me, except an army life—do not know that I am fit for anything else. But my inclinations are certainly in favor of a farmers life or at least to have my children brought up that way. I think a good carpenter a most estimable profession— I can sit for hours and see a carpenter work at his trade—it is clean and neat too, and requires a head and good strength. I do not like blacksmithing, so will not discuss it.

Cannot paint, not knowing colors,

Cannot be an architect nor engineer being too old.

Might teach! Cant sing! Too old to be a dancing master, though graceful enough in all conscience!

Have no money to keep a store.

Am good enough to be a preacher but could not preach.

Might be a clerk in a dry goods store. Might invent something and get a patent. —What can *we* do my dear Emily when we leave the army? do propose something.

Give my best love to Bet & sister Laura who I hope get along well together.

My best love to the boys & my sweet little daughter.

Remember me to all about you & with you and believe me your devoted and sleepy husband. L M[c]Laws

((( )))

Head Quarters Division
[Fredericksburg, Virginia]
February 22nd 1863 [Sunday]

My Darling Wife
It commenced snowing last night about ten oclock and continued uninteruptedly until about five oclock this evening. In consequence we have about a foot of snow over the whole country and this after, just after the thaw of a snow of equal depth. It looks like it will snow again to night, but I suppose it will clear off tomorrow and commence to thaw again, which added to the other one which will now be made available to increase the impassibility of the roads, will render the country a complete quagmire, and all the streams will be swollen beyond fording.

But the enemy are moving away portions of their force. Three Corps have left our front, and embarking at Aquia Creek, were landed at Newport News and Fortress Munroe. These three Corps are those which were formerly under Burnside, and when it is recollected that we have read in the papers that the President had offered him an important command, and had given him one month to think about it[,] [w]e may suppose that the three Corps are intended to operate separately under him. And the question comes up, where will he go[?] As he formerly commanded in North Carolina and gained quite a reputation there for his uniform success, and remained there for some time[,] [i]t is not unreasonable to suppose that if sent to operate independently of their army, in front of us—he will go to North Carolina— The landing at Newport News is regarded as a mere stopping place to re-organize for a trip further south. It is a place too where desertions can be provided against, which has become a matter of importance to them, if reports can be relied on, in regard to the great dissatisfaction said to exist among the troops.

It is stated however that the greater portion of the army is concentrating towards Acquia Creek, and that a large number of transports are collecting there as if the whole army was to be sent away from here— In that case, it may be that another advance on Richmond is intended either by the peninsula again, or from Norfolk and Suffolk, on the south side of James River—or it may be intended to make a grand advance against Charleston and Savannah.

The great desire of the enemy is to get us to so reduce our Richmond army that they can advance against that place with hopes of speedy success. They may have however given up that idea, and intend another scheme for our subjugation. We are all engaged in watching their movements however, and let us pray that our understandings may be so enlightened, as to enable us to conceive their designs and thwart them in their execution.

If the intention is to draw off the mass of the army for operations in another quarter, it will be necessary for them to keep a considerable force in Washington to defend that place. —It is not necessary now, because their army is between us and Washington. We can probably find out when that is done which will be one way to discover their final intentions. We have scouts all through the country, which will be another means, and in addition, it is impossible to move one hundred thousand men without some disclosures from the enemy themselves through their newspapers and letter writers.

So much for military operations. There are a good many other views which can be taken of their plans, but they will not perhaps interest you.

I have not received your letter giving the results of your visit to Sparta. I received yesterday a long well written and very interesting letter from sister, in which she mentioned that it was your intention to move. No she did not mention what your intentions were, but said that you would write me the next day about them. But W^{m}R said in a letter to Hugh that you intended to move by the first of March. —John Edwards will be with you and after consultations I hope you will act in *all things* as seems best to advance your happiness and pleasure. It makes me feel very tired of the war, to think of you and the children, as it were, wandering about the country, in search of a home. —I do so long to be with you, that I am getting very restless and discontented— I think that if you could be relieved from the cares of housekeeping, where everything is so enormously high, and tis difficult to obtain even the merest necessities of life, you would be much better contented. It is objectionable of course not to have a house and home of your own, you and the children will be deprived of many of the liberties and comforts you now enjoy, and will be very much annoyed in making new acquaintances. All these things will have to be considered, and weighed, one against the other, and the preponderance must decide.

You had better take John with you, as he will be I hope a protection and convenience to the children and yourself. —And in a small town like Sparta, I hope there will not be so many temptations and he will be more steady— But all this must be as John E & yourself will determine.

I wish very much that Bet could remain with you. I believe she would be more contented than with her husband even, in Grenada, where he cannot consider himself stationary, and in the event of a sudden move, may be forced to leave her among strangers, or send her back alone—she had better make up her mind to stay with you and wait patiently for better times. If you insist on it she may remain.

John E will I think add his voice to yours, and I will be much more contented to hear of her consenting, both on her own & your account. —The cakes & turkey were received all in good condition. Give my warmest love and thanks to all who contributed. Tell my sweet little daughter that her cakes were very fine and nice and I give her two kisses for each one—all are well including myself. Good night with much love to all. Your devoted husband.

L McLaws

((( )))

Head Quarters Division
[Fredericksburg, Virginia]
April 2 1863 [Thursday]

My dearly beloved Wife
No letter from you to day! is the information daily given me by the mail carrier. I would be very much delighted if it was different but suppose there must be some good reason why you have not written or rather why the letters has not been rec^{d} for I believe you *have* written.

An order has been issued designating the amount of transportation to be allowed to officers and men of the army, which gives two four horse wagons to division head quarters; one two horse wagon to the QMaster & Comsy. My staff will be, One Surgeon, One AdjGen^{l}, one Inspector Genl, one A. D. C.—

one Chf of Ordnance—and myself, will be six officers. Our tents will have to be carried, as well as our cooking utensils, mess shirts, clothing &c, all must go in one wagon as the other wagon will have to be used as a forage wagon— I do not know that there is any particular movement is on foot, but the order is to arrange all things for a movement should circumstances require that one should be made.

The Yankee papers acknowledge that their Charleston expedition was a complete failure—and they are now calling for military success on land, which may force some one or more of their generals to advance even against their better judgement, in which event we may again to the clash of arms in this quarter before very long. But there are no signs of such an event at present. Some few changes are observed on the other side but nothing of sufficient importance to warrant the belief of any general change of base; the warm weather south is now rapidly coming on, when it will be impossible for either Yankee or Southern to operate extensively except in the country removed from the sickly lower grounds and rivers. This may cause a concentration of forces on both sides and desparate battles may be the consequence, but let us pray that the evil be averted, and before that event should threaten even, peace may come to gladden all our hearts, and you and I & our children may be blessed with each others presence— I felt so content and happy when with you all that it somehow seems to me as a dream and I ask myself, is it really so that I have been home? I have but one cause to regret, & that is, that I did not Kiss you more & talk to you more, & try & show you how *mu*ch I love you & the children— Good night my dear wife, love me & pray for me & write me. As I do you, Your devoted husband, L M^c^Laws
Tell the boys that the Kite Lesson is now coming in, or rather is in & they Should learn from this Boys book how to make them. Genl Lee gives no leaves of absence now & I have Sought in vain for a *ch*ance to send anything home.

((( )))

Head Quarters Divisions
[Fredericksburg, Virginia]
April 11th/63 [Saturday]

My Dearly beloved Wife
I have just this moment arrived and found all well. Allie is suffering from a sore throat so he sags and looked so low spirited that I thought really he was sick but I had not been long in the place where he was, when he showed me a paragraph in one of the papers, announcing the marriage of Miss Lucy

Pendleton of Louisa County to a Mr Robert Baylor of the 6th Va Infy instead of to Lieut Alfred Edwards of the Ordnance. And that is the cause of his sickness and his downcast look.

I wrote you from Richmond & subscribed there for the Examiner and the Illustrated News, the latter will be sent to the direction of W H McLaws but is intended for all the children including Ulric, but W. must file it away for himself.

I arrived in Richmond at 8.P.M., after a very tedious journey, and if it had not been for your eggs and biscuit, would have been half starved, as the eating houses *when there were* any, had nothing eatable in them—the time tables have been changed— The r. r trains not being allowed to run over ten miles per hour. So the eating places are all out of place.

I found N. Carolina a much more pleasant state to travel through via Charlotte, Raleigh & Fayette, then by Wilmington[.] [T]he country is rolling, with fine forests of oak and hickory, and fine lands.

I am writing at the r r depot and must now close as my transportation for camp is waiting.

Give my love to all the children and to Bet one or two kisses through Johnny.

Tell Willie to shoot off his gun & keep it fired off when in the house. I have a plenty of powder & shot for him, so he & Johnny must practice with that he now has, so as to be ready for the fall shooting but he must be very careful in loading so as to keep the muzzle away from his body, & in carrying his gun to keep the muzzle up, & in getting over the fences to be very careful not to let the gun point at himself or any one else.

There is nothing occuring as I know of, but I will hear more by tomorrow & will write.

With many kisses & Much love

Your devoted husband
L McLaws

((( )))

Head Qrs Division
[Fredericksburg, Virginia]
April 12th/63 [Sunday]

My Dear Wife
I take the opportunity offered by a few moments of leisure to write you a short epistle, promising longer ones when I have visited my different commands and learned all the news.

I found all my staff well and all were glad to see me which was extremely gratifying.

The enemy are very quiet, and civil, our men not only fish in the river but *seine* it, catching hundreds of fish. The enemy fish with poles but have not ventured to seine as yet.

It is the general belief that we will move before very long, but in what direction is not known. If such is the case my opinion is that we will change our base so as to have the mountains in our rear.

I found my horses in much the worse for wear condition, but John went to work at once and made Dave do something and already they look better, because very much cleaner. Tell Mary Jane that her beloved Dave is a very worthless fellow if he is not watched and made to do—which I do not believe is her case.[3] By the way, I forgot to give Mary Jane anything when I left and herewith enclose fifty cents for her benefit[,] one dollar for the cook of the house and the remainder fifty cents for Johnny who I believe spent all his money to buy me some ground nuts. Speaking of which, makes me suggest that you buy two or three bushels of the raw ones, and have them cooked when you wish them.

The contrast between the weather here and at home is very remarkable. Here there is no vegetation excepting here and there a few patches of green grass in sheltered positions, while at the south, you know, the grasses are green everywhere and the trees are fast getting their summer clothing. The weather is however quite warm now, and the trees & grasses will soon rival those of the more southern states. A large proportion of this country remains still unplanted, and I suppose will continue so, as there are no laborers, nor animals for agricultural operations. This want of cultivation will necessarily cause great suffering among the population heretofore dependent upon the productions of their own farms. Indeed it is plain that an emigration from their present residences will be an imperative necessity with a great many, for the bread and meat will not be here for their subsistence and there will not be transportation to haul it from other sections.

I visited this evening, in company with two of my staff, some houses in the neighborhood where refugees from Fredricksburg are living. In one house with five rooms there were five families men women & children, some with two & three sick. In one little house, with a room about fifteen feet square there resided a widow woman with seven children, who subsisted by wash-

3. Mary Jane and Dave were two of ETM's servants.

ing & by obtaining provisions from the charity fund. The children excepting one daughter [letter ends here]

((( )))

Fredricksburg V[a]
April 13th/63 [Monday]

My darling wife
To day being the anniversary of the attack on Fort Sumpter [Sumter] which was in fact the commencement of the war, we are expecting that an attack will be made by the Yankees this day, and are consequently waiting for tomorrows mail with much interest. For that and because I expect a letter from you, I am very desirous for tomorrow—to be here, I am as full of anxiety as a young married man, and think the time hangs heavier with me than with all the world besides. I am so lonesome is the cause of my anxiety in some measures, I am thinking of something rather else than of my business—but I will not talk so much of my feelings, as the subject must be tiresome to you.

Tell Willie that I am in search of some one going to Georgia to send his powder and shot by. I will send small portions at a time, and when received it must be carefully used, not wasted—a quantity will be necessarily expended in learning how to shoot, so as to be ready for the hunting of next fall. When I speak of Willies ammunition he must recollect that it must be shared by Johnny[,] who I know will be an enthusiastic and good sportsman so soon as he grows big enough and gets strong enough to carry the gun & pull the trigger.

I visited Fredricksburg this evening and found the command there,[4] all in good spirits. The men playing ball, the band playing. Some fishing, and all as unconcerned about the enemy as if there was no war, no enemy within a thousand miles, and yet the Yankees are visible on the other side, parading and drilling and moving about in large masses.

I have not Seen Gen[l] Lee nor any general from whom information can be obtained as to our intentions or those of the enemy as gatherered from their movements and therefore cannot speak advisedly upon those subjects.

Gen[l] Lee has been sick for some six or ten days, but is getting better so I am informed much to my pleasure, as it would be a real misfortune for him to be away from us at this time.

You promised to write me longer letters when you became settled in

4. Brigadier General William Barksdale's brigade.

Sparta and I am looking for them much oftner than before. This is the fourth letter I have written you since leaving home. When you write me, please my dear Em do so in perfect frankness and full confidence, and do not allow any anxieties to weigh on you without letting me know all about them, a full and fair discussion between us will not but soften any distress. Do not allow Bet to think that sister Laura does not like her, for distrust cannot but get dislike. Sister may be jealous of her, because she wishes me to love her in preference and thinks perhaps that such is not the case. I do not think there can be any other reason. If there should be any exhibition of dislike on the part of sister you must let me know and I will write sister about the necessity of being very polite and amiable to one who is as it were an exile from her home. Good night my dear wife with many kisses for yourself and children. I would like to get three or four of the small photographs of myself, as my friends here have asked for them. Kiss master Uldrick for me—my little daughter, my best love to Bet and her husband. Remember me to Wm Stubing and the family.[5]

((( )))

(17)
Head Q^rs^ Division
[Fredericksburg, Virginia]
April 26th/63 [Sunday]

My dearly beloved wife
This the 17th letter I have written since I left home, to yourself, the children & one to Laura & Bet each, all included. The letter to Laura was forwarded this morning

To day has been beautifully clear and cool, the roads are drying rapidly and the bows [boughs] are at last putting forth their leaves.

There is nothing new to be reported about the enemy, in their late raid across the river at Port Royal below this twenty two miles. It is now found out that they captured several of our wagons and took twelve or fourteen men prisoners. The cavalry who were guarding the river fled ingloriously and saved themselves without as it seems giving proper information to all concerned.

They (the enemy) retired after destroying the nets & fishing boats and oyster tongs, and doing some damage to a few houses in the vicinity—it was however reported in Richmond that thirty thousand of the enemy had

5. The Stubing family has not been identified.

crossed the river and that a general engagement was expected— I think it not improbable that the exaggeration was sent by telegraph through the south and many an anxious heart was made to beat for the loved ones in the army.

I am more and more convinced that the telegraph lines should all be under the sole control of the government, and the[n] sensation despatches would not be prevalent.

Nothing is known of our operations at Suffolk or North Carolina, except that General Hill had retired from Washington, and there had been some fighting about Suffolk—no one is informed of the intentions of those generals, nor of the tenor of their instructions. Gen[l] Longstreet's command seems to have gone on a foraging expedition only—& drawn the enemy into Suffolk, & beyond, to give greater security to his trains—[6] It may be that General Hill went for the same purpose—but the newspapers in Richmond had laid down a plan of their own for both Genl L & Gen[l] Hill, and now finding that their views were not carried out, they are abusing those officers for doing what they, the editors, thought was the best.

A considerable cavalry force of the enemy has been reported near Warrenton, but nothing is known as to their intentions. A considerable number of persons are of the opinion that the enemy are leaving the other side of the river, a scout—an officer of the signal Corps reported to day to an officer of my staff, that he had been to Acquia Creek and Evansport and the Yankee troops were debarking in large numbers and going down the Potomac. I would not be surprised however if Gen[l] Hooker is not sending off his two years men at once instead of waiting for the expiration of their time, and has been drawing reinforcements from Washington and other garrisons to fill their places. There is a rumor that Hooker intends advancing up the peninsula as McClellan did. If so the troops from here may be debarking for Old Point.

Give my best love to all with you and many kisses & blessings to our dear children and am very much pleased and proud to hear that they are going to school and are doing well, and are pleased to go. My love to Bet & sister—and all my heart to my dear wife from her "precious" husband. L M[c]Laws

6. On February 18, 1863, two divisions of Longstreet's corps were ordered to move from Fredericksburg to east of Richmond to protect the capital from Federal threats via the Peninsula.

((( )))

Head Quarters Division
[Fredericksburg, Virginia]
April 29th/63 [Tuesday]

My dear Sweetheart
The enemy suddenly crossed below my position about one & half miles, last night—surpising a North Carolina Regiment, capturing near a hundred men and succeeded in establishing themselves on our side, building two or three bridges and crossing a large body of men, before Genl Lee was apprised of the fact. Of Course I was ignorant of it for the North Carolinians not only allowed themselves to be surprised and captured, but failed to notify any one either on their right or left of the circumstances. In consequence the whole line was jeopardized. Fortunately a Georgia regiment was on their right, which gave such stubborn resistance the enemy were driven back & kept at bay until ten oclock this morning, when our troops got into position.

To day Genl Lee came over to my position and we had a long conversation with each other, he was very confident of his ability to beat back the enemy should our troops behave as well as they have usually done, and "General McLaws" he said "Let them know that it is a stern reality now, it must be, Victory or Death, for defeat would be ruinous."

The enemy have crossed above us & below us and the combination of our movements are very intricate. Who is to blame tis useless to inquire now, all we have to do is to keep firm and confident, and rely upon the God of battles as our shield and we will pluck safety & honor from the very jaws of danger.

Upon the eve of great and stirring events; my dear wife, the mind turns from war and its desolations, and seeks consolation in the thought of home, of wife and children, and no one in the world I do not think, has a sweeter wife to think of and to love nor dearer children than I have. But the thought of them nerves me to be more worthy of them.

Your last letter I keep in my pocket and read it over and over, and at every reading I can but think how good and how estimable I should be, to be worthy of you.

I have been riding all day and must be in the saddle before day in the morning . . . so I must try and get some sleep.

Give a thousand kisses to our dear children and my dear wife you know how my heart beats for you.

My love to Bet and to sister Laura, remember me to Sallie & family when you write.

I believe that I forgot to tell you that my trunk had been obtained for me from Wm Benning by Genl Wise,[7] and is now in Richmond at the depot of the Georgia Relief Association.

Good night and many kisses and blessings upon you all is the prayer of your devoted husband.

L M^c^Laws

((( )))

24

To day is the anniversary of the battle of Resaca de la Palma.[8]

Head Quarters Division
[Fredericksburg, Virginia]
May 9th/63 [Saturday]

My darling wife
I received to day your letter of the 1st inst.

The battles are now over for the present, and I write you with freer breath. Let us be thankful my dear wife for the mercies shown us, on this as on many other occasions, God has given us the victory over our enemies once again, and driven them to their stronghold, and may they retire to their country and remain away from us for ever.[9]

I received the letters of Johnny & Willie for which give them my very particular thanks—in a few days I will try and answer them. At present I have too much of the details of service to attend to. Their letters were very good ones indeed, highly creditable, and should be an inducement for them to write more. Seeing how well they can do with a little effort.

You did not write in this last letter what your intentions were, whether to remain in Sparta or to leave for another place—it must be really annoying to you my dear wife, and I feel very anxious and troubled to think that we have no place we can call home. This everlasting war will give our children such unsettled notions about even the most common affairs of life, that I dread to think how the mode of living, the constant changing of residence must add to this evil. —But I really cannot perceive how we can help it—

7. Henry Alexander Wise, Virginia, Washington College graduate and Confederate brigadier general.

8. The Battle of Resaca de la Palma took place in southern Texas on May 9, 1846.

9. LM is referring to the Battle of Chancellorsville.

unless we agree at once to dispense with daily mails and telegraphs & rail roads and retire at once into the country where the want of easy communication prevents these constantly occurring changes, which are the bane of life.

I begin to pine after riches in order that you and the children can be placed above want and in a situation where you will be independent of the fluctuations in the prices of bread & meat. Not that you have ever exhibited any disposition which would warrant the suspicion you were not perfectly content with whatever lot fortune may have given you. But I know you would do a great deal of good with your riches, would be happier in having it in your power to contribute to the happiness of others, and would be more content in having those things about you which, could be called your own, & which tomorrows dawn would not probably take away from you. —I am not like M^{r} McCauben, for I can not look forward to "Something turning up" which will add to our riches. But my dear wife God has given us health and has spared our children to us. And we, husband and wife, are lovers yet, and can see things through a silver veil, which others would look at through a darkened glass. So let us put up with small annoyances, or call all annoyances trifling in comparison to separation from each other, and let us look forward to our being together as the joy to be hoped for. So I Kiss you and quit writing about it.

The enemy are opposite us, but not so arrogant in their display. All things with us go on with the usual monotony, and routine, and before very long I hope to see our army in as good condition and spirits as before the battles.

I am not yet in the frame of mind to write about the battles, but will I hope be able in a few days to commence an account of them for you and the children.

Give the children many kisses for me. Tell my little daughter that when she is able I want a pair of gloves made by herself. Give master Ulrick my best love, and my love to Sister Laura & Bet—remember me to the family of Capn Forbes & Col Johnson & Dr Pendleton.[10] Good night & Gods blessings with you & the children. Your devoted husband L McLaws.

10. Captain Forbes and Colonel Johnson have not been identified. E. M. Pendleton was a forty-five-year-old physician who lived outside of Sparta in Hancock County. Eighth Census, 1860, Mayfield, Hancock County, Ga., entry for E. M. Pendleton, sheet 215, NARA M 653, RG 29.

(copy)
Head Quarters Division
[Fredericksburg, Virginia]
May 31st 1863 [Sunday]

General Hood
Your reply to my communication relating to the reflections made upon my conduct by ——— [Nicholas A.] Davis[,] Chaplain of the 4th Texas[,] referring to my delay in coming to your assistance at the Battle of Sharpsburg has been received.[11]

The whole tenor of the publication is so unfounded[,] so maliciously false that one naturally seeks for a motive which would prompt a writer to turn out of his path to utter a baseless slander. My division arrived in the vicinity of Sharpsburg just after day light on the morning of the 17th and I received an order from Genl Jackson to post it on the right supporting Genl Walker[.] [B]efore doing this I reported to Genl Lee, who directed me to halt my command in the vicinity of the road near his Head Quarters and to rest my men, that I was not then required but he would call for me when necessary. Those of the men who had anything to eat & the majority had nothing made fires & cooked their breakfast—myself and many others took advantage of the opportunity and went to sleep. About an hour and a half or two hours after my arrival or perhaps longer I was aroused and told that my Division was wanted. I immediately mounted my horse and rode to the Head of my command then under way and met you on the field &c &c &c.

My Command crossed the river before day light and Genl Barksdale tells me that he recollects distinctly when a mile from the river he wished to get some water to drink but it was then so dark he could not find the well.

I rode ahead and went into and beyond the town of Sharpsburg looking for Genl Lee or some one from whom to receive information and directions but saw but one or two persons about the place. When returning I met Genl Longstreet & staff going to the front and he told me where Genl Lee was[.]

11. John Bell Hood, Kentucky, USMA 1853, major general, later held the temporary rank of full general. Hood, who favored offensive tactics and was one of the more aggressive generals in the Confederate army, commanded Longstreet's second division. Nicholas A. Davis, Texas, was an ordained Presbyterian minister and chaplain of the 4th Texas Infantry. Davis did not participate in many of the engagements and based his "reflections" on after-battle stories related by several individual soldiers.

[E]verything at that time was perfectly still. I did not hear a gun or sound denoting the vicinity of ~~the~~ a battlefield.

In my report of the operations of my command I stated that some troops were retiring as mine went in but whose they were I did not know.

As regards the publication in the Illustrated News concerning myself, I have never read it but Maj. Goggin my Adjt Genl tells me that your name is not in it.[12]

I have thought it best to be this minute as to the arrival of my command in the vicinity of Sharpsburg in order that you can judge how maliciously false is the publication in the pamphlet of the Texas Chaplain[.] [T]hat pamphlet which is devoted to a glorification of yourself and the Texas Brigade, of which he was a member, is or would be all very well in itself and no one would object to such a harmless production if the writer had not thought proper to enhance the reputation of his favorites by clouding the fair fame of others.

I find that the pamphlet has been industriously circulated and as I have been attacked it has become a necessity for me to defend myself[.] I dislike very much to be drawn into newspaper notoriety[,] nothing is so repugnant to my sense of propriety as a military man.

I am very glad that you have denied that the pamphlet of Mr. Davis was published under your auspices for I tell you frankly that it has been the opinion of many who have read it, that you must have known its contents before publication.

Very Respectfully
[signed] L McLaws
Maj Genl

12. James Monroe Goggin, Virginia, started with LM in 1838 at the USMA but left the academy to fight in the Texas revolution. Goggin was commissioned as major in the 32nd Virginia before joining LM's staff as adjutant general. He consistently won LM's praise in after-action reports, became LM's confident, and was appointed brigadier general to rank from December 4, 1864. The nomination was canceled, and Goggin returned as adjutant general for Major General Joseph Brevard Kershaw in the final months of the war. Compiled Service Records of Confederate Generals and Staff Officers & Nonregimental Enlisted Men: James Monroe Goggin, NARA M 331, RG 109. The *Southern Illustrated News* article on April 4, 1863 (p. 3), did not mention Hood. It did state: "When the gallant part it bore of the heroic deeds it performed, when the true history of this war shall come to be written from official sources, when the vain and silly puffs of particular commanders shall be forgotten, or only remembered to be laughed at— The public will then learn that when the division [McLaws's] did enter into the fight, on a portion of the field which other gallant men had not succeeded in holding,

[note on back of letter]
About
Battle of Sharpsburg
Letter to Genl Hood
June 1/63
& His reply
&
Letter from Chaplain Davis
(Stopped to rest by Gen. Lee's orders)

The letter published in Richmond papers charged that instead of hurrying to Sharpsburg, I stopped my command at the river and around the river to bathe & wash & in consequence, did not arrive on field before 9 oclock A.M., a made up lie for the Special purpose of damaging me, as I arrived there before daylight & was on ground before Sun rise. L McLaws

((( )))

Head Quarters Division
[Fredericksburg, Virginia]
June 2/63 [Tuesday]

My Dear Wife
Your letter of the 24th was received yesterday. You have been a long time waiting for my letters. The principal delay is in the city of Richmond, but we are endeavoring to devise means to correct that evil.

I have written to WmR to see the express agent in Augusta concerning the package with two hundred dollars. How did you get into the valise or satchel[?] The key was placed in the letter containing the money. I will send you some more money to Augusta Georgia, to the care of WmR McLaws, with the request that he forward it by private hands.

Rest assured my dear exacting wife that if Colonel Jack Smith wrote to his wife twice each day, & on one occasion a letter of sixty two pages, that he was perfectly worthless as a Colonel and resigned because he had been notified he would be dismissed for incompetency—he should be conscripted at once.[13]

I have written you every day but two, when not on the battle field, and

they swept it like a tornado, retaining possession of it until the following evening, when with the remainder of the army, the division recrossed the river into Virginia."

13. Colonel Theophilus Jackson Smith.

you do not write more than once a week. There may be wives in the world who write oftener but I do not like to make comparisons.

My poor Willie[,] I do not really know what to do with him, unless he tries campaigning with me. The conviction that if he gets sick, there is no chance of being cared for may of itself act in his favor by nerving him to extra exertion. It is a common remark in the army that the men are always more healthy when there are no doctors about. This is true no doubt, because they do not give way to small ailments, and take more pains with themselves, to keep free from disease.

I have written you advising the purchase of a place in Sparta or elsewhere as you think best. Habersham county is said to be a very beautiful country, and will be very populous and prosperous. A visit to that section would no doubt be a great desideratum. Land is cheaper, and everything to eat more reasonable. When we have achieved our independence or even if we do not, there is no doubt but that section of the state will advance more rapidly in wealth & population than any other.

Give the boys my best thanks for delivering their speeches. Tell them to try & try until they satisfy themselves to keep on trying, & do not be bashful or sensitive.

My best love to sister & Bet. I have written to both, but no acknowledgement has been received. Good day & God bless you. Kisses to my little daughter & Uldrick.

Your devoted husband
L McLaws

((( )))

Head Quarters Division
Raccoon Ford on the Rapidan [Virginia]
June 5th/63 [Friday]

My Dear wife
As you will perceive we have changed our camp, thirty miles from Fredricksburg up the river. The designs of General Lee are of course unknown, as are those of General Hooker. General Lee however acts on his own responsibility and is allowed to be the arbiter of his own actions, where as General Hooker has to be guided by President Lincoln, Genl Halleck and the northern press.[14]

14. Henry Wager Halleck, New York, USMA 1839, general in chief, later chief of staff.

We are all still anxious concerning Vicksburg[.] [T]he information we have received is entirely too indefinite to give satisfaction, and the effect of a disaster in that direction will have such an important bearing on the length of the war, and the general conduct of affairs that everything is kept in suspense until the finality is announced.

I sent you two hundred and thirty dollars by express a few days ago, less the charges to be paid in Augusta—the package was addressed to W^{m}R McLaws Augusta G^{a} and I wrote him requesting that he forward it to you by some safe conveyance.

My present camp is beautifully located, near fine streams of water, and with very fine grazing for our animals. The mountains are plainly visible and at night the air is so cool as to make a blanket very acceptable.

Hu received a letter this morning from Sally saying that she had heard from you & all were well. Your letter acknowledging the receipt of the money arrived yesterday, I am delighted to hear that all are well with you, the children will be delighted visiting Jimmy and I suppose that Sally will take as much care of them as if they were her own.

You have evidently not received my letter relating to the purchase of a place in Sparta. I dreamed one night that you had, and were pleased with it.

Mr Paris my orderly has been discharged from the service on account of his infirmities[.][15] [H]e will leave for Augusta tomorrow and will take this letter, he will carry with him a bottle of powder and some caps (percussion) for the gun, I hope the shot & powder previously sent will have been recd before this. But it should be saved for hunting in the winter time, when there will be plenty of game & it will be fit to eat. I hope to hear of you being supplied with game in abundance by the boys, at least once a week.

John E. sent 100 dollars to Bet this morning, which will I hope relieve her anxieties about the extra expense at the Edwards House. John can well afford to send that amount nearly every month.

You must write me, to "General Longstreets Head Quarters. Army of Northern Virginia." With my best love to the children and those with you, and much love to my wife I remain your devoted husband L McLaws.

15. Joseph Paris was a private in Company B of the 10th Georgia. He served as LM's orderly. Henderson, *Roster,* 2:13.

((( )))

Head Quarters Division
Raccoon Ford on the Rapidan [Virginia]
June 5th/63 [Friday]

Dear W

I send by Parris a bottle of powder and a box of caps for Willie, which you will oblige by forwarding by some safe conveyance. I also send a letter to Emily which contains a little money. Please forward that in the same way.

As you will perceive we are again on the move, our destination is still unknown, but it will be known before very long as whatever our army does next and once very shortly, and if well done it will then be a very important part in our efforts for peace and independence.

The news from Vicksburg is so meager and unsatisfactory that it carries much uneasiness. Its fall would be so discouraging and its successful defense so inspiring that everything concerning it, is looked for with the greatest anxiety.

Hugh is well, as are all my staff.

The weather is warm and dry. We need rain very much in this country[,] as I have understood is the case in Georgia and all other Southern States. But Emily writes me that the wheat crop is excellent and being gathered. I hope it will answer all our demands, and tend to bring down prices and ruin extortioners. The army has a heavy debt to settle with them all over the country & I hope when the war is over, the returned soldiers will settle for all past grievances. I think that if I was a lawyer I would argue that extortioners are beyond the law, not entitled to its protections, and every one has a right to help himself from their possessions. It will need but the prompting to have the sentence executed, and it may be done before the end is decided. Our people are however a law abiding race, and will bear and forbear beyond the point of virtue, if pursuaded. But their reactions will be very great if they decide to be lawless. A full crop and lower prices now may prevent all difficulties. So we must hope for that.

My best regards to all with you.

My address will be "Headquarters General Longstreets Corps, Army of Northern Va."

Good day.

Your brother
L McLaws

((( )))

Head Quarters Division
[Raccoon Ford on the Rapidan River, Virginia]
June 10th 1863 [Wednesday]

My dear Emily
Your letter of the last of May has just been received. You have not received my letter in relation to purchasing a house in Sparta or at least you make no mention of it. I wrote that if you could get a place on reasonable terms, it was advisable to buy, and that I had written to William Walton requesting him to write you advising as to the best course to be pursued and as to the best way to pay for it. In your letters you make no mention of now entertaining the idea.

The Confederate tax will be in force now within a short time, and it is thought that its influence will be to lower the price of not only provisions but of real estate. There may be a time when, under its influence property will fall, our money becoming more valuable, as its representative—by having some one on the lookout for the occasion you may be able to make a purchase upon reasonable terms.[16]

I think it would be better if you and Sister & Bet should get rooms wherever you can. You can visit each other at pleasure and be better satisfied perhaps in being more independent, and in extending the area of your acquaintanceship.

Our army has taken up the advance[,] as you will read of in the papers by the time this reaches you. Our destination is not known of course, but circumstances point to a movement towards the valley of the Shenandoah, or towards Pennsylvania. We may go in that direction, or may turn again. So soon as we unloose Hooker from his present base, threatening Richmond. There are many political reasons mixed up with our advance that tis impossible to argue from the mere position our troops are assuming, where our destination will be, or what we are arriving at. If we are striking for Pennsylvania we are actuated by a desire to visit upon the enemy some of the horrors of war, to give the northern people some idea of the excesses committed by their troops upon our houses and inhabitants. On the other hand does it not seem natural to suppose that if we invade their country it will be

16. The tax-in-kind law passed by the Confederate Congress on April 24, 1863, levied a 10 percent assessment on all agricultural products and livestock raised for slaughter that were in the hands of producers. The Congress expected this tax to fund a significant part of the war effort.

the means of re-arousing the war spirit which is now apparently fast dying out, and give an excuse for the enforcement of the Conscript act, which the President does not now seem inclined to attempt to put in execution. Thus it appears to many—and it causes much discussion.

Our cavalry were surprised yesterday by the enemy and had to do some desperate fighting to retrieve the day.[17] As you will perceive from General Lee's dispatch the enemy were driven across the river again. All this is not true, but it will be better to allow the impression to prevail. The enemy were not however driven back, but retired at their leisure—having accomplished I suppose what they intended, that is they felt our lines to make us show our forces; our infantry was not however displayed to any extent— but I am afraid enough was shown to give notice of our general movement.

It has become very interesting to watch the movements of both armies so far as tis known, and to endeavor to decypher the general plan. I will write you as the opportunity offers and wish you to write often.

I rec^d a letter from W^mR of the 5th inst, telling me of the arrival of Willie & Johnny, on a visit to Sallie & the children & of the arrival of the shot & powder for Willie; &c.

My dear little Uldrick, how hard it has been for him and for you how much harder. I had hoped that you & him would have been both in the enjoyment of good health ere this & that he would be weaned.

My love to sister Laura who owes me a letter. Give my best love to Bet & tell her not to be so low spirited, but to cheer up and get fat. She need not expect even a letter for a month yet, & so must take events as they come and not repine. Your devoted husband L McLaws.

((( )))

Head Quarters Division
Camp near Culpeper CH
[Culpeper Court-House, Virginia]
June 15th/63 [Monday]

My Dear Emily
Last night in the night I received an order to put my command in motion, towards Winchester via Springville, early this morning, accordingly at an early hour my troops were in readiness but they waited and waited for the final order of movement. At last it came and the march commenced—but it had not more than commenced when an order for me not to move be-

17. The Battle of Brandy Station, Va.

yond the immediate vicinity of Culpeper CH was received, and this accounts for my present camp. But I am ordered to move in the morning, and my orders are for the march to be commenced at 4 oclock. —Lieut General Ewells command is now in the direction of the Potomac in the valley of the Shenandoah; and Longstreets is moving in the same direction. Where are we going to? is the constant inquiry. The Yankees are evidently afraid that we will attack Washington, as they have withdrawn from Fredricksburg, and report says are concentrating in the direction of Centreville & the old battle grounds of Mannassas, but appearances do not indicate that we are going in that direction except collaterally.

It is reported that our army will not be allowed to plunder or rob in Pennsylvania, which is all very well; but it would be better not to publish it. As we have received provocations enough to burn and take or destroy, property of all kinds and even the men, women & children along our whole border.

It is absolutely necessary however to our salvation that our army should not become demoralized, which would be the case should our men be permitted to rob and take at pleasure. But it should be and could be restricted like the gold digging in California to special parties, to details made daily for the special purpose to do all in their power to retaliate for the many outrages committed against us. In every instance where we have even threatened retailitation, the enemy have given away—and I am strongly in favor of trying it the very first chance we get. But we are not yet in Pennsylvania, and may before going there have to give Hooker a good sound whipping. It will have to be done either in Virginia or out of it—and I think it is preferable to do it in Virginia.

However we had better not anticipate but take events as they transpire.

The weather has been to day excessively warm, several of the men fainted from heat during our short march. But these things will always happen, at first.

Give my best love to all with you, my kisses in abundance to my little daughter and Uldrick and many to my dear wife.

Address your letters "Major Genl McLaws McLaws Division 1st Army Corps Army Northern V^{a}."

Good day and God bless you is my daily prayer.

Your devoted husband L McLaws

My photographs are received and every one says they are excellent.

((( )))

Head Quarters Division
near Piedmont, on the
Manassas Gap Rail Road
[Piedmont, Virginia]
June 18th/63 [Thursday]

My Dear Wife

My present position is as you will perceive above.

The weather has been exceedingly warm, so oppresively hot that my men fell by hundreds along the road[.] [S]ome cases I am afraid proved fatal, but the majority I hope will be able to come up again and join us before many days.

The operations of our army in the Valley you will learn by reading the newspapers. Winchester has been captured with over three thousand prisoners, and a number of cannon, & Martinsburg also with a quantity of ordnance stores.

Our operations will be given in the papers as they are disclosed by the advance and you must look there for them.

The story about the capture of Milroy is not true. The villain made his escape tis said in Citizens dress.

When Genl Ewell demanded the surrender of the town, *tis said* that Milroy returned answer "When Brig Genls Jones & Imboden of the cavalry wish to transact business with me they must use their own signatures" so entirely was he surprised at the movement of our infantry force.[18] Again tis said that when Milroy found out that it was Lt Genl Ewell with his Corps who demanded his surrender, he sent back word declining to surrender and saying that if attacked he would burn the town, and that Genl Ewell sent word in reply that he would attack and if the town was burned or set on fire, he would hoist the black flag and neither ask or give quarter. —The town was not burned however and I suppose the reported sayings are all lies manufactured to swell the prestige of a Virginian.

I am moving along the eastern slope of the Blue Ridge[,] a very beautiful country to look at, but a bad one for travelling with vehickles or artillery—the hills are blue in the distance, the country rolling and the first fields of

18. Robert Huston Milroy, Indiana, major general of U.S. volunteers, later major general; William Edmondson "Grumble" Jones, Virginia, USMA 1848, Confederate brigadier general; John Daniel Imboden, Virginia, Washington College, Confederate brigadier general.

clover and fine grasses meet the eye in every direction, untouched by man or animal, as there is no one to reap, and no cattle to graze—all this caused by the Yankees. —The people appear to be all true to the south, and detest the Yankees most cordially. Milroy in particular.

I must to bed, as we start early in the morning[,] so with much love to the children & others with you and much more to my dear wife I remain her devoted husband.

L M[c]Laws

I rec[d] letter from Bet[,] a very excellent & interesting one. Congratulate her for me on the arrival of her husband and give him my best rememberances. John E and Ally are all well[,] also Hugh and all my staff.

((( )))

Head Quarters Division
June 28'/63 [Sunday]
Camp near Chambersburg, P[a]

My Dear Emily

My command arrived at this place, this morning at 10 oclock, and joined the rest of the Corps camped near this place.

We left Martinsburg in Virginia on the 26th at five oclock in the morning, and fording the river, camped three Brigades near W[ms]port and one brigade with my artillery near Hagerstown. I camped in an open lot in the town. The ford at W[ms]port is a very good one the men crossing without difficulty. The Chesapeake and Ohio Canal which runs along the river bank on the north side, was dry[,] the aquaduct having been blown up. The track of the Baltimore and Ohio Canal running along the canal was also destroyed—from Martinsburg to the river, eleven miles, the houses were all closed, the curtains drawn and the people either absent or invisible—showing an evident dislike to our cause. It was remarked as we went into Martinsburg that the magnificent farm of the Honl. Charles J Faulkner who was the Adjutant General of General Jackson was in a beautiful state of cultivation,[19] not a stone of his fences injured and the laborers at work with their teams, collecting the clover which has been cut and cured. While on the other side of the road, the fences were down, the crops destroyed, the grounds trampled and everything wearing the appearance of places which had long ago been deserted and devastated. The secret was out, when we visited the town and was

19. Charles James Faulkner, member of Congress.

told that Mrs Faulkner had not long since returned from Washington,[20] and on the evening our troops first entered the town she had issued tickets for a large party to be given to the Yankee officers. Her daughters were also constantly visiting the Yankee families and were being visited by them and the Yankee officers generally, and that the greatest cordiality existed between them.

The farms we saw lying in waste were those of southern families who were not so devoted to Yankeedom. There was no welcome given us in Martinsburg, except by a very few and those of the ladies who exhibited any cordiality I noticed were clothed in silks, and de lames & muslins, and all the finery of a thriving Yankee town. Many women & children made faces at us as we marched along, and although we could not hear them, we could see their mouths moving, and from their expressions knew they were giving us their maledictions[.] [A]s we crossed into Williamsport, the people were more friendly but yet all the shops were closed and the houses generally deserted or exhibiting no signs of being inhabited. One lady said she was delighted to see us. Shook hands very cordially. Said she expected to be sent over the river if the enemy should ever return but did not care. Shortly after I went to the window to get some water and seeing a boy of nine or ten in the room with the blue blouse of a Yankee. I Said "You are a Yankee Sir"[;] the boy said nothing but held down his head. The young lady before mentioned said to him "Speak up buddy and tell him you are no Yankee." ["]Yes but I am one" asserted the boy. And I remarked "Children take their opinions from their older sisters and brothers & they always tell the truth" and rode away. The family within looking as if they had been caught in a falsehood.

I camped three Brigades near W^{ms}port and one near Hagerstown with four batteries and camped in the town myself (Hagerstown) where a good many persons called to see me and I was invited to supper and breakfast. I went to supper and had nothing better than I usually have at home[;] in camp, did not mention the breakfast. Was introduced to Mr Roman formerly Member of Congress from Maryland,[21] and went to his house for a few minutes. Found him a very polished gentleman, and his wife and niece good specimens of southern ladies. I was very glad to meet them as I thus had in my mind to contrast between the southern gentleman and ladies and the very different species I soon encountered. As I crossed the line into Pennsyl-

20. Mary Wagner Boyd Walker.

21. James Dixon Roman, member of Congress from Maryland.

vania. At Green Castle on the road to Chambersburg. Several young ladies were assembled engaged in scoffing at our men as they passed, but they were treated with contempt or derision. I heard of nothing witty said by any of them. It was made evident however that they were not ladies in the southern acceptations of the word. The men I spoke to acknowledged that the brutalities practiced by their troops, upon the southern people, fully justified our retaliating and were surprised at our moderation—the poorer classes told me that our troops behaved better to them than their own did. Arrived at & marched through Chambersburg on 28th[,] a town of five thousand inhabitants perhaps more. And camped two miles east of it on the Harrisburg Road. Then arrived in camp on the 29th & destroyed about four miles of the rail road leading then to Harrisburg. The people of Chambersburg are decidedly. The men dare not show it but by their looks, the women tried to be sarcastic on various occasions but succeeded in being vulgar only. They are a very different race from the southern. There is a coarsness in their manners and looks and a twang in their voices—which grates harshly on the senses of our men[;] the distinction of class, the poor & sick is very marked. Every one speaks for peace at any price, and since war has been brought to their own homes, they look desponding to the last degree, and begin to believe that they have been vastly deceived by engaging in it— I have found no one to speak of Lincoln as a man of either capacity or patriotism, every one even the women think he is under abolition influence entirely, and they assert boldly that freedom should not be the lot of the negro. To day I moved camp seven miles on the Gettysburg Road, to Greenwood a small village, sending one brigade two miles on to Caledonia, where Thadeus Stevens[,] the abolition Member of Congress from Penna who introduced the bill for the employment of negro troops,[22] had large iron works. They were burned by our troops however, and are now in ashes & total ruin—

My division mail rider was caught by the enemy, in Hagerstown on his way here with letters.

When you write, therefore you must be cautious and particular. This may be captured also & I am particularly cautious as you may observe.

You may send this letter to WmR to be returned to you.

Give much love to the children, and ask them to write me, also to sister Laura & Bet. —Good night and much love from your devoted husband L.

22. Thaddeus Stevens, member of Congress from Pennsylvania.

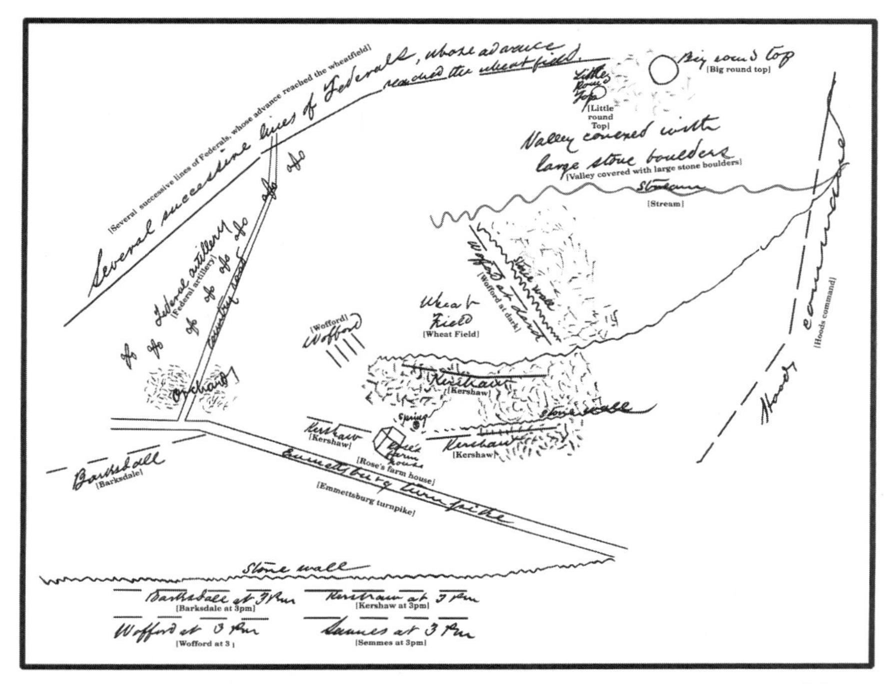

Lafayette McLaws's hand-drawn map of Gettysburg, Pennsylvania, on July 2, 1863. (Courtesy of the Southern Historical Collection, University of North Carolina at Chapel Hill)

((( )))

Headquarters Division
[Hagerstown, Maryland]
July 7th/63 [Tuesday]

My Dear Wife

Since I wrote you last we have had a series of terrible engagements out of which God has permitted me to come unscathed again. On the 1st of July we left Chambersburg and went across the mountains by Fayetteville and Greenwood to Cashtown and camped within five miles of Gettysburg. Where we heard that there had been a considerable battle fought between the forces of the enemy and the Corps of Genls Ewell and Hill,[23] resulting in the route of the enemy with a loss of several thousand prisoners. The next morning we moved around Gettysburg towards the Emmitsburg road, to arrive at the *Peach orchard,* a small settlement with a very large Peach Orchard

23. Ambrose Powell Hill, Virginia, USMA 1847, lieutenant general and commander of the newly formed Third Corps.

attached. The intention was to get in rear of the enemy who were supposed to be stationed principally in rear of Gettysburg or near it. The report being that the enemy had but two regiments of infantry and one battery at the Peach orchard. On arriving at the vicinity of the Orchard, the enemy were discovered in greater force than was supposed, and two of my Brigades were deployed to face the enemy, and the other two in the rear as reserve; ten or twelve pieces were put in position, and fire opened— General Longstreet sent word that he was satisfied there was but a small force of the enemy in front and that I must proceed at once to the assault. On examination it was discovered that the enemy were in much greater force than was expected, and the assualt was delayed, but again delayed and finally I was directed not to assault until General Hood was in position. Gen H had gone around above me to the right, and found that the enemy were very strongly posted on two rocky hills, with artillery and infantry and before he could aid me it was necessary to carry one of the hills—the one nearest to him—which was done by his troops after a desperate encounter, and my division was then ordered in readiness, and as Genl Hoods success became apparent, the Brigades of Kershaw and Semmes were ordered to advance and then those of Barksdale and Wofford,[24] gallantly our men swept the enemy before them, away from the Peach orchard and on to the woods and hills beyond with great slaughter. The enemy in crowds running to our lines. The right Brigades attempted to storm the second hill which was very steep and rocky and bare of trees towards the top, their efforts were however vain and we were obliged to desist. We however occupied the woods beneath the hills, and remained during the night. Genl Barksdale, commanding the Mississippi Brigade was killed, Genl Semmes badly wounded. Colonel Carter of the 13th Miss killed, Colonel Griffin of the 18th Miss & Col Holder 17th Miss. badly wounded, Col de Saussure 15th S.C. killed, Lt. Col. Fiser 17th Miss[.] Wounded, &c &c.[25] —The loss in my Division was near twenty four hundred, the heavi-

24. Joseph Brevard Kershaw, South Carolina, educated at private schools, brigadier, later major general. Kershaw was a planter, lawyer, and member of the South Carolina legislature. LM generally led attacks or assigned key defensive positions to Kershaw and William Barksdale's brigades. Kershaw succeeded LM after the court-martial. William Barksdale, Tennessee, graduated from the University of Nashville before becoming a lawyer and politician. A brigadier general, he commanded a brigade of Mississippi regiments at Gettysburg. William Tatum Wofford, Georgia lawyer and brigadier general, commanded Thomas R. R. Cobb's brigade after Cobb's death at Fredericksburg.

25. James W. Carter, Mississippi, colonel, whose 13th Mississippi was raised from

est of the war, and many of the most valuable officers in the whole service have been killed. Thus ended the battle of the Peach orchard. In place of there being but two regiments of infantry and one battery, the enemy were in very great force, very strongly posted and aided by very numerous arty. I think the attack was unnecessary and the whole plan of battle a very bad one. Genl Longstreet is to blame for not reconnoitering the ground and for persisting in ordering the assault when his errors were discovered. During the engagement he was very excited[,] giving contrary orders to every one, and was exceedingly overbearing. I consider him a humbug—a man of small capacity, very obstinate, not at all chivalrous, exceedingly conceited, and totally selfish. If I can it is my intention to get away from his command. We want Beauregard very much indeed, his presence is imperatively called for. On the 3[d] inst, all our available arty was put in position along our lines, and commenced the most tremendous artillery fire I expect ever heard on our continent. We had several hundred cannon and the enemy as many more[;] finally our troops assaulted the centre, and gained the enemies batteries but were compelled to relinquish our hold and retire to our lines of the day previous to the assualt—where we remained until the next day, when were retired at dark without molestation and reached this place 2 miles from Hagerstown last night about ten oclock. Our men very much fatigued and foot sore, but not disheartened.

The retirement was necessary because it became important to re-establish our communications with the government.

Give a thousand kisses to my dear children, and my dear wife a thousand kisses to you also, and much love indeed. The mail is waiting & I write in a hurry.

Your devoted husband
LM

Be careful in writing as the last mails were captured by the enemy and were of course read by all, & may be published.

Lauderdale, Winston, Wayne, Attala, Newton, Chickasaw, Kemper, and Clarke Counties; Colonel Thomas M. Griffen, whose 18th Mississippi was recruited from Yazoo, Coahoma, Madison, De Soto, and Hinds Counties; Colonel William Dunbar Holder; Colonel William Davie DeSaussure, whose 15th South Carolina was raised from Richland, Union, Lexington, Kershaw, Fairfield, and Williamsburg Counties; John Calvin Fiser, Tennessee, lieutenant colonel and later colonel.

((( )))

Head Quarters Division
[Orange Court-House, Virginia]
August 12th/63 [Wednesday]

My Dearly Beloved Wife
I rode a long distance to day and have returned quite tired and very much heated as the sun must have been hotter or as hot at least as it ever is in Georgia. I must try and send you a map of our theater of operations so that when I mention points, you can locate me—but the conveniences for a drawing are very few, and I am a poor draughtsman as you know—to draw well is a very great accomplishment and I would be delighted to hear that our children had any talent for acquiring the art. Not one has any musical talent. So far as I know. Unless it is your prodigy Uldrick. Willie can make a noise as if he was whistling, Johnny cannot whistle as well as W. And Laura cannot sing, one of them may have a talent for drawing; or they may all have the faculty of acquiring knowledge. It is said that this is a distinct faculty, some persons cannot acquire because they are continually doubting, their own ideas of the subject are constantly obstruding themselves, very often in opposition to those of the instructor and consequently they never say good lessons, but they really know more of the subject than those who are exact in their recitations. The head men of colleges are very seldom heard of afterwards because they have the faculty of acquiring information from others, of absorbing the ideas of others, without having any of their own, whereas the doubter the independent thinker, who was slow with his books becomes the man of mark, who leads the community. The question is are our boys independent thinkers, who are destined to lead their fellows or are they quick in acquiring the ideas of others only—and yet they may be good draughtsman, if they study how to be, when they get old enough.

My head quarters camp is in the yard and on the premises of a Mr Mason, who married a widow with three grown daughters and one grown son & one son about fifteen he himself having several grown children, and some not of age, he has a very little property and she with her daughters have a farm which brings subsistence. The three grown daughters are unmarried and call their father in law "Mr Mason." They are all very stout laborers and apparently are very industrious and contented; a few straggling beaus now and then make their appearance. But no one seems to think of marriage, the times being too hard. The mother appears to be a very kind hearted woman, very quiet and retiring. My Brigades are camped all around the farm, and my pickets cover the whole country for miles. —The family does not appear to have suffered from the depredations of the enemy although Stoneman in his raid,[26] passed within a half mile of the house, and others in the neighborhood lost considerably in negroes, produce and in animals. This excites some suspicions that this family are not sound to the Confederacy; but I expect they are so harmless and without influence[,] they are unnoticed. Hugh is getting very anxious to go home, as indeed we all are, but he stands so well as a Q'master I doubt if he will be permitted to resign—but will be assigned to some post duty. I hope it may be so. Genl Lee will not give any leaves of absence to any one under any pretence, not even for three days.

Good day & much love many blessings to all. Your devoted husband L McLaws.

((( )))

Head Quarters Division
[Orange Court-House, Virginia]
August 14/63 [Friday]

My Dear Wife
To day has been more pleasant than usual winding up with a thunder storm this evening, which has purified the atmosphere, and I hope will give us a little intermission of cool weather. The condition of our affairs is calculated to produce depression in the minds of those who do not calculate the advantages resulting from our reverses, but despond because we have had them, and think everything is lost because we have been unfortunate during one month.

The taking of Vicksburg will release our armies from the onus of defending the Mississippi at certain points, against which the enemy can gather all his vast power at leisure. Its fall & that of Port Hudson releases so much force to be actively employed in preventing depredations, by raiding parties, and will in time by establishing or carrying batteries from point to point, as effectively and more effectively prevent the navigation of the river than ever before, and besides these places Vicksburg & Port Hudson Natchez &c will require a considerable force of the enemy to maintain them[,] thus weakening their army by detachments, while our army will always be concentrated.

Our invasion of Maryland & Pennsylvania was unsuccessful, because we failed in the battle of Gettysburg, which if gained would have given us Balti-

26. George Stoneman, New York, USMA 1846, major general of U.S. volunteers.

more or any other town we may have wished for in the north, south of New York. We did not have troops enough, was the cause of failure—but we are back again concentrated, are in the interior, and are increasing daily in strength and efficiency, have all our old spirit and self confidence, and know that we have fallen back, not from fear of the Yankees but because it was necessary to obtain supplies.

We thus find ourselves not spread out as before over a vast country, but are gradually drawing to a centre, from which our forces can spring against any army coming from the outside. If we should lose Charleston & Savannah, there would be in reality a gain to our military strength, and a corresponding loss to the enemy, for we would be still more concentrated and the enemy's forces still more scattered—so there is no cause for despondency in our situation. We have ascribed importance to places which were really elements of weakness & have been dejected because they have been taken. I believe that our reverses were intended by God to work some great good upon our people, and let us bow to His will, and while nerving ourselves to renewed efforts, wait patiently for the developments of his intentions towards us.

There is nothing new of the enemy, but it is not thought that any thing of importance will shortly occur.

Good night me dear wife and many thanks for your sweet letters of the 8th[,] much love to the children & with many kisses I remain your devoted husband L McL.

((( )))

Hd Qrs Division
[Orange Court-House, Virginia]
Aug 17/63 [Monday]

My Dearly beloved Wife
To day is the 17th of August[,] about the time I left Richmond a year ago to march towards Maryland. Since then how many changes have taken place? and yet we have all returned very near to our former positions. As if life rolled in circles—I commenced my military Career in the Cherokee nation, was ordered thence to Mississippi, back to Louisiana, then to Florida[,] then Mexico, then Missouri, then New Mexico, then back to Fort Gibson—starting again as it were, I was ordered to Missouri, then to Utah, then back to New Mexico, thence I joined the Confederacy, went to Savannah, then to Virginia on the Peninsula, thence to Richmond[,] then north to Maryland, again turning south came to Culpeper and the Rappahannock, again

north to Maryland & Pennsylvania and then back to Culpeper and the line of the Rappahannock & its tributaries. In our next march to be back to Fredricksburg or Richmond, to complete the circle or may be to Savannah, who knows.

I received a telegram from Colonel Lay in Richmond telling me that Hugh would be appointed enrolling officer in the State of Georgia with the rank of Major, or rather Inspector of Conscripts and wishing him to report at once at Richmond. My advice is for him to report at Richmond accepting the office, as it is a very important one, and will give him the long desired opportunity to go home and attend to his business, and I hope he will assist in our small affairs.

I recommended Colonel Bryan to be Brigadier General but there seems to be a hitch somewhere, as his appointment has not been made, although that of another officer recommended at the same time has been forwarded & announced in the papers. The removal of Colonel Meyers Q^{mst} G^{enl} looks as if the Twiggs influence was on the wane in Richmond.[27] Colonel Bryan openly denounces President Davis, and therefore cannot look for favors & should his appointment be refused he can blame no one but himself—he is a capable and gallant officer and no doubt would make a good general. His opponent for the office is a politician from upper Georgia, Colonel McMillen of the 24th G^{a} Regt.[,] Woffords Brigade[,] who is a zealous man, and a gallant old fellow—yet not at all suited for the place, he talks too much, and is quite ignorant of his duties. I would not be surprised however if he got the appointment.[28]

There was quite a number of county ladies assembled this evening to witness a parade of one of my Brigades which did not take place however. I sent for a band of music and after getting them seated around the music I left them and rode to my outside picket posts several miles away. When I returned everything was quiet, as it was quite dark. I inspected a Brigade to day going through the ranks myself, & was very much fatigued when the duty was over—I was three hours on my feet & consequently I am tired & must to bed. So good night & with many kisses & blessings to my dear wife & the children I remain the devoted husband L M^{c}L.

Remember me to Bet & to Sister and Miss Carrie—give my best respects

27. Colonel Abraham Myers was removed and replaced by LM's former commander in Savannah, A. R. Lawton.

28. Robert McMillen, Georgia, colonel. Bryan was appointed brigadier general on August 29, 1863.

to M[r] Gaullard & thank him for me for his kindness to you[,] also M[r] Johnson.[29]

((( )))

Atlanta Georgia
September 19th 1863 [Friday]
6½ A.M.

My Dear Wife
M[r] Dudley who is here proposes to go on and visit you this evening,[30] he is not in the army and is not subject to conscription— I have advised him to get employment outside of the army, in order to keep himself free should our operations extend into Kentucky, when he could either make himself useful in organizing a force to join us, or can communicate with his family without hindrance. I will give him a letter to Hugh, who may be of service to him.

The reception of the troops all along the route was enthusiastic in the extreme, dinner and supper for all comers were provided with the greatest liberality— I was called on several times to "show myself" to the assembled multitude, as the ladies wished to see the Georgia General. The beauty displayed was not very great, but the hearty cordiality was remarkable. The pressure upon me for permits to see their friends has been very great, but I have refused except in a very few cases, presenting extraordinary claims to especial consideration.

I have a room in the Trout house, and was blessed with a very sound sleep last night—not being disturbed but once and that by a *rat,* which I found located under my pillow this morning. I will leave here to day or tomorrow morning early.

Genl Bryans Brigade is coming in and Genl Woffords, will leave in an hour.

Our army is concentrating towards Ringold [Ga.], and the report is that Rosecrans is taking himself out of the state, but I do not believe it. That he will remain at Chattanooga [Tenn.] I think doubtful, but that does not necessarily imply a movement to the rear.

9 A.M.

General Bryan has arrived with his Brigade but I do not think he can leave before tomorrow.

29. Miss Carrie was the future Mrs. Alfred Edwards.
30. William Talcott Dudley of Atlanta, Ga.

I cannot leave before this evening. Everything here is enormously high and rapidly advancing. We must all economise very strictly, I never buy anything but something to eat, as every one laughs about, good naturedly however. Make arrangements for your winter supply of fuel, and for a hard winter—for if our army remains in Georgia the demand for all things will enhance the prices.

I send this by M[r] Dudley. My love to the children—a great deal is expected from my Division and I must be at work. Good morning my dear wife. Your devoted husband L M L.

There is no news from the front this morning. I have just seen Genl Cobb who has been very kind and obliging in his offers to do anything for me in his power—my room has literally been besieged by applicants for leave of absence, if but for one day, for husbands or sons to visit their parents & families, all of which I have had to refuse—many men I am sorry to say have gone off without permission, all of them however to return in a day or two. So I am told and sincerely hope.

((( )))

Head Quarters Division
[Tennessee]
October 1, 1863 [Thursday]

My dearly beloved Wife
No letter for me to day, although the mails have been so much out of order as indeed everything is, that it was hoping against hope to expect one. The Yankees have done nothing but fortify their positions, and we but fortify ours hemming them in, our ulterior operations are not known to me, and those of the enemy must be guided by circumstances.

Yesterday I was honored by a call from Governor Brown of Georgia who came escorted by Genl Bragg and Genl W H T Walker[.][31] [H]e was visiting the camps of the Georgia Regiments to see that the troops from his state were well provided with clothing, and I suppose there was some electioneering strategy in his movement as his election has to be contested within a month or perhaps less. It is only a short time ago that there was any opposition candidate, and his visit to the troops looks something like an electioneering tour. I rode with the Governor to Gen[l] Hoods Division, where there were Georgia troops in Genl Bennings brigade, and then went first to the Brigade of General Bryan, and then to that of General Wofford—at Gen-

31. Braxton Bragg, North Carolina, USMA 1837, general.

eral Bryans he merely paid a visit to the field officers, but when we got to Genl Woffords, a band was in readiness and gave us a musical welcome, the Brigade then formed around the Generals tent, and Governor Brown was introduced by Colonel McMillan[,] Commander of the 24th Ga Regiment, who extolled him as the greatest man in the universe at present, or that ever had adorned any age or country or was ever expected to appear. The introductory of Colonel McM was so long that Genl Bragg said to me, "I thought it was Gov. Brown who was expected to address the troops"! finally Colonel McM, who is a candidate for Congress & wishes to get the influence of Governor B, broke down and got down from the mound of earth where he was standing, and Governor B gave us his views. He told the men that he knew that the majority of them were poor, depending upon their own labor for the support of their families, that they were with few exceptions not slave holders, and that as the cry of many had been, this was a war for the rich, and fought by the poor, he would take the opportunity of showing them that the poor were more interested in the success of our cause than the rich were, and made a very good statement of the ends aimed at by the North, as represented by President Lincoln. He then denounced those who were for a reconstruction showing that reconstruction was not possible, and would not be listened to by the North, that their aim was to conquer us and confiscate our property. He then denounced the faint hearted as being unworthy of the grand mothers even of our revolutionary war with Great Britain, for they never dispaired although all our large towns were captured during that war, and the enemy marched through the country wherever they pleased— finally he gave us his idea of re-construction, which was to build a wall so high between us and Yankeedom that no one could get over it, or even see over it and to pass laws forbidding any Yankees ever to come again in our country— Colonel McMillan then jumped out into the arena and waving his hat, called for three cheers for Governor Brown, which was responded to, and the Governor came down from the stand.

The cry was then for Bragg. Bragg and the Genl stepped on the stand, and gave them a really stirring speech, very short, but very appropriate, which was loudly cheered.

The call then was for Walker, and that General made a few remarks, which were also well recd.

Genl McLaws was then called out and as I stepped forth, the whole Brigade commenced laughing— I merely thanked them for the notice telling them they certainly did not wish to hear me as I was with them every day, but as they wished my views, I would assure them that if they would but carry out the views of their Governor of their commander in chief and the gallant General Walker, all would go well. —[T]he crowd then dispersed with music and shaking of hands and in good humor.

These troops, those in Woffords Brigade are from the northern counties of Georgia, among which there is said to be some disaffection and therefore the address of the Governor, I have no doubt will be very beneficial.

I do not mean to imply when speaking of disaffection, that there is any among the troops, but there is in some of the northern counties. Some of the inhabitants desiring peace so badly that they would vote for reconstruction of for re-union upon any terms.

The enemy have been for the last three or four days sending ambulances and wagons into our lines, to get their wounded & up to, to day about four hundred ambulances and over one hundred wagons have passed loaded with wounded. General Bragg informed me that we had over twenty three hundred of their wounded who could not march, and had been sent into their lines at the request of Genl. Rosecrans, who to his surprise had written him a very polite letter asking that it be allowed.

Hugh will visit you shortly I hope, and if he does, I wish you would send me my stoutest pair of boots; those of the coarsest leather—it has been raining now for over twenty four hours, and it will be I expect so extremely muddy, one pair of stout boots will not be sufficient.

I hope the boys have been very careful with their guns, I am constantly anxious about them. I have been very anxious indeed to hear from Uldrick who was not yet well when you last wrote. I hope for a letter, tomorrow. Give my love with kisses to my daughter & to the children, to Bet and to my dear wife I send much love and good wishes good night. Your devoted husband L.

((( )))

Head Quarters Division
Camp Near Chattanooga [Tennessee]
October 14th/63 [Wednesday]

My Dear Wife
John E. returned this morning, no it was yesterday, bringing me two cotton undershirts, some butter, some apples. My boots and some preserves for all of which you have my best thanks and love and some kisses, if you could get them. And with them came three fine sweet potatoes presents from the children, for those kiss them all for me and thank them for their kind re-

membrance. Thank Mary Jane for her portion of the gift, and tell her that I promise something in return.

I was very much annoyed at your proposition to send Willie away from you. I can understand that your fears had blinded your judgement, and that you were unselfish enough to wish that your children should be away from the danger, and that your first wish carried your thoughts to your first born. But Willie is of all the children, the most helpless, and less able to bear the absence of his mother—he is so retired in his habits and so much wanting in perserverance, of that kind which pushes one along in the world, and so little disposed to make acquaintences, and requires so much nursing that he would suffer more than any other person of the children, by being away from you. And his constant thinking of what might happen to him, and the fear that he would not have those about him who would sympathise in his little peculiarities—would render both you and myself unhappy. I wrote to Bet about the children having notions put in their heads to leave their parents and wander off. Thus making them dissatisfied with their position and condition. In times like these we must all learn economy and try to be contented—try in every conceivable way to make the best of our circumstances, and to act so as contribute to the happiness of each other— I can do but little towards your enjoyment, except that no matter what may be my occupation or my troubles I try always to write encouragingly and cheerfully—my chief pleasure is to hear that you are well and happy and if I find that you or the children are discontented, I feel as if something might happen to let you all know that the bitter cup has not come upon you yet. It makes me tremble to be discontented with my lot, when I look around and see the misery and suffering everywhere else in comparison to which my lot is blessed indeed.

It has been raining nearly forty eight hours without intermission, the whole country is covered with water, the creeks are impassible, and our animals are tied to their stakes without food, it being impossible to cross Chicamauga River, which is between us and the station where supplies can be obtained—many of my command are without tents and hundreds are without blankets and shoes. Added to these wants, the ration is not sufficient, and hundreds are sick. This seems to be a most detestable climate and the men are suffering by the change from Virginia. Where there was order and system and satisfaction and a fine country with a fine climate.

The President has been here for some time endeavoring to settle the difficulties among the generals, I called on him and paid my respects, and rode along in his train when he inspected the troops but I have no acquaintance with him. I have never spoken twenty words to him and to tell you the truth I do not admire him, although he is about the best man we have. He is not despotic enough for the times. His authority is not sufficiently felt to correct existing evils and his manners are cold, and repelling. I hope he may be able to settle the difficulties so as to make the army homogeneous, but I doubt it very much—the recent rains must give us a heavy rise in the Tennessee river and will delay our movements as well as retard those of the enemy. I have never seen a more pertinaceos rain than we now have, it is without intermission.

I believe that now both of the contesting parties are beginning to believe that Chattanooga is the place to strike for ascendancy, and both sides are hurrying forward their forces towards this point. We must wait and see what developments time will make, perhaps the rain now falling is for our special benefit, may be for the enemy perhaps something may turn up in Europe for our benefit, France may recognize us and give active assistance. There may be a political revolution at the North, which will be of some assistance—General Lee may best the enemy in Virginia, or we may damage him here very seriously. There is always grounds for hope, and there are so many instances of good fortune coming to us, when we have no reason to expect any, that the motto should ever be, "Never despair!" so be of good cheer and write often. Keep the children satisfied and do not allow Bet to be coaxing them away to Kentucky or Missouri—if any one of the children should go, it should be Laura, for it is all important that she should be taught a variety of personal accomplishments, and habits, which it will take her some time to learn where she is—it is an old saying that if there is but one daughter in a family and two or three boys, the girl will be rough in her manners, showing the want of female association. The same can be perceived in Laura already, and I ascribe it to that cause. But this is no time to risk her departure, unless under peculiarly fortunate circumstances—but tis now late and I must to bed. Give my love to the children, with much love and many kisses. John E comes back full of Johnnys sayings & doings. My best love to Bet and my devoted love & many kisses to my dear wife from her devoted husband. L.

Give my love to sister if she is with you and if an opportunity offers give my thanks to Mr Dixon for the very fine cheese he sent me.[32]

32. Mr. Dixon has not been identified.

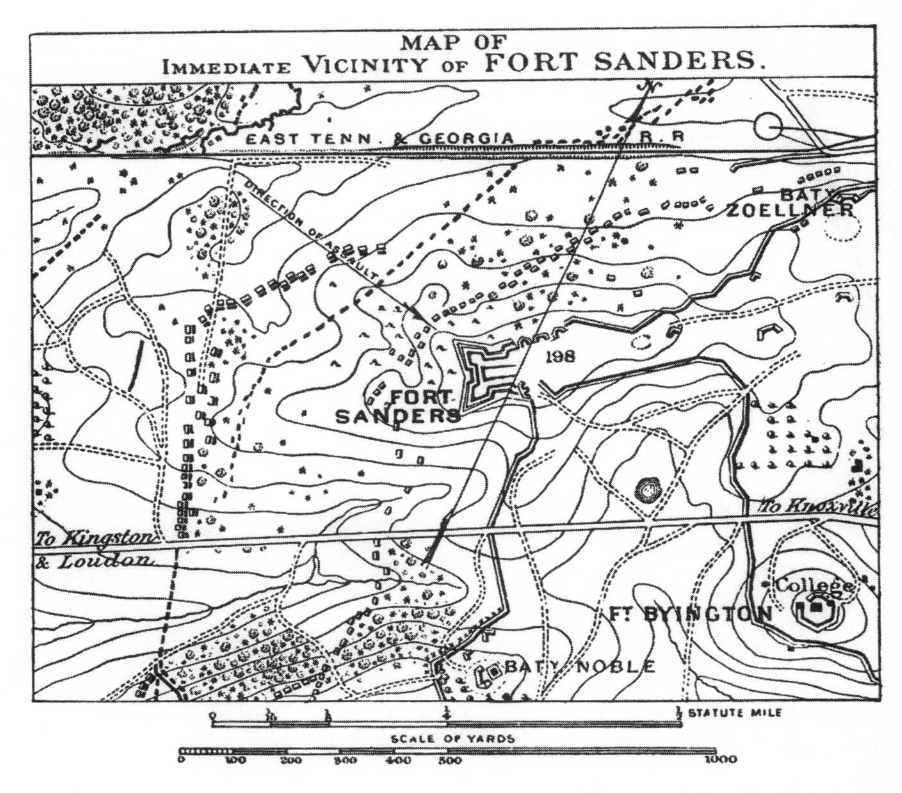

Map illustrating line of attack at Fort Sanders (Fort Loudon), Knoxville, Tennessee, on November 29, 1863. (OR, *ser. 1*)

((( )))

Asheville N.C.
December 21th 1863 [Monday]

Dear W

I arrived here a few hours ago on my way to Augusta Ga.

Tomorrow I will leave on horseback for Greenville S.C. where I expect to take the cars.

Captain Lamar & Willie are with me[,] both well.[33]

I have four horses. One a stallion for Hu, and three of my own.

I was ordered from the Army of East Tennessee by Genl Longstreet because I had exhibited a want of confidence in his plans and efforts and he was

33. George W. Lamar Jr., Georgia, captain. Lamar was a lieutenant and aide-de-camp to LM prior to his promotion to captain and assistant adjutant general.

afraid that my influence would extend to the troops under my command. The order reads as follows[:]

Head Quarters Near Bean Station
December 17th 1863
Special Orders
No 27

Major Genl L McLaws is relieved from further duty with the army and will proceed to Augusta Ga from which place he will report by letter to the Adj & Inspector Genl.

[letter ends here]

1864

I Demanded a Court-Martial

(Copy)
Augusta Georgia
January 17th 1864 [Sunday]

Gen S Cooper[1]
Adj & Inspecter Genl CSA
Richmond Va

On the 15th inst I received from Gen Longstreet's head quarters a copy of a charge preferred against myself with an accompanying letter, being a copy of one which he had forwarded to you, referring to the charges.

To prevent misunderstanding I herewith enclose copies of both the charges and letter.

I beg leave to remark concerning the charges and specifications.

The assault against Fort Loudon which as made by three brigades of my division on the morning of the 29th of November last, had been ordered to be made on the 28th the day previous at I think 2 P.M. perhaps earlier. But at *my request and on my suggestion,* it was delayed until the morning of the 29th to enable me to advance my line of sharpshooters, so as to fire along the enemys works and thus facilitate the advance of the assaulting columns by distracting & preventing the enemys fire.

The enemys pits were taken all along my line, and my sharpshooters advancing beyond them established a new line for themselves, within easy musket range of the main work. This was done, excepting the sharpshooters from Bryan's Brigade, & the exception was made for the following reasons. The sharpshooters of the brigade were arranged from left to right as follows, Woffords, Humphreys, Bryan and Kershaw. Kershaw'[s] line was so far advanced on the right that the connection could not be established with Bryan and Colonel Holt of the 10th Ga who commanded Bryan sharpshooters,

1. See *OR* 31:501–4, 497–98. Samuel Cooper, USMA 1815, spent thirty years in the artillery before becoming U.S. adjutant general in 1852. Born in New Jersey, he developed a close relationship with Jefferson Davis when Davis was U.S. secretary of war. Cooper was appointed adjutant general and was the highest-ranking Confederate general.

came to me some time in the night of the 28th informing me of the circumstances, requested authority to throw the right of his line back so as to protect his right flank, which I authorized him to do, deeming it essential for the safety of his line.[2]

The enemy had not long previous assaulted my line of sharpshooters by coming down on their flank which had not been properly supported on the left by the advance of Hoods division, and had taken their pits temporarily, but were finally driven back with considerable loss by the reserves coming up. I did not wish the experiment to be repeated, and therefore had the right of Bryans line thrown back or rather authorised to be done, but that it had any effect upon the final result, I deny because my loss was about fifty or sixty before reaching the ditch, and the enemy fired but one gun some say, and others but two upon the advancing columns being kept down by the sharpshooters.

To the 2 specifications I merely assert that the 17th Miss, Humphrey's Brigade and Phillips Ga Legion of Woffords Brigade, two as fine bodies of men and as well commanded as can be found any where, were selected to lead and did lead the assaulting columns, and they as well as all others, were ordered to take the work and hold it against all comers, until I arrived to direct otherwise.

My orders were to take the work, that was all for the assaulting columns to do, and I was notified that Gen Jenkins (commanding Hoods Division) would follow my columns and bear down to the left.[3]

I am at a loss to conceive as to what definite instructions further than those I gave could now have been given—as the inside of the work was an unknown quantity, which was what was to be done, after it was taken was to be found out.

If there was no ditch on the left, (the next side) that offered any obstacle & (but little) to the entrance to the work, I have been most egregiously misinformed for I have in my possession a paper which the accompanying one marked B is a copy, from the column of my division which assaulted on the left showing a very different state of affairs.

In regard to the men not being supplied with ladders or other means of crossing the ditch I was assured by Genl Longstreet himself and by members

2. Willis Cox Holt, Georgia, lieutenant colonel, later colonel, of the 10th Georgia, was trained as an attorney.

3. Micah Jenkins, South Carolina, South Carolina Military Academy, brigadier general.

of his staff who made observations of the work, how the heights around on both side of the river by means of powerful glasses, that there was no ditch that offered any great obstacle. I was pertinaceously pressed with the fact that there would be but little difficulty so far as the ditch was concerned in entering the work, and I endeavored to impress that fact upon the men, and in connection with it urged them to rush to the assault with impetiousity and without halting. How well my instructions were obeyed the history of the contest will show, I however contemplated getting bundles of wheat for the men to carry and fill up the ditch, if one was found offering a serious impediment to our advance, but there was not sufficient quantity available for the purpose where I expected to find it.

As for ladders I had no means, nor time, nor material to make any, the idea of obtaining them was entertained, but as I had nothing to make them with I said nothing about them deeming it unadvisable to broach the subject. No one ever mentioned the probability of any necessity for them as it was regarded as a work requiring dash and daring only.

If Gen Longstreet after reconnoitering the works had considered ladders or other means for crossing the ditch were necessary, I suppose he would have made some mention of them at least on some occasion. I should think it was his place to order them: his omission to do neither looks very strange, when he charges me with being criminally negligent in not getting them.

Tis an easy matter after the assault is over to see where errors have been committed but of these I am charged with, where if there was any fact, I do not consider myself responsible and hold myself unjustly charged and I object to being put forward as a blind to draw attention away from the main issue, which is the conduct of the Campaign in East Tennessee under Gen Longstreet.

I assert that the enemy could have been brought to an engagement before reaching Knoxville.

That the town if assaulted at all should have been on the first day we arrived or on the next at farthest.

That when the assault was made on Fort Loudon it was not called for by any line of policy what ever, but on the contrary no good result could possibly have been attained.

You will recollect that on the 29th of December alto [previous month] I forwarded to you a copy of an order relieving me from duty with Genl Longstreets command. Before leaving I addressed a note to his head quarters inquiring the reasons why the order was issued & the reply was "That having exhibited a want of confidence in the plans and efforts of Genl Longstreet throughout [page break] throughout the campaign on which he was then engaged he Genl L was apprehensive it might be extended to the troops under my command, and as he could not leave himself I was ordered to do so. This was the sole reason assigned at that time, yet after my departure charge of neglect of duty with three specifications was forwarded to your office against me, and in the letter accompanying the charges he writes that I was not arrested for the reason he thought I might be of service elsewhere.

I inquired why I was relieved from duty for the reason that if there was any part of my conduct needing investigation, I might before leaving be informed, so that I might make the necessary preparations to defend myself. But as it is now, you can perceive the disadvantage I am labouring under. I must [page break] I must therefore demand that the charges be investigated at an early day by Court of Inquiry or Court Martial or they be withdrawn, and I be assigned to duty at once.

Very Respectfully
Your most obdt Serv
L McLaws
Maj Genl

[note on back of letter]
Augusta Georgia
January 18th 1864
L McLaws
Maj Genl
PACS [Provisional Army of the Confederate States]
In relation to the charge
Made against him by
Lieut Genl J Longstreet
With three [four] enclosures[4]

[new page]

1" Order relieving me from duty with the army in E. Tenne.—the first intimation in any manner or shape, that anything of the kind was in contemplation.

2" Letter giving the reason for the order being issued—which was brought forth by my asking for it.

4. There are four enclosures: (1) the order relieving McLaws from duty, (2) a letter giving the reason for the order, (3) a copy of the letter by Longstreet to Cooper preferring charges against McLaws, and (4) a copy of the charges preferred against McLaws.

3" Copy of letter forwarded to Adj Gen[l] preferring charges against me—no court is asked for, as you will perceive, in my case.*

*I *demanded* a court martial which is the reason why I am ordered for trial.

4" Copy of charges preferred against me

[Enclosure 1: Order Relieving McLaws from Duty]

1" Head Quarters near Bean Station
December 17th 1863
Special Orders }
N[o]. 27 }

Major Gen[l] L McLaws is relieved from further duty with this army and will proceed to Augusta G[a] from which place he will report by letter to the Adj & Inspector Gen[l]. He will turn over the command of his Division to the senior Brigadier Gen[l] present.

By Command of Lt Gen[l] Longstreet
For Maj Gen[l] L McLaws G M Sorrel[5]
Lt Col & Adj Genl.

[Enclosure 2: Letter Giving Reason for the Order]

Head Quarters near Bean Station [Bean's Station, Tennessee]
December 17th 1863 [Thursday]

General

I have the honor to acknowledge receipt of your note to day, asking for the particular reason for the issue of the order relieving you from duty with this army.

In reply I am directed to say that throughout the campaign on which we are engaged, you have exhibited a want of confidence in the efforts and plans which the Com[dg] Gen[l] has thought proper to adopt and that he is apprehensive that this feeling will extend more or less to the troops under your Command.

Under these circumstances, the Com[dg] Gen[l] has felt that the interests of the public service would be advanced by your separation from him; and as he could not himself leave, he decided upon the issue of the order which you have received.

I have the honor to be Gen[l]
with great respect your obt servt

5. Gilbert Moxley Sorrel, Georgia, lieutenant colonel, later brigadier general.

G M Sorrel
Maj Gen[l] L McLaws   Lt Col & Adj Genl.

Twenty nine days [January 15, 1864] after I left East Tennessee I received the following from Genl Longstreets Head Quarters[:]

[Enclosure 3: Copy of Letter by Longstreet to Cooper Preferring Charges against McLaws]

Head Quarters Russelville E T. [Russellville, Tennessee]
Dec 20th 1863 [Sunday]

[addressee]
Official
GM Sorrel
AAGenl
Genl, S. Cooper
A&I Genl
Richmond

General
I have the honor to inclose herewith charges specified against Major Gen[l] L McLaws and against Brig Genl J B Robertson.[6]

I have no authority to order courts martial and have therefore to ask that a court be ordered for the trial of Brig Genl J B Robertson.

Genl McLaws was not arrested when he was relieved from duty here, for the reason that it was supposed that his services might be important to the government in some other position. If such is the case, I have no desire that he should be kept from that service or that his usefullness should be impaired in any way by a trial.

I remain Genl very resptly
your obt servt
J Longstreet
Lt Genl Comg

[Enclosure 4: Copy of Charges Preferred against McLaws]
Charge & Specifications against Major Genl L McLaws C.S.A.

6. Jerome Bonaparte Robertson, Kentucky, physician and brigadier general, was the commander of Hood's Texas brigade. Longstreet filed court-martial charges against him, but Robertson was never brought to trial.

Charge—Neglect of duty

Specification 1"—In this that Major Genl L McLaws being in command of a Division of the Confederate forces near Knoxville Tenn & being ordered by his commanding officer Lieut. Genl J Longstreet to advance his line of sharpshooters at dark on the night of the 28th of Nov to within good rifle range of the enemys works so as to give his sharpshooters play upon the enemy behind his works (it being part of a plan of attack, that the sharpshooters should engage the enemy behind his works, along our entire line, whilst an assault was made upon one of the enemys works) did fail to arrange his line of sharpshooters so as to meet this view, and did allow a portion of the rifle pits, to be sunk about two hundred yards from the point to be attacked under a hill, entirely out of view of the fort aforesaid, thus failing to give his assaulting columns the protection of the fire of his sharpshooters at this point during their advance & attack

Specification 2^{d}—In this that the aforesaid Major Genl L McLaws being ordered by his commanding officer Lieut Genl J. Longstreet to arrange assaulting columns of three of his Brigades and to attack the enemys fort at the north west angle of his works at dawn of day on the 29th of November did fail to organize a select body of men to lead in the assualt, as is customary in such attacks—and did allow his three Brigades to advance to the assault without definite and specific instructions for the leading columns and for the troops that were to enter the fort first. Which are essential to success in such attacks

Specification 3^{d}—In this that the aforesaid Major General L McLaws being ordered to assault the enemys position at the n. west angle of his works at daylight on the 29th of Nov, did make his attack upon a point where the ditch was impassable, and did fail to provide any of his assaulting columns with ladders or other means of crossing the ditch and entering the enemys works and did fail to inform his officers that the ditch on the west side of the fort was but a slight obstacle to his infantry and that the fort could be entered from that side with but little delay. Thus failing in the details of his attack to make the arrangements essential to success. All this near Knoxville Tennessee on or about the 28th & 29th days of November 1863.

J Longstreet
Lieut Genl

((( )))

[LM to ETM with no address or date.
The letter was written after LM left
Tennessee en route to Sparta.]

Concerning the first specification, I have abundant evidence to show that it is not true, nor founded on fact. &

The same concerning the 2nd specification

The third specification contains two very very contradictory points viz[:]

First, it is stated that, being ordered to assault the enemys position at the north west angle of the fort, I made my assault at a point where the ditch was impassable, and did fail to provide any of his assaulting columns with ladders or other means of crossing the ditch and entering the work. It so happens that I did assault the enemys works at the north west angle, just where I was ordered, and just where the ditch was impassible. So, the point of assault having been designated for me, I am not responsible for going there nor because the ditch was impassable there, the only fault than can be found is that I did not provide ladders and other means of crossing the ditch—and I did not provide them because I was assured by Genl Longstreet himself and his staff generally that there would be but slight obstacle in entering the work so far as the ditch was concerned. The second point is—that I failed in not informing my officers that the ditch on the west side of the work offered but a slight obstacle to the infantry in entering the work, to this I answer that I did not know then, nor do I know now that the ditch on the west side of the fort offered but a slight obstacle to entering the work[;] on the contrary I believe that it was not the case and have abundant evidence to prove it—and in addition, if Genl Longstreet knew that the ditch on the west side of the fort offered but a slight obstacle in entering the work, why did he not order the assault there, instead of at the angle, (the north west), where the ditch was impassable[?] I did not know before the assault that the ditch was impassable at the n.w. angle, nor that it was easy to be passed on the west side, I do not believe the latter to be the case now, as I have said before, but Genl Longstreet must have known the depth of the ditch at both places—or why does he charge the facts against me[?]—and if he did know, he is the criminal for ordering the assault in an impracticable place, and not informing me of it, so that ladders might be prepared to overcome the difficulty.

The night before the assault was ordered, I advised Genl Longstreet not to make the assault, but to delay it, because it was currently reported and believed that General Bragg had been defeated & driven back to Dalton

[Ga.]. I wished him to put off the attack until we could hear ~~from~~ definitely the fate of Genl Bragg for if GenlB had been defeated we could not expect to take Knoxville. If Genl Grant was defeated as some said, Knoxville would be ours as a matter of course, without a fight.

If Bragg was defeated and we pressed the enemy in Knoxville, they would retire to the opposite side of the river, and bidding us defiance, wait there until re-inforcements could be sent them, and then the tables would be turned on us, for we [would] be compelled to retire towards Virginia—leaving an immense number of wounded—for it would necessarily have been a severe battle, to have assaulted the numerous works about the town & the town itself—and then we would be retreating without ammunition or with but a very limited supply[.] —[U]nder these circumstances I thought the assault was highly injudicious to say the least of it—and I believe that an indictment for murder against Genl L would stand before any impartial jury.

This it is that has induced the charges—the result has shown that I was right and he was wrong. —Bragg was whipped—Grant sent re-inforcements to Burnside and we had to retreat towards Virginia.

I am charged with not having ladders to cross a ditch, which if crossed could have given us no advantage—and the superior who failed for lack of sound judgement in the whole campaign receives the thanks of Congress.

I wish you would share this paper to those friends of mine who you think would be interested in my vindication—I wrote the facts principally for Mr Harris, if he will honor me by reading them.[7]

Your devoted husband
L McLaws

((( )))

[LB1][8]
Near New Market, E. Tenn.
February 17, 1864 [Wednesday]

My dear wife.
Is anxious to hear from Sparta where wife & children are.

I have been following the court martial to this place, from Russelville to

7. LM might be referring to Isham Green Harris, former governor of Tennessee who served on Braxton Bragg's staff.

8. LB1 refers to letter extracts from McLaws's Letter Book, 1858–64. Virginia McLaws is the most likely editor and begins the extracts writing in the third person.

Morristown [Tenn.] & thence to New Market [Tennessee]. On the 14 I received notice that the court had adjourned indefinitely because of a letter received from Gen. Longstreet giving an a intimation of certain contemplated movements, to carry out which the services of all were needed & the same day I received an order from Gen. Longstreet head quarters directing me to repair to Abington [Abingdon] Va. 113 miles East of this and there await orders of Maj. Genl. Buckner, president of the genl court martial. I have not moved from here because the weather has been exceedingly stormy & cold & because my business here has not been completed with the qmaster of division in relation to the wagons, ambulances & mules left in Georgia and because my stay here was necessary to obtain the deposition of witnesses for my defense. If my trial does not (obtain) shortly I will send copies of the depositions of witnesses to the Adj. Genl. and demand that I be put upon duty at once, or that the charges be investigated at once. I am tired of this delay, of this uncertainty and wish something positive, something definite to occur. It appears as if Genl. Longstreet intends making an advance against Knoxville, but I do not suppose he contemplates an assault upon the place. The weather is so extremely cold that I doubt if any movement can be in contemplation for some time to come as the suffering of our men would not compensate for the prospective & doubtful advantage. However, I shall push everything towards the trial and hope to have the case decided before very long[.] [U]ntil then, let us hope on, hope ever, & put our trust in Providence.

Sends letter recd of pie plant by an officer who goes by S.C. [South Carolina] route which is quicker then the R.R. [railroad] via Lynchburg & Petersburg. Sends love to Willie, Johnny, Laura and Uldrick and my dearly beloved wife knows how dearly she is prized to look for any particular message assuring her of it—my best love to Sister.

((( )))

[LB1]

Near New Market [Tennessee]

Feb-18-1864 [Thursday]

Is busy getting depositions of witnesses in order that he (Gen McLaws) may be prepared for any emergency & can publish a history of the assault on Knoxville, should events so order that the trial does not take place.

The depositions are all favorable to me, & I am unable to conceive in what particular my duty was neglected. I received a letter from Hu giving a short account of a trip he had down the Chattahoochee with Gen Bragg who said that he had no doubt but the prosecution against me was because of my friendship for him, that I must be very much on my guard, as Buckner was a most perfect Jesuit & totally unreliable.[9] He laid the whole blame of the last fight at ~~Knoxville~~ Chattanooga upon Genl. Longstreet, & said also that his orders were for Genl. Longstreet to engage the enemy before reaching Knoxville. He was severe upon both L. [Longstreet] & Buckner.

((( )))

(March, 1864)
[no location or exact date]

Dear Hu
I propose to give you a succinct narrative of the Campaign in East Tennessee under Gen[l] Longstreet; so far as my knowledge and information of the movements enable me to do so.

We crossed the Holston River over a pontoon bridge, thrown across below Loudon, near Haughs ferry and marched, Hoods division leading, towards Knoxville. My division was halted at the point where the road leading to Lenoir Station [Lenoir's, Tennessee] on the R R leaves the main road we were on which lead to Campbells Station [Tennessee]—an old indian trading post or station, not a R R station. There I learned that Hoods Division had turned towards Lenoir station where the enemy was in force, what force however, was not known.

I was then ordered to relieve Genl Benning from picket duty on the road towards Campbells Station, which was done at once as Genl B had just been posted.[10] I then rode towards ~~Campbells~~ Lenoir Station and found Genl Longstreet upon a hill overlooking the Station. Genl Jenkins comdg Hoods Division was engaged in forming line of battle, as if to attack the enemy at Lenoir Station. I could see the ~~enemy~~ RR train moving from that station towards Knoxville & also batteries of Arty. It was getting dark however, and I had no idea that an attack could be made on that day, if one was intended, and getting an order from Genl Longstreet to camp my command where it was, I rode back to the forks of the road, arriving after dark & it was very dark, and gave orders to bivouac for the night.

If Genl Longstreet was in pursuit of the enemy it was not possible to bring

9. The Chattachoochee River is north of Atlanta, Ga.

10. Henry Lewis Benning, Georgia, Franklin College, was a lawyer by training. As a Confederate brigadier general, he attempted to obtain leave to defend LM at his court-martial. Henry L. Benning to LM, March 3, 1864, SHC-LM.

him to an engagement by turning towards Lenoir Station, at the time he did, but he could have done so most effectually by pushing on six or seven miles to where there was a road that led to the RR and gave a strong position, This could have been done by dark or a little after without difficulty, or he could have marched ahead of the enemy to Campbells Station.

14th at 8 oclock received orders to push on to Campbells Station. This was done without a delay of five minutes, and we reached the neighborhood of Campbells Station just after Genl Jenkins advance arrived at the same place. There my command was halted, and forming line advanced through the woods, to within sight of Campbells Station. One brigade Humpheys, was sent to the left. The others making a continual line, connecting with Hoods Division on the extreme right. After various marching & countermarching, I was ordered to form line across the valley & advance against the enemy which was done gallantly[.] [T]he enemy however retired as we advanced & took a position firing on us with two batteries farther to the rear. Genl Jenkins I had understood was to make a flank attack on the right, but he did nothing.

My line was halted about a ½ mile in advance of Campbells Station & remained until dark when we were ordered to camp for the night. I omitted to mention that my advance had been skirmishing with the enemy during the entire day up to the moment of halting.

The next morning about 8 oclock advanced rapidly, skirmishing, driving the enemy until we came in sight of them ~~enemy~~ upon a hill about two miles from Knoxville. Our skirmishers drove beyond Armstrongs house & occupied the house & a line in front of the enemy. Confronting as believed a line of entrenchments compised of fence rails, Kershaws Brigade occupied the front & right, Bryan supporting him about 400 yards in rear. Humphreys on the left of Kershaw and Woffords Brigade commanded by Colonel Ruff supporting Humphreys.[11] Hoods Division in the mean while was marching to the left, so as to envelope the city, the cavalry on the extreme left.

On the 17th Genl Kershaw was ordered to assault the enemy's line of rail entrenchments, which was done with great gallantry & with loss [o]f about 150 men.

From this time forward, no attempt was made against the enemy's position, but they were allowed to strengthen their positions without hinderance.

11. Solon Zackery Ruff, Georgia, colonel, killed at Knoxville.

Notes on my defense [handwritten by McLaws on the side panel] [letter ends here].

((( )))

Abingdon Virginia
March 1/1864 [Tuesday]

My dear Sweetheart
I am still at Abingdon waiting for action.

I wrote you that I had written Genl Bragg and to the Adj Genl in relation to my case. No answer has as yet been received. I expect one tomorrow or next day.

To day Major Edwards arrived here on his way to Richmond. He is ordered there to arrange about supplies for the Army in East Tenn^e^.

I gave him a written statement of the difficulties between myself & Genl L & he will show them to Humphrey Marshal, and get his opinion in relation to them.[12]

When Ally was in Richmond he showed Humprey Marshal the letter from Genl L assigning his reasons for relieving me from command with the Army in East Tenn^e^ and Humphrey remarked it was a "d—d piece of foolishness."

The weather has been very mild for some days past, even now, although it is snowing it is warm enough to do without fires—the season altogether is said to be very mild, and free from storms. Such has been the case throughout the whole South and in consequence the enemy has been moving against us in various quarters,

1" Across Mississippi, threatening Mobile & Selma
2^d^ Across Florida
3^d^ Against Genl Johnston, at Dalton

It has pleased our heavenly father that our forces should be successful against our enemies in every instance thus far, and let us hope his favors will be continued.

I received a few days ago a letter from Mrs Susan Archer Voce Weiss, formerly Miss Susan Archer Talley,[13] the lady about whom I wrote when on the Peninsula—she asks for my photograph— I have replied that, being far away

12. Humphrey Marshall, Kentucky, a former brigadier general, was a member of the Second Confederate Congress from Kentucky.

13. Susan Archer Voce Talley Weiss.

from all artists, and not having a "carte de Visite" with my portrait, I must decline, or rather, regretted to inform her that I could not comply with her request.[14]

If you will give your consent, & will send me one from Augusta, I will forward it to Mrs Voce Weiss.

Her letter is enclosed for the edification of Sister Laura and yourself.

John E. will find out in Richmond whether or not it will be better for you to sell your gold & invest in Confederate "four percent bonds" and will telegraph me accordingly, or will write to you on the subject.

You wrote me that Walker Taylor was with Genl Wheeler. The Qmaster of my Division [J. J. Middleton] informed me that he had given him some eight thousand dollars wherewith to buy horses, when we were at Chattanooga, & had not heard from him since—[15] I doubt the story very much—and wish, if you can reach Walker, you would copy what I have written and send it to him, with my request that he would answer in letters to yourself—Major Edwards and myself—and do so at once. Major Edwards has written him to the care of Genl Wheeler. but the letter may not reach him—if you can be pretty sure of your letter getting to him, write at once.

My dear wife, I send you a thousand kisses and love from my whole heart. Do write me often and tell all about yourself and the children to whom give much love and many kisses—my best love to sister, and best respects to Mrs Sasnett & Mrs Little &c[,] your devoted L.[16]

I sent to W^{m}R, Willies pants (forwarded by Capt Forbes) and a piece of calf skin which I hope you will get. I expect Willies letter daily.

14. A carte de visite was a small photographic image pasted on the back of a card.

15. Joseph Wheeler, Georgia, USMA 1859, Confederate major general; Jonathon J. Middleton Jr., major and quartermaster.

16. Mary Sasnett was a planter in Sparta, Ga. In 1860 she had real estate valued at $20,300, and the value of her personal estate was $60,000. She had two sons living with her at the time of the census, Henry, age 15, and Joseph, age 13. Eighth Census, 1860, Mayfield, Hancock County, Ga., entry for Mary Sasnett household, 586. Mrs. Little has not been identified.

((( )))

Abingdon, Virginia
March 6th 1864 [Sunday]

My dear Wife
Your letter of the 26th reached me this morning, about eight days coming. The one of the 14th by Mr Middlebrooke was recd yesterday[,] nineteen days on the way—so the mail is quicker than private conveyance.[17]

In relation to Willie— It will be too far for him to walk as the summer comes on & if he desires it and you think it proper—I would either not let him walk, but stay at home when the weather is too warm and he cannot ride—or I would change his school. There is no difficulty about it, I am sure! From your account of Willies studies at Johnstons, he would be no worse off at Mr Smiths in that regard and would be better off in being more convenient to the school house. I preferred Mr Johnston in one respect only, I thought the society of larger boys after Willies residence in the army would be more agreeable to him and also more instructive, but if there are other reasons in favor of Mr Smiths outweighing the advantages offered by the other. Why not my dear wife let the scales go down on the Smith side and let Willie go to Mr Smith.[18]

I bought a grammar yesterday from a store in town called "Quackenbos' first lesson in English composition"[;] it is the only book I have ever seen which is understandable for a child.[19] I will try and get another, and also some "Readers." 1" 2d 3d Readers for Laura—Johnny—& Willie, and perhaps can send them to Augusta by express. The Quackenbos book is certainly a very instructive one, the learner is gradually led into understanding the subject and by the force of his own reasoning. In the old grammars, for instance, we are told that "adverbs qualify verbs, adjectives and sometimes other adverbs and then follows one or two examples—but in this "Quackenbos" [t]he subject of adverbs is commenced as follows[:]

17. R. Middlebrooke.

18. Mr. Smith and Mr. Johnson have not been identified. It is possible that LM was confused in hearing ETM's description of events that took place in Sparta. There were three Smith households: one headed by a planter, the other two by overseers. An eighteen-year-old teacher named Mary Johnson lived with the George Smith family. The Smith home was relatively close to the Sasnett home, and the children Mary taught were slightly younger than Willie. Eighth Census, 1860, Mayfield, Hancock County, Ga., entries for George Smith and Mary Johnson household, 524.

19. G. P. Quackenbos, *First Lessons in Composition* (New York: Appleton, 1862).

Quest[n]. What is the sixth part of speech[?]
Answer. The adverb[.]
Q. What is the meaning of adverb[?]
A. Joined to a verb.
Q. Why are adverbs joined to verbs[?]
A. To modify them.
Q. In the sentence "George struggled hard[,]" [w]hat word tells how he struggled?
Answer—hard
Question—Then hard is joined to or modifies what word?
An—The verb struggled
Ques[tn]—What part of speech then, is "hard"?
Ans—An adverb
Ques[tn]—Are adverbs ever joined to any other words besides verbs?
Answer—Yes, adverbs modify verbs, adjectives & other adverbs &c &c—

Thus the learner is gradually lead up to understand the rule—and then numerous examples are given, and lessons for him to supply the words & then point out others until the subject must be *under*stood, with but very slight explanations from the teacher.

I received a letter from Hu this morning telling me that he had heard Gen[l] Cobb was applying for my Division— I cannot conceive that such is the case unless Gen[l] C wishes it transferred to Georgia, for I have more confidence in his patriotism than to suppose for a moment, he wishes to command troops in the field. But I think it probable that Gen[l] L wrote to Gen[l] Cobb informing him of my being ordered away, and as Gen[l] C has no command he thought it a good idea to have my Division ordered to Georgia, or down somewhere in the south west to defend the country against the attacks of the enemy now promising to be more frequent, as the enemy have a large and increasing force of negroes, which they would like to find employment for, and there would no force better calculated to give confidence to the people, than a Division of old troops. I think it probable that such is the real state of the case—but Hu hearing that Cobb had made application to get command of my Division (which may be untrue after all) has thought that there was some conspiracy against me, and denounces it & the parties concerned.

Such money as you have on hand and cannot invest in—five dollar bills had perhaps be better invested in four per cent bonds or paying all your debts up to the month of April, however.

You say that you are getting more fleshy every day?!!!! What must *I* do?

I know two persons in this place besides the gentleman at whose house I am staying, but have a very pleasant room, and a good table for which I pay ten dollars per day.

John E is expected back to night and will give me all the news which I will write you tomorrow or the next day—

I am writing in a hurry to be in time for the mail.

So good night my dearly beloved darling—give much love and kisses to all the children and love to sister—my best respects to Mrs Sasnett & Mrs Little & family.

Your devoted
L.

((( )))

Abingdon V^a
March 8th/64 [Tuesday]

Your letter of the 20" of Feby was received this morning.

Let me thank you very sincerely and with twenty kisses for it, and again for the others lately received giving me so much pleasure. It is a long time since I received a sweeter letter than the one of this morning.

I am very glad that the papers containing an account of my difficulty should have given satisfaction. That the charges are malicious I am more and more convinced every day, but on that point there need be no discussion until after the trial.

I will leave this place tomorrow to attend the court which is ordered to assemble on the, 10th, day after tomorrow at Greenville E.T., and will write you from time to time from that place.

Tell Laura that Hu writes me that Dr Ganahl was considered one of the most promising young lawyers in Georgia and it was necessary for me to have one because I was not with the command. Genl Longstreet ordered me away from my witnesses and it was necessary for me to have some one to look at my interests and to counteract the many evil reports and false impressions which which were being put in circulation by my enemies. Doctor G has already silenced several slanders, and had done me considerable benefit by correcting false impressions made by Longstreets emissaries.[20]

20. Joseph Ganahl Jr. was appointed surgeon on June 17, 1862. He was mentioned on September 30, 1862, as a major and surgeon in Longstreet's corps, where he was

You know that it is a device of lawyers, to create a general impression in a community favorable to their views before a trial takes place or to at least prevent the opposite party from prejudicing the public mind against them. You have in your own experience no doubt, noticed how a community is prejudiced with very little effort when there is no one present to represent the other side.

Now by having Doctor G, who has gone into the business with his whole heart and devotes his whole time to it, to create correct views as to my case and disabuse those who have been falsely informed and is watching the manuevers of the opposite party, and Genl Benning to add to this favorable influence by the weight of his character, I am at least as well taken care of as if I had been allowed to be present myself and Genl Longstreets scheme to injure me will lose nearly all its effect. It was absolutely necessary to have some one to watch over my interests, and when I sent for Doctor Ganahl there was no one else, with whom I was acquainted, who had any reputation for talents or independence of character as Genl Benning was away and would not return until after the trial—as was there to be conducted.

I wrote you that, hearing Genl Bragg was in Richmond, I had written him a letter giving a short synopsis of my case and asking his advice—but that learning he was appointed to conduct the military operations of the government, under the President—I had written him another letter recalling my first. Yesterday I recd a reply from Genl B of which the following is a copy.

((( )))

Head Quarters Armies of the
Confederate States 4 March 1864

My dear General,
Your two comm[s] [communications] reached me by same mail, but the case was so extraordinary and involved so much calculated to destroy the integrity of the service—that I determined to use the information.

Orders have been given to the President of the Court, evidently a tool in interest against you that will most probably secure you from further delay and annoyance.

---

assigned to the 10th Georgia. Ganahl took sick leave after the court-martial and on January 20, 1865, was transferred to the office of the medical director in Charleston, S.C. LM and Ganahl exchanged four letters from 1890 to 1897 that can be found in SHC-LM. Compiled Service Records of Confederate Generals and Staff Officers & Non-regimental Enlisted Men: Joseph Ganahl, NARA M 331, RG 109.

The irregularity already committed cannot be commented on until the official proceedings are recd. They will not then escape attention.

This matter has been carried so far that self defense may require you to attack, and I can assure you the evidence in my possession is ample to convict of disobedience of orders, neglect of duty, and want of cordial co-operation and support, which resulted in all the disasters after Chicamauga. This matter is worthy of your consideration.

Genl Law has seen me on the subject, as far as his command is concerned—

Genl Benning I hear is equally sore and under the ban of authority because he prefers his country to a faction.

Wishing you every success and happiness.
I am truly yours
Braxton Bragg

((( )))

Maj Gen L M^c^Laws
Abingdon V^a^

General B speaks very plain and to the purpose.

His advice I think of following in relation to the attack.

But yet I will not join a faction in doing it but will make my own movement and on my own responsibility.

My dear sweetheart[,] your letter is so kind and loving and encouraging that I can not express how much pleasure it gives me.

I have applied to be ordered to Augusta when the court adjourns, and will I hope find you well and happy, and I hope we may be together some days. If fortune so favors me, you must be prepared and be as kind to me as my bad fortune of late requires to restore my equanimity and eveness of temper.

I recd a telegram this evening from Buckner to appear before the court on the 10th at Greenville. I wrote you a long letter on yesterday relative to Willie & the children. Many kisses & much love [for] you. L

I wrote you to remove Willie to Sparta if you thought it tiresome for him to walk, or let him stay away from school on those days.

My love to Willie and Johnny and Laura & Uldrick & to Sister.

((( )))

Greenville, E.T. [Tennessee]
March 12/64 [Saturday]

My dearly beloved wife
I have received no late letters from you but suppose the cause is my change of residence from Abingdon to this place.

I rec[d] from Hu however a very long letter, giving me advice principally. He mentions of having heard from you, and that everybody was well—for which thank heaven.

This is the season for kites and I hope that our boys are engaged in that pastime. I never could make a kite that would fly unless I ran with it very hard against the wind, but then in my boy days there were no books which taught how to make kites. I suppose that Willie & Johnny with the assistance of the boys own book can fly as high a kite as any body. I hope to hear of them trying at any rate.

My trial commenced yesterday and two witnesses were examined for the prosecution, both of whom testified as strongly as possible in my favor.

One of the witnesses[,] Col now Brig Gen[l] E P Alexander[,] chief of Arty of Genl Longstreet[,] was introduced by the J.[udge] Advocate, with a grand flourish, as having been formerly an officer in the Engineer Corps of the U.S. Army, a graduate of the West Point Military Academy, Chief of Arty of Gen[l] Longstreet and one too in whom Gen[l] had all confidence, confiding all his plans to & consulting him on all occasions. He then put some well digested formal questions to him, which were answered in the most precise terms, and then the witness was turned over to the defense—whereupon Gen Alexander gave his testimony in full and as strongly as possible in my favor. He declared that he made a reconnaissance of the enemys works, and the result was his conviction that there was no ditch at the north west angle of the enemys works that offered any obstacle to entering the works[,] that he repeatedly declared this to Gen[l]. Longstreet and myself and repeatedly advised that the assault be made at that point and that it was his opinion which he expressed openly, there was no use for ladders or fascines to get over the ditch.[21]

The other witness, the next, was Surgeon Cullen, who visited the fort

21. Edward Porter Alexander, Georgia, USMA 1857, colonel, later brigadier general. Four postwar letters between LM and Alexander can be found in SHC-LM.

under a flag of truce[.][22] [H]e testifies that the ditch at the angle where the assault was made was not more than than four feet deep but that along the sides of the work it was *ten* feet deep and ten feet wide at least, and yet I am charged with not informing my officers that the ditch at the sides offered *no* obstacle to entering the work.

Thus by two witnesses for the prosecution I am fully acquitted of the third specification, concerning which my friends had more concern then for any other.

Your statesman Buckner I think evinces a sincere desire to have me convicted and also to get Longstreet in a scrape for the evident purpose of getting command. I believe that Genl Bragg is right in his estimate of his (Buckners) character.

I will write you from time to time my dear wife as the trial progresses. But there is an evident intention of Buckners to put off the trial if he can have it done by any hocus pocussing.

Willies letter has not been received.

Hu wrote me that he had told Mr Hazelhurst that he could have the horse for 1600 dollars—[23] I can hardly advise you, whether to dispose of him or not, but unless you are convinced that it would be better it does not seem to me that there is anything to gain by selling until after the first of April and then for available funds—my best love and kisses for my contented little daughter and the mischief making master Uldrick.

My best love to Willie & Johnny.

Give my best respects to Mr Harris & family & to Mrs Sasnett & Mrs Little & all with you. I leave this morning for Blue Springs, 9 miles from here, to which place the court has adjourned[;] address your letters however to this place. I recd Sisters very welcome letter which will be answered very shortly. [letter ends here]

((( )))

[LB1]
Burkesville Va
May 16-/64 [Monday]

I reached here on Fri. evening last & found all conn[ection] with Richmond cut off by means of raiding parties. I took command, have been busily engaged in trying to keep main points secure from their depredations & have

22. Dr. J. S. D. Cullen.

23. Mr. Hazelhurst has not been identified.

fortunately been successful up to this time. The news [about] Richmond is very cheering indeed[.] Beauregard has succeeded in repulsing & defeating Butler. Breckenridge has defeated Seigel in the Valley. Johnston repulsed the assaults in Georgia.[24]

((( )))

Savannah Geo.
June 5th 1864 [Sunday]

My dear wife
Your letter of the second has been received[;] it came this morning, for which accept my sincere thanks.

My health is all right again & I am on duty as well as ever.

Tell Laura that I called on Aunt Eliza and Mrs Thomas & family and found them all well—the Thomas family[,] particularly Miss Eliza and Captain Thomas whom you saw in Sparta[,] expressed their unfeigned? regrets that you were not with me and that you would not live in Savannah. I sympathised with them for their great deprivation, and hoped that circumstances would permit your coming occasionally—groundnuts were handed around and I put some in my pockets and left having done my duty.[25]

There is a great deal of care and responsibility resting with the commanding officer here. The line is so extensive and there are so many salient points, all of which are vital in their nature—and there are so few troops to defend any one of the points that one is kept anxious all the while.

The enemy lying at Tybee Island and around Fort Pulaski and at Hilton Head [S.C.] can at any time make irruptions upon points of our coast along the numerous inlets, and owing to the scattered conditions of our troops a great deal of damage could be inflicted before an available force could be collected to drive them back.

Major Genl Hunter so the prisoners say has been placed in command at Fort Pulaski, and General Foster of the Department—as they are both negro men—not in color but in principle—this looks as if it was intended to make

24. General P. G. T. Beauregard kept Major General Benjamin Franklin Butler's Army of the James at bay near Drewry's Bluff, Va. Major General John Cabell Breckinridge defeated Major General Franz Sigel, commander of the Department of West Virginia, at the Battle of New Market on May 15, 1864. General Joseph E. Johnston attempted to repulse Major General Joseph Hooker at Resaca, Ga., on May 14–15, 1964.

25. Mrs. Thomas was Ella Gertrude Clanton Thomas of Augusta, Ga. The journal she kept before, during, and after the war provides remarkable insight into home front issues and life in Augusta. Ella G. C. Thomas, *Secret Eye.*

a campaign with the negro troops against some point of our coast—all this depends however upon the result of the struggles now going on in Virginia and Northern Georgia—[26] If we are successful there, we will have nothing to fear.

I dined yesterday with Genl Henry R Jackson of this place, in company with Colonel Brown A D C of President Davis and Superintendent of Conscripts of the State of Georgia, and had a good chicken & a good glass of wine.[27]

Captain Lamar has rented a house with four rooms, which will be cleaned out, and whitewashed tomorrow prepratory to our occupation—we will not have much furniture—nothing beyond the fine chairs I brought with me, and my cot— Captain Lamar may however get something from his numerous relations.

I am staying at the Pulaski house, eating my substance up very rapidly, and therefore am anxious to commence housekeeping.

My trunk and contents arrived all safe— I found the vest inside & have been wondering ever since until your letter came, how it got there.

Captain Lamar has no children and therefore proposes to bring his wife down to keep house[;] of course I cannot object, although I would prefer it should be otherwise.

Mention to Mrs Sasnett that I will—that it is my ardent desire to look after and advance her sons if it can possibly be done. Their being attached to an artillery company is however a decided obstacle, as artillerists are always much needed, and their duties are specific so much so that the absence of any one impairs the efficiency of the whole company.

My command here will be much more responsible than it ever was before, and my force larger.

I took the pay account from W^{m}R in order to have it cashed here but I am told that there is no money in the Q^{r}Mr Department— I will however try tomorrow, and will at once send you what you desire.

Tell Willie that I am very much obliged to him for going to Mr Smith—my time has been so much occupied ~~however~~ that I have not been able to write him as was my intention—but hope to do so in a few days. —I hope

26. David Hunter, Illinois, USMA 1822, major general of U.S. volunteers, later retired brevet brigadier general, U.S. Army; John Gray Foster, New Hampshire, USMA 1846, major general of U.S. volunteers, later major general U.S. Army.

27. Henry Rootes Jackson, Georgia, Yale 1839; William M. Browne, Georgia, colonel, later appointed brigadier general by Jefferson Davis, but the Confederate Senate refused to confirm the appointment.

Johnny is no longer suffering with his stone bruise in the foot and in his head and arm and that he and Willie will stay out of the sun and away from the branch.

Master Uldrick and Laura I hope are contented and happy—give both of them much love and many kisses.

My best love to Sister, and my best respects to Mrs Sasnett & family.

Keep Yourself healthy and happy my dear wife and I'll be content.

Your devoted L.

I send Bets letter, which Mr Pratte got from John Edwards, with a short note on it from M^r^ P—you will remark that he has the hoop &c in viero.

((( )))

Savannah G^a^
June 23 1864 [Thursday]

My Dear darling Wife
As I leave in the morning to inspect Fort McAllister on the Ogeechee river & will be gone two days, I write you to day so that you may hear from me before Tuesday.

I will write to Hu who owes me thirty dollars and ask him to subscribe for the Constitutionalist for you.[28]

Colonel J. C. Fiser of the 17th Miss Regt[,] formerly of Barksdales Brigade under my command[,] has been assigned to duty with me as Inspector. He has just come from Richmond and says there is a perfect feeling of security there—in regard to Grants army.[29] Col F. tells me that it [is] the universal opinion that Longstreets charges against me were of a purely malicious character and that great injustice has been done me. I am glad to be getting my old companions in arms about me; I wish there were some more of them, as the officers here, generally, are wanting in experience and the prestige which long service in the field gives. The Colonel has lost an arm in the service, and is one of the most gallant men in the army.[30]

There is so much manueuvering among the people here in relation to command and positions. —The officers who have been in command here were natives of this town with large family influences, and the ramifications are difficult to follow & the manifold abuses arising from this state of affairs

28. *Savannah Constitutionalist.*

29. Ulysses Simpson Grant, Ohio, USMA 1843, Union lieutenant general and future U.S. president.

30. Colonel Jonathan C. Fizer lost an arm in leading the attack at Fort Loudon, Knoxville, on November 29, 1863.

you can well imagine. It will require some time for me to shake myself clean from the cliques and act independently, or as I really would desire.

Captain Lamar and his wife have not yet appeared in my house, and I have been eating alone, until to day when Colonel Fiser arrived[;] he will mess with me.

There is such a demand for houses in Savannah that it is very difficult to obtain a room even—we were lucky in getting a whole house. The town is crowded and those who have island residences are moving into them.

I wish I could see my way clear enough in the future to enable me to have you and the children with me, but at present everything appears in a state of uncertainty and confusion. By the time winter sets in, I hope to be in position to ask you down, the unhealthy months here are September and October—to provide as much as possible for myself I have been trying to engage a house upon one of the sea islands, which would be far preferable to the town, but fear I will not be fortunate enough to make everything suit.

I intend to have Malcomb Johnson, son of Col J, detailed as clerk in the Office of my Inspector. The Colonel having but one arm, needs a young man with him, who is well educated, a good writer and of quick intelligent mind, & I have thought that Malcomb would suit him perhaps better than most any other one.[31]

Concerning the horse, I have thought that perhaps he had better be advertised for sale, but will write to Hu to night and ask him if he knows any one who wants to buy.

You must try and be contented my dear wife and make the children so, or at least do not let them long too much to come down—away from their home. The Yankees are it appears aware of the depletion of our coasts—of the great majority of our troops[,] and as their navy is unemployed[,] [t]hey may at any moment attempt some movement. I am thus continually on the alert, either travelling about or in my office, and therefore could give but little of my time to amusing them or taking care of them—and then the sun is so exceedingly hot, it would be a great risk for them to be exposed to it. And again there is absolutely no place to fish within a long distance of the town, and I would have no time to go. Again the Malaria from the rice fields is considered fatal you know for residents of even one night. These things can be shown to the children and they can perceive the great anxiety I would

31. Malcom T. Johnson; Lieutenant Colonel Thomas C. Johnson. Fiser had been transferred from the Invalid Corps to LM's command on June 16, 1864; LM assigned him as chief inspector on July 27. NARA M 331, RG 109.

have about them should they be here with me. All of which you have no doubt impressed on their minds already.

After this long homily, I must close and wish you a good evening, with many happy thoughts. Your must write me what the boys are doing with themselves and how the little one gets along and what my little daughter says & does—suppose you take Uldrick to Dr Steiner in Augusta or Dr Paul F. Eve and let them see what can be done—I think it not improbable that it would be better to use the knife at once.[32] With all my best wishes and much love, I remain as ever your devoted L.

((( )))

Savannah G[a]
June 28th 1864 [Tuesday]

My dear Emily

I assure you that there are but few persons who can write like Miss Susan Archer Talley, although it is not so much to be wondered at for besides being a woman of very rare gifts as a writer[,] [s]he has cultivated her powers by constant practice, and wrote in fact for her sustenance in life—she made it her business in life—in addition she was forced to write, for she could not talk— [W]e do not wonder at a professional writer expressing herself well, any more than we would at a professional dancer, dancing well—or a professional singer, going through all the scale of the gamut—their proficiency in their several avocations please us, and we applaud but there we stop and think no more of them. It would be a bore for me to write to Miss Talley, for I would feel compelled to be very particular in expressing myself, be anxious about my english and my orthography—and cease thereupon to take pleasure in the correspondence-she would write very free and easily expressed letters and mine would be constrained and unnatural— I therefore do not write Miss Susan, unless to keep up her good esteem which I gained by being polite on the two occasions we met while on the Peninsula & and on the last, advising her against the attentions of a man, who I knew was courting her for no honest purpose— I gained her good will, and the man, a Major Hawes, promised to shoot me.[33] I however treated him with contempt, and there ended the matter between him & me at least thus far.

I neglected to call on Miss Talley when in Richmond, in fact forgot to do it, and I am sorry for it, for she appeared to be a good friend of mine. If I

32. Dr. J. Paul Eve of Augusta, Ga.

33. Major Richard Randolph Hawes.

had another photograph I would send it to her. Since you have recalled her to my memory; although you are jealous because she writes me and wishes my photograph.

I can recollect far enough back in my childhood to remember that I always thought that holidays were for play and not for study, and thought it very hard that I should be called to my books, when I was just at that time always in the best part of my play. So I do not wonder at my boys grumbling at having to study. But I do not suppose that you are very hard upon them during these hot days.

Yesterday was so exceedingly hot that I was steaming all day and far into the night. It is my intention to ask Mr Sasnett to mess with me so soon as Lamar and myself commence housekeeping in earnest, which will happen in two or three days.[34] Richard has a leave of absence for ten days which he will take advantage of in a few days.

I saw the programme of the concert in Sparta, it must have been a grand affair. I would have been very much pleased to have attended and heard Miss Ballard[;] the other performers mentioned, I do not know.[35]

We have sent scouts upon the different islands along the coast and from all that can be found out, there is no raid in contemplation—nor have I been able to discover that there was even any intention to make a raid—it is believed by many that the report of a raid was gotten up by [Governor Joseph E.] Brown to keep the reserves from being ordered to Savannah or was invented by the Augusta reserves themselves for the same purpose. It is always better however to be on our guard, and be ready to meet the foe, let him come from whatever direction and at what time they choose. In regard to the horse—if the prices have very much decreased since I was there, will you please ask at what price I can obtain a horse from that section, a good riding animal for myself.

Sister writes me from Augusta that Hus child, the youngest, is in a low state of health, with the summer complaint. I was told yesterday that salt and water taken freely, but not in sufficient quantity to produce vomiting was one of the very best remedies. That it seldom required more than two or three doses to cure it—and that it was a certain cure for chills and fever, without too producing the bad results of quinine. You may be sure that I will try it, [s]hould I be so unfortunate to be attacked with any of those complaints.

34. Harris H. Sasnett, a member of the Terrell Light Artillery. Harris and his brother R. W. Sasnett were sons of Mary Sasnett. LM refers to both men several times.

35. Miss Ballard has not been identified.

Tell the boys that I sincerely thank them for the little study they do in their holiday times—even for that—and hope they will at least enjoy themselves, and keep healthy. I think they might write me a line or two now and then, just to keep up acquaintainship— I hope my little daughter is doing well and keeps herself busy and in full enjoyment, and tell Master Uldrick that when I come to see him I will try and bring a heap of cake provided he is a good boy, and gets his Ma to say so—my best respects to Mrs Sasnett and the family[,] also to Mrs Harris & family. Good night my dear wife, take care of yourself & write me. Your devoted L.

When you try I think you write a much sweeter letter than Miss Susan could to save her life.

((( )))

Savannah G^a
July 9th 1864 [Saturday]

My Dear Wife
I am off for to day on a trip to visit some fortifications about eleven miles from town and will be gone all day. I expected to write you a long letter this evening but may not be able.

I have been unable to obtain a bed or bedstand or mosquito bar from Mrs Huegenin (Aunt Eliza) or any body else, and will write to Hugh and see if he can spare one, otherwise I think we will have to meet at the half way house on the Sand Hills, and see ourselves for a day or two at a time.

There is an amount of heat in the atmosphere of this place surpassing ordinary comprehension, and I am in a semi fluid state all day. I still keep on my thick clothes, for they are generally regarded as the most healthy when a change of climate is made.

My time is very much taken up, and I am exceedingly annoyed with the reserve troops. All other kinds, excepting artillery, has been taken from me, and my dependence therefore is placed on a mob of unarmed, undisciplined, undrilled, crowd of men—who are as ignorant of the art of war as if they were young children.

The attack upon Charleston seems to be a determined affair but as it has not succeeded up to this time, I am in hopes it will be destined to end in disastrous failure[.] [T]he 1st G^a Regulars, the one in which I first entered service—then a state regiment has been engaged on Johns Island, and repulsed the enemy at every assault.

W^mR is at Turners Rock on Whitemarsh Island with his company and I have no doubt is very much pleased, as it is the coolest place in my command, and noted for its fishing and crab qualities. In addition he has a fine garden to draw from; which in connection with the other advantages will make his residence as delightful as a visit to Newport or any other sea coast watering place. He has been asking for my big tent, and does this perhaps with the intention to send for his wife. He was annoyed when I told him that Genl Jackson who commands the reserve forces, informed me that he desired to retain Captain Dyes company in Savannah.

You perhaps have received my letter sent by Harris Sasnett with five hundred dollars enclosed, and I am patiently (a little impatient) waiting your answer.

Our bedding will all have to come from some other place besides Savannah, if you decide on a visit. I have no sheets to my bedding, it has all disappeared under the combined influences of my stupid and ignorant & conceited fool of a boy John & the mistress no 2 of Bills house. So I have merely my old blanket and buffalo robe & counterpane bed, and the house top shaped mosquito bar—if you come however you shall have it, and I will sleep somewhere in the vicinity.

The children must bring their own accomodations.

Have you not a bedstead and bedding at Hughs, or Marys? besides the iron bedstead?

The pleasure of having you with me would be very much dampened by the thought that you would be uncomfortable. But my dear wife we must try and meet somewhere, for it seems many years since we were together before.

I think I wrote you that Mr Sasnett would bring the grey horse with him to Savannah, where I can sell him to more advantage than in Sparta, and can keep him for our use, if we decide to keep him, without expense.

I started to make the visit referred to in the first part of my letter, but the steamer got out of order and we were compelled to return before going one fourth of the way. It was an unexpected accident and I looked upon it as all for the best, expecting a letter from you on my return; but that part of the best is exploded for I find no letter. It has been several days since one of your sweet epistles have been received.

Hu spoke to me about you and the children coming down to see him; but I told him that you were not anxious to come; I did not believe until you were certain of meeting me there—and until the difficulties at Charleston were settled I did not feel authorised to leave my command—all the regular forces have been withdrawn from me, and in their places the reserves came tumbling in—my chief engineer has also been withdrawn to Charleston; which leaves me in a state of anxiety not at all pleasant. I suppose that in a few days, if the enemy find that they cannot take Charleston—they will withdraw from their present positions before that city—but they may then make a dash at this place, supposing that I have no troops here or may attempt some other point along my long and thinly guarded line which makes constant vigilance absolutely necessary for our safety.

I intend at trying to get Hugh appointed as my Chief Qmaster with the rank of Lieut Colonel. An energetic and honest man who is well acquainted with the country is very much needed, and I know of no one better suited than he is, to supervise the Qmaster Department in Georgia where it is believed there is so much peculation & speculation.

Give my love to the boys and to my dear little daughter and to Sister L. I wait in anxiety for your letters my dear darling wife. So write me often as your letters are my only pleasure.

My best respects to M[rs] Sasnett and family and to M[rs] Harris. Your devoted husband L.

((( )))

Savannah G[a]
July 27th 1864 [Wednesday]

My dear Wife
I am becoming really alarmed at not hearing from you. I have not rec[d] a letter for over a week and it seems to me unaccountable if you are well. There are daily occuring circumstances which [obliterated] me confined to Savannah which prevents me from being off duty, without neglecting my duty. Otherwise I would run up to Hu's & find out what in the world can be the matter.

The reported raids to Columbus and digression towards Andersonville [Prison] and then the threatened attack on Augusta and Macon & Milledgeville [Ga.] and on the Oconee Bridge and then the arrival of six or seven hundred Yankees taken confined in Savannah and the necessity for my being here all the time to carry out the orders constantly being received upon different subjects which have to be complied with at once—prevents my going away.

I have written you four or five letters and no answer comes—what can I think but that you are sick or some accident has happened which prevents your writing.

Now is indeed the crisis in our affairs and it behooves every one to be on duty all the time so as to advance the interests of the public, whenever the opportunity offers.

I asked Hu to keep you with him until I could see you again and he said that it was his wish you should remain until Sally was through with her difficulty at least—as for the boys going to school. The affairs of the country are in such an unsettled state that it is next to impossible to do anything now. And I am willing for them to run about until we find out whether it will or will not be necessary for them to run away from the Yankees. If Gen[l] Hood should be driven off from Atlanta he may be forced back towards Macon. And then the Yankee raiders will have plenty of room towards Augusta, and might make a dash upon Sparta—but the finale of this must be known in the next few days. Six or seven—and we can wait that long.

I was quite un well one day this week, but the doctor gave some active medicine and I was well again next morning, indeed I did not have time to lie down, and did not do it— But if I had not been well on the next day I would [sentence stops here]

The regiments raised about Savannah are now for the first time in the war and in consequence are experiencing the horrors of it, by the death of a number of the first young men in the county. Write me my dear wife and with much love to the children and to yourself with many kisses for all I remain ever Your L.

((( )))

[LB1]
Head quarters Savannah [Georgia]
Sep-14-64 [Wednesday]
Afternoon 3¼ P.M.

My darling wife
I propose that I go from here to Augusta next Friday evening the 16th arriving in A. [Augusta] on Sat. 17th and that you engage a seat in the stage at Sparta, beforehand, & leave there on Saturday morning & reach A [Augusta] the same evening of the 17th & meet me at Wm R. McLaws's house or leave Sparta on Friday morning & arrive in A. [Augusta] the same day & wait for me until next morning. You would be with me a few hours more.

In regards to the flour & meat you have purchased, can you not freight them to me in Savannah & keep on purchasing meat[?] I can have the articles placed in commissary store here & kept until called for.

The armistice will last until the 21st int. & there will be no danger from raids until you return & there will be ample time for you to do so before the 21st. The armistice will begin on the 12th.

((( )))

Head Q[rs] Sav
[Savannah, Georgia]
Sep 23/1864 [Friday]

My dear wife
I hope you arrived safe and well at Hus and found them all content, and in a good state of health.

I would have written you to Augusta but doubted if you will receive it.

Nothing new has transpired since you left, except that the press of business upon me, caused by my temporary absence has kept me close confined until now, and now I am away from my office because I am tired of the ding dong system of complaint, which every one is indulging in, and which they think advisable to pour into my ears, just as if I had ten thousand men at my beck & call, ready to go anywhere at any mans bidding.

I never have been more anxious since the war commenced than I am now as to the conditions of our affairs. I can form no plan of operations for the future, that has not so many doubtful prospects mixed up with it, that it is too unsatisfactory to be pushed to completion.

Sherman told a gentleman named King who was retained in Marietta [text obliterated] had frequent intercourse with [text obliterated] was his intention to fortify Atlanta so as to make it an impregnable fortress, easily held by fifteen thousand men.[36] That he intended to provision it with rations for his whole army, sufficient to last them one year. And that with the rest of his forces his intention was to operate against Augusta[,] Savannah and wherever cicumstances might warrant him to go. That in the event of being forced back he could retire to his stronghold and bid us defiance. That he would have to burn and otherwise destroy a great many houses, to be sure, but that was a military necessity which he was in no way responsible for. His duty was to look to the safety of his army and provide for its most active operations in the future, and he intends to do it, regardless of all our remonstrations.

If Sherman is allowed to do this; to fortify Atlanta and collect his supplies, I have no doubt but that he will ruin a large portion of the state, by enticing our slaves from us, and raiding upon us, and making our property and lives so insecure within a hundred miles of his base that the people will

36. William Tecumseh Sherman, Ohio, USMA 1840, Union major general, later general and general in chief of the army under President U. S. Grant.

not live there—will abandon their homes and crowd to the lower sections of the state or to other states.

If he does these things, Sparta will come within the sphere of his outrages. [Obliterated] will suffer in its corn and bacon.

On the other hand, there are indications and reports that it is the intention of the Navy to attack Charleston or Savannah [s]o soon as the usual gales of the Equinox have passed over. Genl Jones is apprehensive of an early attack on Charleston, and is making his preparations accordingly—but yet under great apprehensions as to the result.[37]

There are no indications as yet off Savannah, so far as we can discover except some fortifications on Tybee Island which are being constructed. Yet there are rumors of movement[s] which make me anxious.

Both Charleston and this place are crowded with prisoners, which demand all our troops to guard them, which takes so much from our strength and in fact adds that much to the force of the enemy.

If lodgements could be made either here or in Charleston, the enemy would have points on the coast towards which they could direct their efforts, and thus have auxilliaries in the rear of any of our armies who might attempt to oppose the advance of their forces.

If a judgement was once effected here then we could not dislodge them.

We have already fortified Savannah & Charleston to such a degree that if the enemy once gets in, with their resources of men & munitions of war it would be impossible to make them take water again.

So between Shermans advance and the threatened attack here—with all the uncertainty of the issue in either event, I feel anxious, and undetermined.

I have heard nothing from the Calico, nor the shoes.

The Yellow Fever has become an epidemic in Charleston and has gotten in among the Yankees so I understand. The people here are discussing the propriety of establishing a quarantine between the two cities—the disease may reach Augusta, and in the present crowded population it may commit sad havock.

We hear that Pres Davis was in Augusta and delivered an address to the people. What the purpose of his remarks were, we have not heard. It is rumored that Beauregard was with him, which I hope is true.

I hope you have well considered the comparative advantages of the two

37. Samuel Jones, Virginia, USMA 1841, major general.

localities and will give me an early decision— Col Fiser told me this morning that Lamar had told him that himself & wife would stay at their uncles. If so, how are you off on cooking utensils, plates & knives &c &c[?]

Give my love to all, to the children many good wishes & blessings, write me as soon as possible. Your devoted L.

((( )))

Head Q[rs] Sav[a] G[a]
[Savannah, Georgia]
Oct. 1–64 [Saturday]

My dear Wife
I have understood that movements are on foot which will force Sherman to retire from Atlanta before many days; and either give battle to Hood or scatter his forces in an effort to retreat, or surrender or make desperate efforts to reach one of the seaports. In other words Sherman will have to do something desperate within a very short time. His forces I am told are very much depleted by the expiration of the terms of service of the Kentucky and Tennessee troops under him & from various other causes. His army is said to be on half rations, his horses dying from starvation, and his men and officers very much alarmed at their perilous position. If such is the case we may begin to be hopeful provided our army is in a condition and are willing to fight, and if they are not, I cannot imagine there can be any inspiration to be derived from the implorations of their parents and kindred, the voices of their commanders, of the President himself and the appeals of Beauregard & other distinguished men. That patriotism and every other inspiring virtue is dead within them if they do not fight now, cannot admit of question. But I believe that by getting rid of Hardee, the one most dangerous element of discord is put out of the way, and the others will be so overruled that they will be powerless, and now instead of being split into factions intent on the personal aggrandisement of particular individuals; or striving to detract from the merit of some rival chieftain, they will unite in advancing the public good & in driving our enemies away. How any one can be patriotic under the leadership of Hardee is beyond my comprehension. It is said that Beauregard, A P Hill & the President are with Hoods Army. So a woman tells me who reports herself this morning as a government spy and tells me that three days ago, she took dinner with those Generals at a place called Palmetto on the Atlanta & West Point R R.

October 2 [Sunday]

Since writing the above I have had a long interview with the woman and am satisfied that she is more of a cheat than a Confederate spy. For instance she showed me a letter which she said had been written by Genl Polk in her presence, but on comparing it with a letter from Genl P. written to Bishop Elliott, the hand writing is very dissimilar. Again she says that she was at breakfast with the President, Genl Cobb &c on Sunday last - I telegraphed to Charleston and learned that Genl B. arrived there on Sunday last at 8 oclock A.M. She also stated that she breakfasted with Genl Cobb, on the 29th—I telegraphed to Genl C, & he replies that he never heard of Mrs Meeker, as the woman calls herself. Mrs Amanda Meeker. She has various papers about her, purporting to be from different persons of distinction, but I am happen not to be acquainted with the signatures of any one of them—she claims to have done great service to the Confederacy by her accurate and important information. But she is an illiterate woman, for I managed to get her to write me a plan of cypher by which we could communicate should she go into the Yankee lines—& many of her words were spelled ridicuously for one instance, the word such was invariably written "Sick" &c &c— I intend to pretend to employ her as a spy and send her to communicate with the enemy—but will have her arrested at the last moment and searched.

Young Harris Sasnett has invited me to his wedding on Monday next, and if nothing happens I will attend—he informed me yesterday that his mother had written him that if I desired my family to remain in Sparta during the coming year, she would rent her house to you— I told him that I was very much obliged to his mother and himself, but gave no other reply. There is one thing I will do, which is—the family here, the boys go to their companies, so soon as you leave Mrs Sasnetts. The rent of this house is one hundred dollars per month, with the prospect ahead of it being increased to two hundred, following the rule of Augusta—which would *necessitate* my removal to Thunderbolt or into camp. But these things have not been decided on. I will make it a special subject of inquiry on Monday, tomorrow— I heard but last night that the rent was to be raised again.

I will give you timely notice whether to move or not to move— If Sherman is forced to leave Georgia, as every one thinks he will have to do, rents will be cheaper, as families who have been driven from their homes will return to them.

I wrote Willie a long letter on yesterday which I suppose you will receive in good time.

Much love & many kisses to the children & to my dear wife.

I forgot to mention that I have three more pair of shoes for Uldrick— there were none large enough for any of the other children. My love to Sister. Your devoted L.

((( )))

Hardeeville S.C.
Dec 24th/64 [Saturday]

My dearly beloved Wife
I send by Mr McNish three sacks of flour, one bundle of bedding and several bundles of other articles.[38]

The entire furniture was sent to the ladies where Colonel Fiser was staying [at] Misses Ker, and to Mr LaRoche.

Mr LaRoche was married the day or rather the night we left Savannah to Miss Richards, a lady who was sometimes seen in the house, and he remained among the Yankees and perhaps will take the oath.[39]

A gentleman who came from Sava the night after the evacuation tells us that the streets were filled with Yankee flags when the Yankee made their appearance, floating from very numerous houses. That but three Regiments came into town and they acted as Provost Guard, keeping everything very quiet and orderly. That about thirty of the most prominent citizens had been arrested. He did not state their names however.

My orders are to defend the line of the Combahee River, as I wrote you, indefinitely, the other evening. I expect to leave for that place tomorrow (Christmas).

WmR is with me, very quiet and fat, is very well and very military in his conduct.

I hope that we may be together again before very long. That is if Sherman does not keep pushing us from the coast— I will write you my views to night about the future of our country— so far as it relates to our own personal prospects.

Give my best love to all the dear children & to all with you. —Write me in detail concerning your trip and your ideas of the future & write often[.] Your devoted L.

38. Mr. McNish has not been identified.

39. Isaac LaRoche married Marie A. Richards on December 19, 1864.

((( )))

Pocataligo Station
[Pocataligo, South Carolina]
December 27th/64 [Tuesday]
10 [A.]M. to 7 P.M.

My dear Wife

After evacuating Savannah I came to Hardeeville and was ordered to take command there and hurry on supplies and then move my troops to Pocotaligo and assume command of the line of the Combahee—called by the people the "Combee"— [A]fter removing everything from Hardeeville, I reported the fact and was ordered to *march* my command at once to Pocataligo and report for orders[.] [A]ccordingly my command, about thirty five hundred men, was put in motion on Christmas day and marched to Grahamville. That night it rained very hard indeed, rendering the roads exceedingly muddy and tiresome for the men who resumed their march the next day, and camped before dark within three miles of this place— I Sent Captain Elliott to Pocataligo Station and he reported back that I had been ordered to assume command of the troops from Hardeeville to Pocataligo— I came into this place and finding the telegraph order waiting me, directing as Elliott had reported.[40]

General Jones (Sam) and General Taliaferro were here waiting for me, and anxious to get away.[41] I arrived after dark and they left early in the morning.

I have between eight and ten thousand men under me and have all the trouble of attending to the removal of stock and negroes, &c &c besides defending the line, when everything is in confusion.

Officers who went into Savannah under flag of truce report that everything is perfectly quiet, guards are stationed over the city, who repress the least disorder. No citizen has been arrested and nothing burned by the enemy.

The Yankee officers say however that Sherman will not disturb the women & children but will make all the men leave who do not take the oath. — They reported that Genl Foster would before long occupy the city with negro troops. They say however that those troops are under more strict disci-

40. Captain Richard W. B. Elliott was serving as LM's assistant adjutant general.

41. William Booth Taliaferro, Virginia, College of William and Mary, studied law at Harvard, brigadier general.

pline than the whites—but they told M[rs] Genl Anderson, who is a Northern woman not to leave at present, for although the occupation by negro troops would be disagreeable; principally because of the effect they would have upon the servants, yet they would not advise her to leave the city at present.[42] They promised to let her know when it would be best for her to do so. — Which looks as if they did think there would be a time when it [would] be undesirable for a lady to live in Savannah.

Captain [H. D. D.] Twiggs went over under flag of truce and was, so he says[,] treated with marked courtesy by officers & men[.] [H]e stayed there four hours I believe and was allowed to walk about at pleasure.

One of the Captain Commissaries, Captain [D. H.] Baldwin remained in town and is said to be very friendly with the Yankee army generally.

Captain Hardee[,] a nephew of the generals[,] remained also.[43]

D[r] Willis is with them & perfectly delighted.

A General officer is staying at Captain Metters. General Slocum is at the British Consuls house. The brick one near the park, which was closed when we were there— General Sherman is at M[r] Greens, was invited there.

I wrote you that M[r] LaRoche was married the night of the evacuation and remained in town.

It is reported that the Irish mob ransacked Charles Lamars house and also Colonel Jones, (C C Jones) but it is not believed.[44]

M[rs] Elliott remained in town— M[rs] Hartridge went to Augusta.

Sherman says no one shall go to Savannah unless in order to leave the county and to remain absent—but any one may come from the place to stay away.

The designs of Gen[l] S are not known[.] Sub [the subordinate] officers in Savannah told some of the ladies (M[rs] Genl Anderson &c) that Sherman would shortly march on Charleston and then on to Wilmington, but I do not believe [page ends here, and perhaps a page or more is missing; letter continues in LM fashion on the first page of the letter in the left margin].

My best & warmest love to the children and all. Address your letters to

42. Mrs. Anderson is believed to have been the wife of Robert Houston Anderson, Georgia, USMA 1857, brigadier general, who was recommended for promotion to major general by Joseph Wheeler. The recommendation was not acted upon.

43. Captain Hardee is believed to have been T. S. Hardee, who was aide-de-camp to William J. Hardee.

44. George Lamar's father; Charles C. Jones, Georgia, colonel and future author of several histories of Georgia and Augusta.

Genl Hardees Head Q^{rs} Charleston SC[.] I will send a special messenger daily to Charleston for the mail[.] Your devoted L.

Not having heard from you that I cannot entertain definite ideas upon any subject—until I do. Bishop Elliott promised to call and let you know about myself & I pray for a letter from you to day. L.

1865

What Will We Do? My Dear Wife, Let Me Know Your Views

Pocataligo [South Carolina]
January 12th/65 [Thursday]

My dear Wife

I have written a letter every night for some time past, either to you or Hu or to the children. I wrote last night to Hu, thanking him for his kindness to you and the children. I sent by my courier Arthur a box of flannels, the fine piece of grey cloth which was presented to me, and my blue long tailed coat. I thought you could have a nice cloak or some kind of female apparel made from the grey cloth and the flannels would be useful about the house. I sent also a pistol box, with no pistol in it, which you could use or turn it over to the boys for their little traps or to my little daughter for her dressing or sewing case. There was a pair of large pistols with holster in the bundle which you did not mention as having been recd—none of our furniture or bedding nor anything was sold by Captn Thomas as he was ordered over the river the next day on the very day we saw him and did not have time to bring away any bedding or clothing for himself— I sent everything however to Mr LaRoche or to the ladies at whose house Colonel Fiser was staying and hope they will be taken care of—but I had to leave everything to Wright and to take his word for what he did with everything as I had no time to attend to anything but the minutiae of the evacuation of my lines.[1]

The news from Savannah is that the negroes are becoming impudent and are leaving their homes. Four hundred refugees were to arrive in Charleston to day and I suppose we will get the particulars of the state of affairs there.

The belief is that Sherman will move on Branchville and up this side of the Savannah river. It may be so, and I am afraid he cannot be easily prevented from injuring us very much. There is great alarm all through the country, and a strong disposition to give up, among the old residents even, and with the females especially.

1. Ambrose Ransom Wright, Georgia, lawyer by profession and major general, was assigned to the defense of Georgia on November 26, 1864. After the war, he acquired the *Augusta Chronicle and Sentinel.*

And what will we do? My dear wife, let me know your views and I will try and comply with your wishes—do you regret having left Savannah? I sometimes think that it would have been better if you had remained; but again when I think of the many indignities which may have been offered you & the children and the chance of your being in want and dependent upon the kindness and charity even of the Yankee officials, and the ban to all intercourse with the outside world, and the impossibility of seeing you, I feel grateful that you are away—you state that Mr Greenwood had offered you the old place; what old place do you mean? and what facilities does it possess of wood and water and other necessary comforts and conveniences—does he mean the old Greenwood place? How do you like the idea of living there [letter ends here]

((( )))

[LB1]
Salkahatchie
[on the Salkhatchie River, South Carolina]
Jan-17-65 [Tuesday]

The Yankees are taking everything from the people & from the negroes old & young[,] taking the food & clothing & shoes from the negroes & turning them lose [loose]. They have been especially severe on a number of free negroes who had settled a short distance from Pocataligo, taking everything they had.

The fall of Fort Fisher is a death blow to blockade running & will perhaps result in the loss of Wilmington with a large amount of valuable stores. But it will but concentrate our armies & bring events to a crisis by bringing on a general engagement which must decide the fate of both South & North.[2]

((( )))

[LB1]
Fort Stevens Depot
[St. Stephens Depot, South Carolina]
Feb. 22nd 1865 [Wednesday]

Gen. Wright who is president of the Senate leaves here for Augusta this morning—(carries this letter)[.] Charleston was evacuated on the night of the 18th. The enemy entered the city about 12 next morning. Gen. Hardee

2. Federal forces captured Fort Fisher, N.C., on January 15, 1865, effectively cutting off Wilmington, N.C., as the last blockade-running port in the South.

being sick, I was ordered to Charleston to take his place & arrived there during the night of the evacuation— All orders had been given & I had nothing to do, but to leave & join my command here now, but expect to leave & join my ~~commission~~ division in a few days.

The enemy have taken Columbia & it is said, are advancing towards North Carolina. Rumors afloat are—Columbia has been burned and the soldiers turned loose in the city,[3] others say that the utmost quiet & order was preserved. I believe the latter for I have had scouts in the rear of the enemy since they left the lower Salkahatchie, especially for the purpose of learning the conduct of the enemy towards the people, and the reports agree in that the white troops have been invariably well behaved! Rudeness was rare—but there were few inhabitants in that section. I have always endeavored to persuade the inhabitants not to leave their homes. To send off the male slaves but keep their women & children. The men to take the woods when the enemy approached—the white females to remain always.

When houses were deserted they were burned generally—though there were exceptions.

((( )))

Ft Stevens Depot
[St. Stephens Depot, South Carolina]
February 22nd 1865 [Wednesday]

My dear Sweet Wife
How sweet the name sounds and how dear my wife is, cannot be expressed. I can only call you my sweet wife and leave the comprehension of the full meaning to your own expression of my own dear husband[.] [W]hen we were in Savannah and you used to sit by me with your hand in mine I felt more content and happy than I had done in years, and I now recall those pleasant hours with a sigh and a feeling of discontent of my present lonesome condition which but the hope of again being similarly happy enables me to endure without absolute despair. I am constantly wondering how are you situated? What are you doing? What are your circumstances? How is your health? What are the children occupied at, how is their health. What do they talk about—do they think of me often—until my dear wife I am tempted to run away, leaving military fame, military honor, and all other considerations behind me to take care of themselves, to be coloured as my worst enemies might desire, all to be sacrificed to the gratification I would experi-

3. Columbia, the capital of South Carolina, was burned on February 17, 1865.

ence in clasping my wife once again in my arms and have our children with us. How little do we prize the blessings which are dayly showered upon us and around us, until we are deprived of them and have their opposites to contend against—the sweet welcome of my wife and her sweeter kiss of love, and the unaffected welcome of my children, now so highly appreciated were once regarded as too much a matter of course; the value of those blessings I did not sufficiently appreciate! but now what price could buy them, how much would I sacrifice to obtain them? And what have I to compensate for or replace them? My time is occupied with caring for others who do not care for me, who give me no smile of welcome but seldom—and the feeling or expectation of gaining love is never thought of—we laugh and appear joyous because we know that it cannot bring but discontent and discouragement should we do otherwise, we do not laugh because we are joyous at heart, nor contented[;] even we laugh because it is our duty, and from half recklessness—but my dear darling, this letter will be sent by Mr Thomas J Black a Son of Edward J Black, whose mother you saw on her plantation when travelling from Savannah to Augusta—he appears to be a very straightforward honest man and bears a character which is respected by all— I have asked him to call and see you and learn all about you and the children so that he can answer all my questions when he returns— I wish you my sweetheart to write me a long sweet letter and give a long account of yourself and the children and of Hu and his family. How long it will be before I hear from you is a matter, of course, for conjecture, but I hope that the courier I sent you from Four Hole Swamp will be before long on his return, and that Mr Black will be with me again in ten days. I write whenever I hear there is a chance—and I try and send couriers whenever I hear the way is probably passable.

From all accounts the Yankees are burning the houses of the rich and leaving the poor comparatively free from molestation. They take all horses and beasts of burden, and what cattle they wish for food—they take or destroy where there is a great abundance, but in the generality of cases will leave enough for the bare subsistence of the family. The South Carolinians have suffered very much[;] the rich rice planters who had surrounded themselves with every luxury and lived in lordly magnificence, upon their princely estates, have been left without lands or houses, or negroes and are wanderers. But they do not but in a few instances, appear to be downcast or repine over their fallen fortunes, but on the contrary are in high spirits and appear anxious to engage the enemy, in order to be revenged.

I heard a scout relate this evening that he witnessed the burning of two of the most magnificent homes on the coast, and saw the negroes rushing up to the Yankees shaking hands with them and dancing about them, shouting and singing—I fear this will be the case all along the coast.

But my dearly beloved darling, I must to bed as I start tomorrow morning for Kingstree [South Carolina] on the N Eastern R R. I travel by rail for five miles and then ride fifteen & wish to be there by two oclock[,] so good night and with unnumbered blessings and kisses wafted to you and our children and with much love to all, Hu and his family W^{m}R & Sister—I remain your devoted L.

((( )))

[OB2]
[St. Stephens Depot, South Carolina]
February 23rd [1865] Thursday
[page] 7

Left St. Stevens Feby 23rd-'65 Thursday[,] arrived at Kingstree same day at 5 P.M., stopped at Gourdins depot. Telegraphed about impressed negroes having no agent to receive them—about the arms & ammunition lying exposed at depot, also hospital stores & and sick soldiers. Came on by horse back crossing Black River over a good bridge ten miles from Gourdin [South Carolina][,] five from Kingstree—Gen Robertson along with his staff— Saw Gen Hardee who appeared to be recovering rapidly—lodged at Saure House. My Division moving rapidly to Cheraw [South Carolina]—Conners Brigade [had] not [started] off—[4] To leave in morning for Cheraw by train—Recd a note from Taliaferro that the enemy had burned the bridge over Santee [River]. Commenced moving toward dark.

((( )))

[OB2]
[St. Stephens Depot, South Carolina]
February 24th [1865] Friday

Rainy dark day. Recd notice from Allen of Texas escort that enemy were in large force at Columbia on Monday 20th & were reported as moving heavy force towards Camden [South Carolina].[5] Heard Genl Hardee say that it

4. Beverly Holcombe Robertson, Virginia, USMA 1849, brigadier general; Conner's brigade, part of Kershaw's division, formerly LM's division commanded by Brigadier General John Doby Kennedy.

5. There were four Allens in the 8th Texas Cavalry; LM is most likely referring to Second Lieutenant Rowland A. Allen.

was his intention to send prisoners now at Florence [South Carolina] to Monks corner [Moncks Corner, South Carolina][,] tis faster about 11 or supposed to be. Left for Cheraw on train, with portion of Conners Brigade—raining hard—trains crowded in and outside—one car broke in[,] no one hurt—much delay on road—arrived at sundown at Florence—started again at 8 oclock—left those who were on top in camp, on account of wet & exposure after much delay arrived in Cheraw next day twelve or one P.M.—found road completely blocked—gave Kennedy (Col) permission to visit Columbia & gain information of movements of enemy—he & Capt [C. R.] Holmes started about two P.M. & returned after daylight on 26th reporting the enemy at Kings twenty seven miles from Cheraw & across Lynch's creek & also on Darlington road—Major [John H.] Screven QM.

((( )))

[OB2]
[Cheraw, South Carolina]
[February 26, 1865, Sunday]

26th—[W]ent over river reconnoitering after hearing Kennedy's report. With Col [John J.] Clarke, Col [George P.] Harrison[,][6] Capt [Abram] Huguenin. Bluff on Cheraw side [is] low flat country.

[page] 9

Col Kennedy & Capt Holmes went yesterday as far as Kings on Camden Road twenty seven miles from Cheraw. Found the enemy encamped within a few miles of Wm Kings. Stretching across the Cheraw & Darlington Roads, leading from Camden. They are reported by persons in the neighborhood to be in Considerable force. Infantry and cavalry. No arty reported. Col K and Capt H saw some of the camp fires (said to be)— Capt [Francis D.] Lee of the Engineer Corps reported that two gentlemen of veracity whom they met on the road Friday told him that the enemy had entered Camden in force on Thursday. Col K left Kings place at twelve oclock last night— Some of the enemy had appeared at Blairs Mill ten miles above ~~Belains~~ Tillers Bridge, Wm King did not know if army had gone in the direction of Chesterfield C H [Chesterfield, South Carolina].

6. Colonel Harrison commanded the 32nd Georgia Infantry.

((( )))

[OB2]
[Cheraw, South Carolina]
[page] 11
H Qrtr Cheraw
Feby 26th 65 [Sunday]

Captain [William M.] Tunno
I wish you to proceed back on the road towards Florence and hurry on the wagons and artillery coming to this place. The enemy were reported to be thirty miles from here on the Camden Road, covering the road to this place and that to Darlington. As Darlington is nearer to their position last night than this place[,] [i]t is probable the road which our wagons are travelling may be occupied before our trains can pass unless hurried forward rapidly—I wish you would use your utmost efforts to have them brought to this place with the least possible delay. The enemy tis said crossed Lynchs Creek at Tillers bridge or from whatever direction the enemy may be found moving, and therefore send you the order for impressment leaving the name blank, to be filled by yourself, the officer selected to receive positive orders to keep his party between this place and the enemy and to be notified himself & men that upon their vigilence we are relying for an early notice of the approach of the enemy. The men from the 8th S.C. are particularly mentioned as I understood from you that many of that regiment are natives of the section of country to be guarded and consequently are acquainted with the roads & approaches &c. I would like the party to start as early tomorrow as possible, say at daylight. I wish you to notify me if you can obtain a suitable body of men, giving their names.

Very Resptly
L McLaws
Maj Genl

((( )))

Sent to Colonel Kennedy 2½ P.M.
[page] 13

To day an order was received from Genl J E Johnston assuming Command of the Department of S.C. Ga & Florida and of the Army of Tennessee. (By direction of the General in Chief [Robert E. Lee].) The appointment appears to have been received with general favor by officers and troops. Perhaps now as the enemy are along Lynchs Creek there will be a concentration at Cheraw, instead of in a more northerly direction.

Visited Col Kennedy— dined with him—his brigade inspected—drill—serenade by Col Harrison & field officers of Brigade— Recd an order during the night to send Fisers Brigade to Chesterfield C.H. and Harrisons Brigade to Perins Bridge over Thompsons Creek.

~~Got notice~~

((( )))

[OB2]

[Cheraw, South Carolina]

[February 28, 1865, Tuesday]

28th—Col Henderson arrived from below—got an order at 1½ P.M. to march my division to Perins Bridge as Colonel Harrison had reported the enemy had appeared (with cavalry) two miles in front of the bridge. Ordered Kennedy[,] Blanchard and Henderson to march at once—[7] Kennedy moved first—then Blanchard and then Henderson who arrived just before dark—ordered two batteries to accompany the command—went myself & staff ahead of Kennedy— The enemy had retired when I arrived at Col Harrisons which was in advance of bridge about ⅓ of mile— Found Col Harrison had his reserve ⅓ of mile from Bridge—one regiment on Chesterfield road where Old Camden Road crossed it, another on Chesterfield where New Camden Road crossed it— A regiment of mounted infy [infantry] had come up & engaged our troops, but were repulsed with one man killed[,] none of ours hurt— Kennedy was put in position so as to enclose the head of Perins Bridge & entrenched the position— Some prisoners sent in by Butler's Cavalry—camped Blanchard one mile in rear of bridge, right bank.

[page] 15

Henderson moved across the bridge & camped with Kennedy—after dark went to head qtrs at a house which proved to be that of Capn R. C. Gilchrist['s] Step Mother. Capn G himself was there. D & myself & Huegenin inside of house, Lamar & King not invited to enter.[8] —Mrs Gibbs[,] name of lady—the house being too distant from my command I moved back to

7. Albert Gallatin Blanchard, Massachusetts, USMA 1829, Confederate brigadier general; Colonel Robert J. Henderson, who commanded Cumming's brigade.

8. Major General Matthew Calbraith Butler; Captain Mallory P. King, assistant inspector general on LM's staff.

hill in front of Blanchards camp & pitched tent. Dark and rainy weather, roads full of water. Saw Genl Butler[;] he reported 17 Army Corps (Blair) as advancing against Cheraw.

((( )))

[OB2]
[Cheraw, South Carolina]
[March 1, 1865, Wednesday]

March 1—[J]ust before day Major Pringles train commenced to arrive & followed by D Pass & Kanninpaux batteries under Capn Kanningpaux—[9] Major Pringle with train saw no enemy, reported nothing behind Gallairds battery coming on train—that to the front, no enemy reported, indications of their retiring.[10] Another scout came in & reported them as advancing & engaging our skirmishers. Saw Genl Butler & talked some time about affairs. He sent out scouts and also his entire force—which during the day brought in a N° of prisoners. Genl Hardee came over to inspect the ground, went back under the impression that the enemy would not advance to day. I advised through [Lt.] Col [Del.] Kemper, against wanting an attack on opposite bank of river, with nothing to cross on but one wornout & not very strong bridge. Genl Hardee wrote in reply that it was necessary to hold the advanced position in order to protect the passage of our trains & arty from Florence & below & therefore if Harrison was attacked I must reinforce him. My understanding with Genl H. was on seeing him this morning that Genl Butler should retire across the bridge in case the enemy advanced in force & the infy should burn the bridge. Genl B understands it in that way— Genl Hardee in note from his headqts during night of 28th said that he wished me to notify

[page 17]

wagons not to come on Chesterfield road but to turn to left and come onto Camden Road near to the bridge on road leading to Cash Station on RR— I wrote back that I had no cavalry & therefore could not qive notice to trains. Col Harrision wrote that he could hold advanced position against cavalry, but could not against Infantry in larger force, unless correspondingly reinforced— Capn De Sassaure wrote that Elliotts Brigade was ready to support me—Elliott having gone scouting and posting troops to defend cross-

9. Major Motte A. Pringle; Captain J. T. Kanapaux.
10. Captain Christopher Gaillard commanded the South Carolina Santee Battery.

ings did not come himself— Capt De. S. called himself also M[r] Jervy—M[r] Story—&c &c—[11]

((( )))

[OB2]

[Cheraw, South Carolina]

[March 2, 1865, Thursday]

March 2d—Remained in position at bridge on Thompsons Creek. Enemy reported as advancing[,] drove in our pickets and forced one line from its position at the cross roads which retired a half mile— Col Henderson commanding line in advance withdrew Blanchard who was in reserve to picket line—strengthened line of works enclosing head of bridge. The bridge was well prepared with rosin for burning— The enemy ceased to advance and retiring went towards Chesterfield[,] everything being quite I went to town calling on Genl Hardee. Cannonading was heard in the direction of Chesterfield[,] [t]he enemy having pressed the cavalry there across the bridge over Thompson Creek[,] Colonel Fisers Brigade which had been several days detached to Chesterfield, and fired shells at our troops on left bank of Thompsons Creek— Fiser reported during the evening that his position was a critical one as the enemy had crossed above him & his forces were in the bend of the river, and asked for instructions. Genl Hardee thought his instructions were specific enough for him to retire on his own discretion. I read the instructions and did not think they were. Positive orders were given to withdraw four miles. Orders were given for Taliaferro to send Elliotts Brigade to support Fiser & Butler was ordered cover the retirement of infy across Pee Dee [River].

[page] 19

Orders were issued for evacuation on next day. The wagons & arty to be sent at once across the river. My command to move at four o'clock & cross the river excepting Fisers Brigade which was ordered as before stated—twenty of Butlers Division was ordered to remain at Perins Bridge over Thompsons Creek. To wait for orders to destroy it— The object being to wait for Collocks cavalry which was expected from below & to arrive at 10 oclock next day.[12]

11. Captain Louis D. Desausure; Stephen Elliott Jr., South Carolina, brigadier general and son of Bishop Elliott.

12. Colonel Charles J. Colcock commanded the 3rd South Carolina Cavalry.

((( )))

[OB2]
[Cheraw, South Carolina]
[March 3, 1865, Friday]

March 3d—My troops moved of[f] as directed arty & wagons having been sent forward the night previous & crossed the bridge road on left bank of river [the evacuation went] very bad indeed— Commissary depot at L W Harrington ~~The bridge of~~ Perins Bridge not being burnt the Yankees came over & Fiser had difficulty in withdrawing and the bridge would not have have been destroyed if Fiser had not have driven the Yankees away ~~with~~ by Fisers Command. Butlers men and also Capn Fielding and many others claim the exclusive credit of having burnt the bridge— Orders were given to halt at commissary depot at Harringtons and issue the surplus rations which can not be taken by the commissary train to the troops for them to carry, on their person. But on arriving at Harringtons found that the supply train was just being loaded & there was so much confusion the troops were marched on to within three miles of Sweats Mill and camped for the night— empty wagons were sent back to bring up the surplus supplies. The enemy pressed on Fiser retiring and his troops were withdrawn with difficulty. He ~~supported~~ protected the cavalry bringing up the rear, where as the order was for the cavalry to bring up the rear of infny. But the pressure from the enemy came from those who crossed at Perins Bridge

[page] 21

not from other side. Fiser thought his brigade had been badly treated, imposed on both by cavalry or by Genl Butler and by superior authority— Enemy shelled our troops on left bank of river—we lost guns & ammunition left on other side.

((( )))

[OB2]
[Rockingham, North Carolina]
[March 4, 1865, Saturday]

March 4th—

Came on ahead to Rockingham and camped on left bank of Hedgecombs Creek—roads very bad in places— Mr. Leak, took dinner & Supper— Hardy's Brigade was at Mills Ferry & guarding other points of river. Enemy reported as having crossed the river at Cheraw, one brigade according to Butler, one regiment by scouts from Conners Brigade reports of crossing at other points not credited. Cannonading heard occasionally. Summoned to counsel at Mr Leaks. Orders given to march on towards Ashboro camp to be three or four miles beyond fair grounds 10 miles from Rockingham, one brigade of Taliaferros under Anderson to lead the advance then the reserve arty.[13]

[skips to unmarked pages out of numbered sequence]

& supply trains, the Taliaferros division train, then rest of division of Talieferro. Movement to commence at 2 A.M. of 5th— My division with arty & wagons to commence the march at 7 oclock.

Went to ride after dark and found that side road leading directly over hill was the best. Found out roads to Mills ferry other road to Rockingham the river road &c. Old Mr Cole horses impressed equivalent to stealing by Sgt of Daniells Battery—[14] The engineers have been working for days with nine hundred men on a bad road when the one next to it required no working & was the best of the two.

((( )))

[OB2]

[Bostick's Mill, North Carolina]

[March 5, 1865, Sunday]

March 5th—The rear of Taliaferros command passed my camp at 1 +10 M[inutes] A.M.— My march commenced at 1½ P.M. Marched on—heard that enemy had crossed river at Mills Ferry & were advancing upon our forces advancing on Ashboro. I rode forward & found Hard[y]s Brigade—Blanchards & Hendersons in line of battle &c— This proved to be entirely a false alarm. Marched on & reached fair grounds ten miles, thence by left hand road to Martins, on banks of Job Creek which in conjunction with Adams Creek forms Little Mountain Creek. Heard enemy were crossing at Society Hill [N.C.], one corps—and two corps at Cheraw— One corps not accounted for, Mrs Martin daughter in law of old Martin offered a room in house—left sick in house very disloyal

[returns to numbered pages]

neighborhood—all men who had been in army had returned— Many bushwackers So tis said in the country. Negro girl R. Genl Hardee camp on beyond, reached camp late at night— Genl Taliaferro turned to left &

13. Hardy's brigade, commanded by Colonel Washington Hardy.

14. Georgia Regular Battery D, commanded by Captain Charles Daniell.

camped at Bosticks [Bostick's Mill]—passed "fair grounds"—well of water at Martins water near top although on high hill.

((( )))

[OB2]

[Baldwin's Mill, North Carolina]

[March 6, 1865, Monday]

March 6—Marched to Baldwins Mill six miles, got into camp considerably after dark owing to detention by Genl Taliaferros troops & trains—bad crossing at pond—recd no instructions as to marching on 7th— Genl Taliaferro recd definite orders—was not inconvenienced. I was told to send all my baggage train by Carthage—he was told to take all his with him— Galvanised Yankee & Capt. Lamar.

((( )))

[OB2]

[New Gileud, North Carolina]

[March 7, 1865, Tuesday]

March 7th Marched without instructions as before stated across Lumber river, took wrong road went over McKenzies Bridge instead of Pattersons— Lost distance.

[page] 23

Lumber River an inconsiderable stream, not over twenty feet broad. I took Fayetteville Road on hill after crossing Lumber River, left hand road leading to Carthage. Fayetteville distant 45 miles, Carthage 19— Many deserters from S.C. troops[,] some from N.C.—130 from S.C. —Sgt Shot in Rhetts Brigade by sentence of Drum head C M [court martial] for mutiny—[15] Camped three miles from New Gileud. Arrived in Camp late—last troops encamped at ten & half— Recd notice from Gen Hardee to March next morning at 6 A.M.—afterwards changed to 7 or 8 at my discretion. Weather good. Country exceedingly barren, but one house in ten miles—rained slightly during night— Supper at Browns wine— Texas Scouts came in jealosy—negroes unreliable.

15. Sergeant O'Keefe of Company B, 1st South Carolina Artillery, was charged with mutinous conduct and inciting the men in his company to riot. He died by firing squad in New Gileud, N.C.

((( )))

[OB2]
[Solemn Grove, North Carolina]
[March 8, 1865, Wednesday]

March 8th—Started at 7— Texas Company ordered to its regiment, by order addressed to Lieut Ferguson direct—no other order recd.[16] Genl Hardee was notified & order asked in the case. No answer recd but Genl H told me not to send the company until further orders.

((( )))

[OB2]
[Monroe's Crossroad, North Carolina]
[March 9, 1865, Thursday]

[LM circled text indicating that this section should be part of March 9]

[March] 9th[—] Conners Brigade was ordered to turn to left and go on to road leading from Carthage to Fayetteville in order to protect wagon train & reserve arty, which had been ordered around by Carthage to Fayetteville— It would have been better to have ordered it across Cape Fear River crossing Deep River & Haw River by bridges near junction of those streams, which united form Cape Fear River. ~~Remainder of~~ Command marched on an[d] camped near Monroes house about X roads [Monroe's Crossroad]. Rainy day & same bad roads. Taliaferros Division leading—bad place reported in road ahead.

March 9th—See above about Conners Brigade— Stackhouses regiment sent ahead to work road, no bad place as reported.[17] The regiment ordered to join its brigade by cross road, firing heard to our right—cannon & musketry— Met Hamptons Scout (Ashby) who reported enemy in force on our right five miles, having crossed at [space] bridge & moving with whole force on Fayetteville,[18] went to rear & shortly returned reporting [. . .]

[page] 25

Squadron of enemys cavalry about one & half miles in my rear. Fisers Brigade being in my rear, he was directed to march with strong rear guard & to take precautions against surprise, load his guns &c— Nothing happened however—roads very bad as we approached Fayetteville. Rotten gail— Arrived in camp very late, rain pouring in tremendous torrents, everybody wet

16. First Lieutenant J. W. Ferguson.

17. Colonel Eli T. Stackhouse commanded the 3rd South Carolina.

18. Colonel Henry M. Ashby commanded the 2nd Tennessee Cavalry.

& disgusted—delay owing to Taliaferros trains— Never experienced a more disagreeable night.

((( )))

[OB2]

[Fayetteville, North Carolina]

[March 10, 1865, Friday]

March 10th—Found a road which avoided the bad road we were upon, by turning to left & going to plank road from Carthage— Sent troops on direct road as I was ordered to relieve Taliaferros troops posted on the Cumberland Plank Road leading from bridge, wagons sent around, went around myself[,] met Kennedy with his brigade and ordered him on at once, found road blocked with Taliaferros ordnance, passed it with arty. Sent Brooks on to Plank Road.[19] Harrisons Brigade marched by side road & came in on plank road near point it was intended it should occupy, about 3½ or 4 miles from town—relieved Rhetts Brigade by Harrisons— Sent Shells battery to front with it—[20] Changed the position of Harrisons men so as to place them in rear of field instead of across it. Met Gen Hardy & with him selected a new ground for line of battle. Taliaferro ordered to conform to it on left— Conners Brigade occupied the line—wagon trains all ordered across the river, enemy not advancing went into town that evening. The old or main place built on plain immediately upon river. The new town or its extension on the hills around, a very pretty place, picturesque. Visited arsenal, everything in confusion[,] Genl Hardees head qrts there—Col or Major White drunk. Genl Hampton in town, enemy reported with whole force within 5 miles of place, which was not fortified & nothing but a rickety bridge over which to cross to other side. Ordered to retire that night, arty and wagons to move at once, my command to bring up rear of infantry. Hamptons cavalry the rear of everything else. Miss Keyser near my hd qts—[21]

[page] 27

A close shave to get out of town— Got a bridle from Major Taylor of ordnance— Could get no clothing for troops— Hampton had difficulty in crossing his cavalry, had to charge the enemy to effect it. Report says he killed two with his own hand, but the chivalry have fallen so deep into the pit of

19. Captain John W. Brooks commanded the Georgia Terrell Light Artillery Battalion.

20. "Shells battery" is believed to be Company F, South Carolina Palmetto Light Artillery, commanded by Captain Frederick C. Schulz.

21. Lieutenant Colonel D. G. White; Lieutenant General Wade Hampton.

"want of chivalry" that they are constantly inventing Munchauseus as to the prowess of those from the state, or defaming others in order that thereby they may appear elevated by their contrast—

((( )))

[OB2]
[Across from Fayetteville, North Carolina]
[March 11, 1865, Saturday]

March 11th—Crossed the bridge over Cape Fear River and turning to left, marched about two miles and camped in an open field, rested until 8 A.M. and then marched ~~over Silver Run & Taylors Hole Creek~~ across a mill race, mill on right hand, camped ~~a~~ ¾ mile beyond, next to house of woman whose husband was in the army, & sent a guard to save her fodder—just after Crossing Cape Fear River the main road to Clinton crosses Looks Creek over a high bridge. The road to Goldsboro [Goldsborough, North Carolina] turns to the left branching immediately, one running along river bank, and other across the bend, within about ten miles from bridge— Sent a brigade to McNeils Ferry (Cummings Brigade) with Abells Arty, 17 miles distant, Fiser to Smiths Ferry, Harrison to McKethains[.] Smiths Ferry crossed river & had two landings on right bank, one above the other below Lower ~~deep river~~ Little River. These movements were made. Those of Fiser & Harrison on Sunday, the 12th the rest of the command consisting of Conners, Hardys & Blanchards Brigade remaining in camp. Old woman washed [clothes] on Sunday & satisfied her conscience by charging double price.

((( )))

[OB2]
[Across from Fayetteville, North Carolina]
[March 12, 1865, Sunday]

12th Remained in Camp— See record of 11th—road from my camp turned to left and led into river road. Some steamers lying above it in locks, the river it seems is rocky & not navigable above Fayetteville, but with difficulty & at high water, an attempt was made to improve navigation by lock and dam. The boats from Fayetteville were run above the locks to save capture. I think the steamers were burned, although Genl Hardee gave orders for them not to be, but disabled only. The enemy were reported as crossing the river at various points during the day, but the accounts were very much exaggerated.

((( )))

[OB2]
[Averasborough, North Carolina]
[March 13, 1865, Monday]
[page] 29

13th—Marched the next morning, relieving Harrisons Brigade at McKethains as I went, & ordering Fiser at Smiths Ferry to be ready with wagons ready to turn into road as Taliaferro reached it, and camped my command at the different branches above Smiths Ferry. Covering all roads leading across Bridge (Garrys) over Black Creek. My head quarters were near Mrs Parker*s*? —Mr [Farquhard] Smith a man of wealth with several pretty daughters lived near camp of Col Harrison.

((( )))

[OB2]
[Averasborough, North Carolina]
[March 14–15, 1865, Tuesday–Wednesday]

14 & 15 Remained in camp, went over to inspect the place where Taliaferros command was. Rhetts Brigade in advance in tolerable position, with a field in front— Elliott was camped in rear across a small creek in a bad position. A Mr [John C.] Smiths house in front of Rhetts & on right flank. Rode across Black Creek examining roads, went to Mr Gancys, a man with withered & deformed foot. Justice of Peace. Two roads to Smithfield[,] one called New Road went across head waters of Mingo Creek, twenty miles to Smithfield—The other along Goldsboro Road across Mingo Creek at deep ford, & turn to left to Smithfield. The first road has bad crossing over the banks before reaching Mingo Creek—about fifty yards. Genl Hardees Head Qrs next to Averasboro [road], just across a deep bottom run & just beyond Hardys Brigade— Enemy made demonstrations against Taliaferros front but were repulsed easily— Colonel Rhett advancing beyond picket line was captured prisoner taken afterwards stated that he had been paroled by Genl Jefferson [C.] Davis and was riding with him & staff.[22] I did not select any position for my command, did not know the status of affairs. Never thought about making a stand about Averasboro. Enemy reported to be in our front with two corps, our effective force was about eight thousand men. Commenced

22. Colonel Alfred M. Rhett. Davis, a Union brigadier general recommended for major general by both Rosecrans and Grant, never attained the U.S. regular army rank.

raining during ~~night~~ evening of 15th. All wagons had been ordered to rear by Genl Hampton or some other stampeder, ordered my wagons back to same place came back after dark. Went myself to the house of Mrs Parkers; bad Cholic, had my bed

[page] 31

placed there[,] slept all night—raining hard.

((( )))

[OB2]

[Averasborough, North Carolina]

[March 16, 1865, Thursday]

March 16th—Genl Hardee rode by early stating that he was going to front, enemy was advancing, wanted all my force to the front. I dressed at once and rode to front, placed Conners Brigade under Kennedy across the main road, Harrison on his immediate left, Fiser next and then Hardy. Blanchard was sent back with wagon train— The enemy commenced by assaulting Taliaferros lines which were considerably in advance of mine & not in view, on account of the woods. Producing however no particular results. My time was employed in fortifying and extending my lines. Hardy immediately on his arrival called for re-inforcements saying his left was being flanked &c.

Major Black reporting about 2 P.M. that the enemys cavalry were about flanking Taliaferros left flank. I ordered the 32 G^{a} of Harrisons Brigade immediately forward to engage them, the regiment went on at once and Soon became engaged— Taliaferros forces then deserted or retired from their lines, and came into mine, Conners Brigade in the mean while had been ordered to right to oppose a threatened advance in that direction, his brigade & Wheelers extended to river— As Taliaferros forces came up, mine extended to the left, Harrison taking Fisers place[,] Fiser [taking] Hardys & Hardy extending to a swamp on extreme left, a section of Brooks Arty was placed with Fisers Brigade— The enemy made repeated dashes with heavy lines of skirmishers all along our lines, supported in some Cases by lines of battle, but their advance was checked in every instance easily and with but little loss— The enemy also assaulted Conners Brigade (Kennedy) which was on the right of Taliaferro, but were easily repulsed. They assaulted Taliaferro also, with no success— As the enemy advanced they felt along towards the left and probably would have turned that flank, if the day had not been so far gone—Butler (Rhetts) [. . .]

[page] 33

Smithfield & ~~Averboro~~ Averasboro

Brigade was thrown to left to meet the contingency of a flank movement in that direction. It however numbered but four hundred (400) men— So Colonel Butler informed me—[23] Immediately at dark (raining) [t]he arty was ordered to rear and infantry commenced moving at 8½ P.M.— My command withdrew by a road to left, which led into Smithfield & Averasboro road about two miles beyond Averasboro, avoiding the deep mud and ruts & steep hills—arrived in that road long before Taliaferros Division which had started ahead of me. Cap^{n} [L. J.] Smith lost two or three wagons loads of ammunition—Lieut Richardson one or two caissons, all stuck in the mud. Richardson was arrested for it—marched troops several miles on road beyond the point where I came into it, and halted there for the night with orders to come on in morning, went myself across Black ~~Creek~~ River, which was over the banks on both sides of bridge, no footway for soldiers. Roads very bad. Found [Lieutenant Colonel J. Welsman] Browns camp, three & half miles from bridge although he had reported it to be one & half miles, every one very mad & disgusted—went to bed after eating a little supper about 4 oclock A.M. Harrisons Brigade was in rear with orders to bring up the rear of all things except Wheelers Cavalry.
[hand drawn on page with fingers pointing to right]
Skip to Second leaf beyond this!

((( )))

[OB2]
[Elevation, North Carolina]
[March 17, 1865]

March 17th

Fisers Brigade & Blanchards continuing their march towards Elevation [North Carolina] were ordered to guard Bridge over Hannah Creek without notice being given to me about the movement— The rest of command went on to Elevation [midway between Averasborough and Smithfield]—where we remained a considerable time— Then were ordered to junction of Raleigh Road with Averasboro & Smithfield Road. Got Some pear &c from Tunno at Elevation. Camped troops, Fiser still absent, also Blanchard. Head qr at corner. Rode around over ground. Found a tolerable position for an engagement to defend X roads. Harrison came up as day advanced, no

23. Colonel William Butler commanded Rhett's brigade.

enemy reported in pursuit, the impression was general that the enemy had been decidedly checked & with considerable loss—horse stolen from [entry continues below]

Bentonville—March 18-1865

old man—had Funnel tent pitched— Saw Mr [James J.] Whitehead of Navy who had sent to me at first camp from Fayetteville to get transportation for himself, from Smiths house, near Smiths Ferry, near battle ground. He had obtained transportation.

((( )))

[OB2]
[Bentonville, North Carolina]
[March 18–19, 1865, Friday–Saturday]

March 18th–19th

Wagons were sent across Black Creek tributary of Neuse [River] and orders were recd from Genl Johnston to assemble Genl Hardees force at Bentonville, on Mill Creek, from sixteen to 18 miles South— Marched in front of Taliaferro. Went down Wilmington & Raleigh Road, to the point where Fayetteville & Smithfield road crossed it—then turned to left down that road. Then cut across the angle to another main road—~~Camping however near Sandy & Lees after dark, 4 morning next marching~~ at dawn that to a certain distance, then across to nearer Smithfield Road & camping however before reaching that road, near a Mr Sneeds[,] a strong union man[,] & a Mr Lees and then on 19th moving across Mill Creek to Bentonville. Saw Genl Johnston & Bragg there— Shook hands warmly with Genl Jhstn [Johnston] & Genl Brg [Bragg] also—19th command rested about the church at Bentonville, waiting for Stewarts Corps

[page] 39

to get in position—[24] Finally I was moved to the left, with orders to connect with Genl Hokes left—moved up and did so with great difficulty, through a very dense swamp[;] the officers who were sent to guide me to Hokes left,[25] lost their way every time. Finally Colonel Stackhouses regiment S.C. Ken-

24. Alexander Peter Stewart, Tennessee, USMA 1842, Confederate lieutenant general.

25. Robert Frederick Hoke, North Carolina, graduate of the Kentucky Military Institute, Confederate major general.

nedys Brigade, was sent to Hokes left and a connection was made by pickets from my right— Kennedy occupied the main road and field in his front, Fiser his right[,] then Hardy & then Harrison held in reserve— Field works were constructed along this line & advanced picket works also. Some time after twelve oclock I was notified by Genl Bragg that General Stewart would attack the enemy in flank and I must be ready to strike a blow if an opportunity offered— I went forward & reconnoitered the ground—not long afterwards I was notified by Genl Bragg that Stewart had turned the enemys left and was driving him towards my position. I moved the 32nd G^{a} forward with a section of arty and advanced a line of skirmishers in a direction towards the rear of the firing—before the skirmishers had gotten well into line— I recd an order from Genl Hardee to bring my whole division immediately to the right, which was commenced at once, without a moments delay— On arriving on the right I Saw Genl Johnston—Genl Bragg & Genl Stewart in an open field from which the enemy had been driven[,] so I was told. A brisk cannonade was going on just above. The shells from the enemy bursting over the field we were in, my command was formed in two lines. Kennedy & Hardy in front & Fiser and Harrison in rear— The enemys fire became so troublesome that the troops were moved forward to the slope of the hill & behind some works which, it is said had been deserted by the enemy, but they looked very much like our own, as they

[page] 41

looked the other way, towards the enemy. The musketry fire ceased temporarily and the opinion was that the attack was over, and orders were given to collect arms—but immediately the musketry recommenced with great fury, and I was ordered to send two brigades towards the firing. Harrison & Kennedy were accordingly sent in and also Hardy. The sun was declining rapidly and the smoke settled heavy & dense over the country. A fog also came on, which added to the smoke made it impossible to see but a very short distance. The firing was very rapid and continuous for some time after my Brigades went forward, but gradually ceased as the darkness increased. I then had fires built all along my rear and stretched out Fisers Brigade, so as to stop all men coming to the rear, and tell them where to form— The line in my front being occupied nearly entirely by other troops who were in position

[page] 42 {March 18th—continued}

before I entered. I withdrew my command gradually beneath the hill and formed them in line in rear of the positions they had occupied, having skirmishers to the front— I was not long after ordered to withdraw my command and place them in position out of reach [of] shells— I accordingly withdrew and camped for night in rear of my position of the morning last.

((( )))

[OB2]
[Bentonville, North Carolina]
[March 20, 1865, Sunday]

March 20th—[W]as ordered on extreme right, having Taliaferro on my left, established my line, Kennedy on the right—Fiser on his left—Hardy in front occupying an advanced position. Harrison on left. I had ridden forward

[page] 43

in the morning with Genl Hardee to a mill on our right, by which several important roads passed, then occupied by some Cavalry— It was deemed an important place and Genl Blanchard was ordered there with his reserves, with a section of arty.

Before our lines of defense were completed an order came for my command to move back upon the same road and take position upon left. Kennedy and Fiser went around by the Mill & Hardy and Harrison on the same road they came. I went by mill and saw Blanchard fortifying along the mill race and mill pond, neglecting the high ground immediately in his rear— Hurried on and ~~was informed~~ found Kennedy in position forming a line some hundred yards in rear of Hoke & in echellon, on his left— Harrision was soon ordered forward to form line on left of Hoke. While on the way, I met Genl Hampton who directed me to halt two brigades at the X roads, as the enemy were reported moving direct upon Bentonville—Harrison and Hardy were halted accordingly. I reported the fact to Genl Hardee who went to see Genl Johnston about it— In the mean while I had been ordered to send Harrison to take post on the left of Hoke & ~~Line on his left~~—Kennedy. Fiser & Hardy building a second line, extending to the swamp on the left— After dark I was ordered to relieve Genl Wheelers men who were dismounted and had been skirmishing on Harrisons left, by Fisers Brigade, which was done by Capt Elliott— Everything remained in this status until morning. Hardy was then put on the left of Fiser, and he immediately sent word that there was firing on his left, which was exposed. I had expected it & had ordered Kennedy to send a couple of regiments on Hardy's left to connect with Wheelers Cavalry[,] one division of men dismounted ~~men of our division~~

[page 45]

having been sent forward early to resume the skirmishing on the left. Two more regiments were sent afterwards, leaving four behind the reserve line—Hearing firing still on the left, and not being satisfied with the position of my left—I made a reconnaissance of the ground across the swamp to the left of the reserve line and considering a strong position I sent Cap^{n} Lamar to extend the reconnaissance to the left & to see where Genl Wheelers cavalry were. I went in company with Major Black reconnoitering the ground afterwards and returning met Captain Lamar who had gone as directed and had met Wheelers skirmishers & Genl Wheeler himself, who occupied a road which started about a ~~quarter~~ ¼ mile from town ran around into the Goldsboro Road[.] I went with him then and seeing at a glance the importance of the position returned & reported the result of my observation to Genl Hardee at Genl Johnstons head quarters.
[at this point the journal returns to page 34, with no other entries from the Battle of Bentonville]

((( )))

Near Smithville N.C.
March 25 1865 [Saturday]

My dear Wife
I arrived here to day after our three days fighting near Bentonville and take this opportunity of acknowledging the receipt of two of your letters, one of the 2ndFeby and another of the 27th—the first from Augusta, at Hus place, and the other from Washington Wilkes County. I rec^{d} the other day one, the first from your new house, and acknowledged it by a note in pencil.

At the last days fight near Bentonville, it is said we had the whole of Sherman's Army to contend against, but every assault was beaten off with but slight loss to ourselves, although the odds were perhaps four to one. Sherman had been so undisturbed in his march through Georgia & South Carolina that our daring to fight him so discomposed his troops that their assaults were feeble and they did not pretend to stand a direct charge—our men were confident to the last, although they knew their opponent outnumbered them very largely, and were in fact enthusiastic for the fight.

We are fast concentrating our resources in men and material and if we can gain three weeks, I believe Genl Sherman will be chased out of the state. I think it probable that I will be ordered back to Georgia as I have been informed unofficially, I can be, if such is my desire. My present command is composed mostly of troops which belong to other organizations. Conners Brigade is, in fact, a part of Kershaws Division. Blanchards is composed of reserves which will probably be ordered home again. Harrison's is composed mostly from the Army of Tenn. Hardys, of Regiments from Army of Tenn & Army of V[a]—Fisers of G[a] Reserves which will be sent home probably—so when this army is re-organised as it will be, there will be in truth, no command for me—without the rights of others are trampled on. The Army of Tennessee is in fact our only reliance, and it has to be humored to get it assembled, and when assembled it will be best commanded [letter ends here].

((( )))

[OB2]
[Goldsborough, North Carolina] 1865
[March 27, 1865, Monday]
[Page 34]

Near Goldsboro 1865

March 27th—Remained in camp, quite unwell with dysentery, took Peregoric on going to bed—received a present of hair bridle reigns from Texas company. Got two letters from my wife, one of the 9th Feby & one of 2nd March. The first contained notes from Willie & Johnny—recd telegram from WmR in Greensboro asking where his regiment was[,] dispatch dated 26th—[Sergeant of Scouts T. M.] Paysinger reported captured & killed 68 Yankees, enemy massed about Goldsboro.

((( )))

[OB2]
[Goldsborough, North Carolina]
[March 28, 1865, Tuesday]
[page] 35

Report of evacuation of Richmond

March 28th—Wrote Hu—remained in camp. Called on Genl Johnston, had discussion in relation to the efficiency of scouts. Showed Paysingers account of operations, since Jany last he had killed, wounded or captured two hundred and forty five men—ordered him to report to Genl Johnston to be attached to his head quarters. Paid Capn Bell PM [postmaster] eleven dollars for dispatch sent to Augusta announcing "All Well"—ordered that patrols be sent daily to arrest men absent from camp—five roll calls per day to keep men in— Report of evacuation of Richmond & adoption of interim lines of defense, Augusta & Columbia to be fortified. I suppose that Raleigh and Danville will be in the line of defense, moved camp of head quarters—

Texas company left for their regiment—staid for breakfast. Genl Hardee still absent in Raleigh.

((( )))

[OB2]
[Goldsborough, North Carolina]
[March 29, 1865, Wednesday]

March 29th—Remained in camp, issued orders for drills and for sinks, two drills per day[,] company drills in morning[,] battalion in the evening, brigade drills twice a week in place of battalion drills. Yesterday sent Serg Paysinger to report with his party to Genl Johnston, because there was so much jealousy in Conners Brigade in reference to the employment of the party as scouts. Paysingers record showed two hundred and forty five Yankees killed or captured since January last, he had eight men with him—shot at squirrel in tree, cut tree down, &c Harrison moved camp.

((( )))

[OB2]
[Goldsborough, North Carolina]
[March 30, 1865, Thursday]

March 30th—Remained in camp, weather bad, commenced raining last night[,] rained all day, but warm— Lt. Bennett & Pvt Phelps of Company B 8th Texas came in from Raleigh.[26] Stayed with Capt Lamar over night. Weather cleared off towards evening, bright star seen before sunset in West. Kennedy forwarded a comm [communication] to Genl Johnston to find out his status. Whether a Brig Genl in fact or both Colonel & Brigadier— Genl Hoods report received of operations of Army of Tenn while under his command. Forage very scarce.

((( )))

Augusta Ga
May 23/65 [Tuesday]

My dear Emily
We arrived safe and found all well. I have not however seen Hu, he is said to be planting his swamp place. The negroes have all left him but Annie and

26. LM may have confused names and ranks. There was a 3rd Lieutenant Edwin M. Phelps and a Sergeant James M. Bennett, both members of Company G, 8th Texas Cavalry.

Seeuhronia. The woman who had charge of the little negroes had left but I have not heard what has been done with the little negroes. I will try and go out tomorrow if the cars run—it is said that they do not run more than three times per week.

This morning Cloe & her two children left Mary, leaving Green (who goes off in the morning and returns to supper and bed)—Susan and Annie. W^{m}R has however a white boy[,] one of his old regiment who is to be a boy of all work. I have spoken for one for our use and hope one will turn up.

An order has been issued forbidding officers to wear their uniforms after next Thursday—or should there not be any other clothing in possession of the parties, all insignia of rank, buttons &c must be taken off.

No officer will be permitted to remain in the city, unless it [is] his residence for a longer period than twenty four hours without special permission.

I have obtained authority to keep one double barreled gun—one single do—one rifle[,] one carbine and two Colts pistols & ten pounds of powder and two sacks of shot—swords do not come under the order.

Mr George Lamar[27] was fined one hundred dollars for shooting at a negro who was engaged in stealing from a neighbour, and he was a witness against himself as he mentioned the circumstance incidentally ~~again~~ to illustrate the condition of society in his neighborhood.

I received a letter from M^{r} LaRoche written evidently under fear of a Court Martial & Provost Martial. I send it for your consideration. It was brought by the captain of the steamer which runs between this & Sav^{a}.

Mr Bruce[,] the Member of Congress from Ky[,] has persuaded Cap^{n} Phillips to go onto Ky. and he proposes to leave by next Monday.

I will go out to Hu? and then decide as to coming down here—try and get a white woman in your section—get ready to come down any how— Dr Todd has never left my pistol as he was to do last Sunday.

I do not think we can start down before next Monday. I will start up on Friday, if nothing happens.

My love to all—adios with much love to children.

Your devoted L.

27. George Lamar Sr.

Appendix

Letters Received from J. B. Hood and N. A. Davis

[copy]
Rapidan Station [Virginia]
May 24th, 1863 [Sunday]

Major Genl. McLaws—
Your note of the 20th inst. has been received. The book you refer to was not written under my auspices, and today is the first time my attention has been called to the paragraph you refer to. I have never read the book, and regret it was published. Had I seen it sooner I would have written you on my own accord on the subject.

Any information as to my official report of the battle of Sharpsburg received by Mr. Davis, was obtained from my Adjt. Genl's office.

In my report I cast no reflections on you, or your command. I state that I called upon Genl. D. H. Hill several times, and repeatedly upon Genl Longstreet, for reinforcements, before your arrival; but I received no assistance. I gave my opinion that [with] your arrival by 8 or 8 1/2 A.M. I believe our victory would have been complete, on the left. But I certainly have no right or desire to blame you or Genl. Hill. I had been fighting since sunrise that morning, and my ammunition was exhausted an hour and a half before your arrival. I notice in a sketch of your life in the Southern News, that your troop regained all the ground that I lost at Sharpsburg.

My fighting was done on the left of St. Mumma Church, and in front of the pike. I did little or no fighting in the woods I marched out of for ammunition on your arrival.

I don't think your troops gained the meadow in advance of the pike, as I returned about 12 o'clock and took my position in the woods, again on the right of Genl. Ransom,[1] and our line of battle was on this side of the pike.

Very respectfully,
(signed) J. B. Hood
Major Genl.

1. Brigadier, later Major General, Robert Ransom Jr.

((( )))

Division H^d Qrt [Virginia]
June 3rd 1863 [Wednesday]

General
Your letter of May 31st has been received. I wish very much I could see you on the subject.

Never was there a more unjust construction placed upon the book of Mr. Davis in regard to myself.

As I told you in my last note, I did not know your name was mentioned in the book until I received your note. You say you have been attacked and must defend yourself. I think you are right. But think Mr. Davis should correct it.

He is now absent in Texas. But should be back soon. On his return I think you will find him ready to & glad to correct his statements.

If he does not return soon, and you desire it, I will have someone write to him, or will do so myself in regard to this matter. This will save you from the disagreeable necessity of doing so yourself. I abhor as much as yourself pamphlets or newspaper publications.

I trust you will do me the justice to correct the idea prevailing in the minds of any of your friends that I had anything to do with the book of Mr Davis. You will see from the enclosed that I have other authors in my command of whose productions, I knew as much as, I did about Mr. Davis book.

Resply
J B Hood
Major Genl McLaws

[note on letter]
Gen. J. B. Hood
denies any connection with
statements made by chaplain
Davis—*untrue* at Sharpsburg
1863

((( )))

Camp 4th Texas
Near Culpeper [Virginia]
July 30th 1863 [Wednesday]

Maj Gen. McLaws
Army of Northern Va

Sir
On my arrival from the West I am placed in possession of information which satisfies me that I did you injustice at the battle of Sharpsburg in my journal (Campaign from Texas to Maryland) published early this Spring.

I therein stated what I believed to be the facts in the case as reported to me by gentlemen from the field. But from information since received I feel that I have done you injustice in the severe remarks connected with that statement, and I hereby frankly admit the same. For it was not my wish to do any one injustice and especially in an hour like this. And if I have in any way wronged any one I am ever ready to make an honorable amend for that injury.

I expect soon to revise that publication for a second edition and will take pleasure in correcting the matter referred to by special note.

You are at liberty to use this communication as you please.

Respectfully
Your Obt Servt
N. A. Davis

[note on back of letter]
Parson Davis
Apology for
lying at Sharpsburg
acknowledged the
injustice of his statements
His mistake

Bibliography

UNPUBLISHED SOURCES

Augusta, Georgia

Birth Registry for Richmond County

James and Elizabeth McLaws

Burial Records for Magnolia Cemetery, Richmond County

Mary Ann and William Raymond McLaws

Meta Telfair McLaws

Burial Records for Summerville Cemetery, Richmond County

Anna Laura McLaws

James and Elizabeth McLaws

Brazoria County, Texas

Deeds of Sale, County Clerk

Alfred and Carrie V. Edwards

Mrs. Bernard A. Pratte

Chapel Hill, North Carolina

Southern Historical Collection, University of North Carolina at Chapel Hill

Captain Henry Lord Page King, C.S.A., Diary, June 4–November 16, 1862

Lafayette McLaws Papers #472

Durham, North Carolina

Duke University

Lafayette McLaws Papers #3417

Effingham County, Georgia

Effingham County Records, Deed of Sale

Louisville, Kentucky

The Filson Club, Jefferson County Marriage Registers, Licenses, and Bonds

New York, New York

Major Dr. Henry Orlando Marcy, Diary of a Surgeon, U.S. Army, 1864–99

Richmond County

Board of Education Minutes

Savannah, Georgia

Georgia Historical Society

Lafayette McLaws Collection #2087

Virginia McLaws, "A Sketch of the Life of General Lafayette McLaws," "Emily

Allison Taylor McLaws," and "Children of John Gibson Taylor and Elizabeth Lee Taylor"

Washington, D.C.

National Archives and Records Administration

General and Special Orders Issued and Received, 1842–52, Vol. 1 of 1, April 19, 1845

M 266, RG 109, Combined Service Records of Soldiers Who Served in Organizations from the State of Georgia

M 331, RG 109, Compiled Service Records of Confederate Generals and Staff Officers and Nonregimental Enlisted Men

M 347, RG 109, Unfiled Papers and Slips Belonging in Confederate Compiled Service Records

M 432, RG 29, Records of the Bureau of the Census, Seventh Census of the United States, 1850

M 437, RG 109, Letters Received by the Confederate Secretary of War, 1861–65

M 474, RG 109, Letters Received by the Confederate Adjutant and Inspector General, 1861–65

M 522, RG 109, Letters Sent by the Confederate Secretary of War, 1861–65

M 523, RG 109, Letters Sent by the Confederate Secretary of War to the President, 1861–65

M 567, RG 94, Records of the Adjutant Generals Office, Letters Received, Main Series, 1822–60

M 593, RG 29, Records of the Bureau of the Census, Ninth Census of the United States, 1870

M 627, RG 109, Letters and Telegrams Sent by the Confederate Adjutant and Inspector General, 1861–65

M 653, RG 29, Records of the Bureau of the Census, Eighth Census of the United States, 1860

M 665, RG 391, Returns for Regular Army Infantry Regiments, June 1821–December 1916

Regimental Returns, 6th U.S. Infantry, 1833–44

Regimental Returns, 7th U.S. Infantry, June 1844–December 1859

M 2037, RG 94, Register of Cadet Applications, 1819–66

RG 15, Records of the Veterans Administration, Unindexed Bounty Land File, Mexican War Pension File

RG 94, Records of the Adjutant General's Office, Records Relating to the U.S. Military Academy

RG 109, Adjutant and Inspector General's Office,

General Orders, March 25, 1861–March 24, 1865

Special Orders, Vols. 204–12, March 7, 1861–April 1, 1865

RG 391, General and Special Orders Issued and Received, 1842–1852, Seventh Infantry, October 21, 1844

T 9, RG 29, Records of the Bureau of the Census, Tenth Census of the United States, 1880

T 623, RG 29, Records of the Bureau of the Census, Twelfth Census of the United States, 1900

NEWSPAPERS

Augusta Daily Chronicle and Sentinel
Savannah Evening News
Savannah Morning News
Southern Illustrated News
Tampa Tribune

PUBLISHED SOURCES

Alexander, Edward Porter. *Fighting for the Confederacy: The Personal Recollections of General Edward Porter Alexander.* Edited by Gary W. Gallagher. Chapel Hill: University of North Carolina Press, 1989.

Augusta Genealogical Society, Inc. *Summerville Cemetery: Augusta, Georgia.* Augusta: McGowan Printing Co., 1990.

Bauer, K. Jack. *The Mexican War, 1846–1848.* New York: Macmillan, 1974.

———. *Zachary Taylor: Soldier, Planter, Statesman of the Old Southwest.* Baton Rouge: Lousiana State University Press, 1985.

Blair, William Alan. "James Longstreet." In *The Confederate General,* edited by William C. Davis, 4 vols., 4:90–95. Washington, D.C.: National Historical Society, 1991.

Bonaventure Historical Society. *Bonaventure Cemetery: Savannah, Georgia.* Savannah: Bonaventure Historical Society, 2000.

Busey, John W., and David G. Martin. *Regimental Strengths and Losses at Gettysburg.* Hightstown, N.J.: Longstreet House, 1986.

Cashin, Edward J. *The Quest: A History of Public Education in Richmond County, Georgia.* Augusta: Richmond County Board of Education, 1985.

Davis, Nicholas A. *The Campaign from Texas to Maryland.* Richmond: Presbyterian Committee of Publication of the Confederate States, 1863.

Dowdey, Clifford. *The Seven Days: The Emergence of Lee.* Lincoln: University of Nebraska Press, 1993.

Evans, Tad, ed. *Baldwin County, Georgia, Newspaper Clippings: Volume 5, 1843–1847.* Savannah: Tad Evans, 1995.

Falk, Peter Hastings, ed. *Who Was Who in American Art.* Madison, Conn.: Sound View Press, 1985. Compiled from the 30-volume *American Art Annual* (1898–1933) and its subsequent 4-volume *Who's Who in American Art* (1935–47), originally edited by Florence N. Levy.

Ferrell, Robert H., ed. *Monterrey Is Ours! The Mexican War Letters of Lieutenant Dana, 1845–1847.* Lexington: University Press of Kentucky, 1990.

Freeman, Douglas Southall. *R. E. Lee: A Biography.* 4 vols. New York: Scribner's, 1934–36.

French, Samuel G. *Two Wars: An Autobiography of Gen. Samuel G. French.* Nashville: Confederate Veteran, 1901.

Gallagher, Gary W., ed. *Chancellorsville: The Battle and Its Aftermath.* Chapel Hill: University of North Carolina Press, 1996.

Georgia Attorney General's Office. *The Attorneys General of Georgia, 1754 to Present.* Atlanta: History of the Attorney General, 2000. Internet source: <*http://www.ganet.org/gaahistory.htm*>.

Graber, H. W. *Sixty-Two Years in Texas.* Austin: State House Press, 1987.

Haddock, T. M., comp. *Haddock's Augusta, GA: Directory and General Advertiser.* Augusta: E. H. Pughe, 1872.

Harsh, Joseph L. *Taken at the Flood: Robert E. Lee and Confederate Strategy in the Maryland Campaign of 1862.* Kent: Kent State University Press, 1999.

Henderson, Lillian. *Roster of the Confederate Soldiers of Georgia, 1861–1865.* Hapeville, Ga.: Longino and Porter, 1959.

Jones, Charles C., Jr. *Memorial History of Augusta, Georgia: From Its Settlement in 1735 to the Close of the Eighteenth Century.* Syracuse: D. Mason and Co., 1890.

Krick, Robert K. "Lafayette McLaws." In *The Confederate General,* edited by William C. Davis, 6 vols., 4:128–31. Washington, D.C.: National Historical Society, 1991.

Leonard, John William, ed. *Woman's Who's Who of America.* New York: American Commonwealth Co., 1915.

MacLaws, Lafayette. *The Battle of Gettysburg.* Savannah: Confederate Veterans Association, 1896.

———. *The Maryland Campaign.* Savannah: Confederate Veterans Association, 1896.

Meade, George Gordon. *Life and Letters of George Gordon Meade, Major-General United States Army, by George Meade.* Vol. 1. New York: Scribner's, 1913.

Myers, Robert Manson, ed. *The Children of the Pride: A True Story of Georgia and the Civil War—Selected Letters of the Family of Rev. Dr. Charles Colcock Jones from the Years 1860–1868.* New Haven: Yale University Press, 1972.

National Society, Daughters of the American Revolution. *Daughters of the American Revolution Lineage Books.* 152 vols. Internet source: <Ancestry.com>, 1998.

Smedlund, William S. *Campfires of Georgia's Troops, 1861–1865.* Sharpsburg, Ga.: William S. Smedlund, 1995.

Stiles, Robert. *Four Years under Marse Robert.* Marietta, Ga.: R. Bemis Publishing, 1995.

Thomas, Edward J. *Memoirs of a Southerner.* Internet source: <*http://www.geocities.com/Heartland/Ranch/3631/ejt.html*>, pre-1923.

Thomas, Ella Gertrude Clanton. *The Secret Eye: The Journal of Ella Gertrude Clanton Thomas.* Edited by Virginia Ingraham Burr. Chapel Hill: University of North Carolina Press, 1990.

Thorpe, Thomas Bangs. "Sugar and the Sugar Region of Louisiana." *Harpers New Monthly Magazine,* October 1854.

Timanus, Rod. *An Illustrated History of Texas Forts.* Plano: Republic of Texas Press, 2001.

Unruh, John D., Jr. *The Plains Across: The Overland Emigrants and Trans-Mississippi West, 1840–1860.* Urbana: University of Illinois Press, 1993.

U.S. Geological Survey. *Map of Harpers Ferry, VA.—M.D.—W. VA,* 1988.

U.S. War Department. *War of the Rebellion: A Compilation of the Official Records of the Union

and Confederate Armies. 128 vols. Washington, D.C.: Government Printing Office, 1880–1901.
West Point Alumni Foundation, Inc. *Register of Graduates and Former Cadets of the United States Military Academy.* West Point, N.Y.: Association of Graduates, U.S. Military Academy, 1980.

Index